NOT BY THE BOOK

Recollections of Peace and War

NOT BY THE BOOK

Recollections of Peace and War

Nicholas S. Mair

The Pentland Press Limited
Edinburgh • Cambridge • Durham

First published in 1993 by
The Pentland Press Ltd.
1 Hutton Close
South Church
Bishop Auckland
Durham

ISBN 1 85821 093 3

Typeset by CBS, Felixstowe, Suffolk
Printed and bound by Antony Rowe Ltd., Chippenham

For Hélène
whose book this is, as much as mine

ACKNOWLEDGEMENTS

I am deeply indebted to my old Glasgow friend, Morris Smith, for reminding me of times past, to Denis Rice for his patience and constant encouragement, to Doug Bankson for lending me his critical support and to Jan Sparling for the title of this book.

When an acquaintance won a prize for a work of non-fiction my wife, Hélène, said to me, "You have led an eventful life. Why don't you write a memoir for your grandchildren?"

"Alright," I replied. "I will emulate Frank Harris and write *My Life and Loves.*"

"That," said Hélène, "will fall into the category of fiction."

But everything I have written here is true, in so far as letters, records and the vagaries of memory permit.

"He appears so great a lover of rhyme, that there is scarce a page but where he quotes some verses, and, sometimes inserts his own, so that often he leaves us in doubt, whether he be a better physician, or a poet. And he has this peculiar excellency, as to make the reader not a little merry."
John Friend (1675-1728) on John of Gaddesden (1280-1361)

"Doctor Mair, you never did anything by the book."
(Eric Fox, Chief Technician, Leicester Public Health Laboratory)

CONTENTS

LIST OF ILLUSTRATIONS

FOREWORD

I am privileged and delighted to be asked to write a foreword for this account of the individual and joint lives of two people, whom I hold in high regard.

For those of us who are fortunate we meet during life one or more individuals who make us feel better for knowing them. It is not common and even less so, to encounter a couple who have this effect both in their own right and together. I suspect the appropriate term of description for them is saintly, but Nick has enough mischief in him to be well named.

Each has had a complete life; both before and after they met. They have enriched the world of microbiology, and again have complemented each other: Nick in bacteriology and Hélène in virology.

Each of us will have thoughts on our own lives as we get old. Blessed are those, like me, who can say I knew Nick and Hélène Mair.

Sir Robert Kilpatrick
The President
The General Medical Council

Chapter 1

Immigrants

On the afternoon of Tuesday, 18th September 1917, eight days after my fifth birthday, King George V, who was visiting the disaffected industrial areas of the Clydeside, passed down Stockwell Street in an open car. Our tiny flat, three floors up, overlooking the street, was crowded with friends come to see the spectacle. I can remember distinctly being held precariously over the sill of the kitchen window so that I should miss nothing. I watched with excitement as the royal car approached. In the back seat I could see a bearded man in khaki uniform with a lot of ribbons on his chest. Behind him came other cars, some with soldiers in them, others with men wearing ordinary new suits. The noise from the crowded street came up to and past our window. The account of what happened next I owe to my mother. Watching from the next room, she was startled to hear screams coming from the kitchen. Fearing the worst, she rushed in, only to find the screams turned to laughter, and me at the centre of a group of admiring women. Apparently I had asked, "Who is the man in the motor?" When told he was the King, I had said, "Why is he no at the Front?"

From scraps of adult conversation this little boy had gathered that the Front was an unpleasant place where men were sent while the women stayed at home to look after the family. In the eyes of these women, I had, at my tender age, nailed my red flag to the mast in true Clydeside fashion. The flag is now tattered and its colour somewhat faded, but it is still flying.

While all this was happening, the royal car passed over the Clyde by the Stockwell Bridge into the Gorbals, the Jewish quarter of Glasgow, where the teeming population, according to the official account, shouted with loyal fervour. This is my earliest recollection.

Many of those who cheered with loyal fervour had good reason to do so. Like my parents, they had fled the persecution of Czarist Russia. For more than a hundred years, the vast bulk of Russian Jewry had been confined to the Pale of Settlement, the territory along Russia's western border. They lived there in poverty and despair, in uneasy symbiosis with their gentile neighbours, while periods of cruel repression alternated with periods of comparative tolerance. The latter came to an abrupt end in 1881 with the first of a series of pogroms – instigated by the Government and aided and abetted by the police and the military. Thereafter, Jewish emigration, which had been a trickle, became a flood. Between 1881 and the outbreak of the First World War nearly two million Jews left the Russian Empire for the United States. Thousands more found refuge in Canada, the United Kingdom, Argentina and South Africa. My progenitors, still unknown to one another, were among those who sailed no further than Leith, crossed the narrow waist of Scotland, and settled in Glasgow.

What sort of people were they? As I write this, I have before me the registration certificate of an immigrant, which the holder was required to present to the police at each change of address. The certificate was issued at Glasgow on 26th December 1919 and was apparently a replacement for an earlier one. The particulars in it read as follows:

Name: Sophia Ferrer
Nationality: Russian
Born on: 1849   In: Anikst
Previous Nationality: -
Profession or Occupation: Wife
Residence: 13 Thistle Street, Glasgow
Arrived in United Kingdom: 1897
Address of last residence

outside U.K.: Anikst, Kovno, Russia
Passport or other papers
as to Nationality or Identity: None
Signature of Holder: Cannot write

A distinct large left-thumb print identifies her, her photograph even more so. She is shown standing with her left arm resting nonchalantly on top of a chair and her right arm by her side. She is a small, sturdy, broad-faced woman wearing a black dress and a very large black floral hat held in place by ribbons tied under her chin. She is looking at me, confidently. She is my maternal grandmother.

Her husband comes back to me as a bowed, slender man with a white beard trimmed in the Romanov fashion. He always wore a broad-brimmed felt hat whatever the weather. I never learned his fore-name because he was always known to his grandchildren as "The Zaide". He was a withdrawn, gentle, much-loved man. His wife, "The Bobbe", provided the necessary aggression. She was the dominant member of her family as my mother was of hers.

Uncle Morris, my mother's brother, also had his fair share of these dominant genes. He began his new life in Scotland peddling sponges in the mining villages of Lanarkshire. He could not pronounce the name of the commodity he was selling, but he knew its price. In fact, Uncle Morris knew the price of everything. He became a prosperous business man turning rags into shoulder-pads for tailors and under-felt for carpet stores. Together with his son Louis he helped found the Jewish Golf Club, which owed its existence to the refusal of local clubs to accept Jews as members. Uncle Morris's club had not only one course but two. Gentiles were welcome.

I never met my paternal grandmother, although she lived just across the river in the Gorbals. I am told she was a formidable woman. Apparently, she did not approve of her elder son, my father, marrying a girl whose only dowry, apart from her good looks, was her invisible genes. So against her determined opposition they fled to Greenock and were married in a registry office among strangers. Grandmother was

furious when she learned of their elopement and excommunicated them
as effectively as a pope. She never came to see her grandchildren nor did
we visit her. We saw her husband surreptitiously from time to time, but I
think he was as much afraid of these meetings as we were.

This is all I know about my ancestors. Recently, I read about a
Chinese-Canadian journalist who was able to trace his family back
thirty-three generations and 1,000 years. Painstakingly, I have traced
mine back two generations and nearly 100 years. It is unlikely I can
delve further into the past with any hope of success. Those relatives who
did not emigrate, and their records if they ever existed, were swept off
the face of the earth when the *Einsatsqruppen*, the execution squads of
the Nazi S.S., arrived in Lithuania in June 1941.

After the fugitive marriage in Greenock my parents set up house in
the little cold-water flat in Stockwell Street on the other side of the river
from the Gorbals. Perhaps they felt safer with the Clyde between them
and my irascible grandmother. My brother Henny was born in 1907 and
my sister Ray three years later. Stockwell Street, where I spent the first
fourteen years of my life, has a history going back 1,000 years, when it
was known as the Fishergait, the road to the fishers. But when I was a
boy progress had caught up with this ancient street and much of its
length was darkened by a railway bridge nearly 100 yards wide which
carried the trains into St. Enoch's Station. What was left of the open
street from the bridge to the river bank was occupied on one side by the
Metropole Theatre, the oldest music hall in Scotland, the Scotia pub, a
favourite watering-hole for the theatre patrons, and lastly a huge, black
crumbling tenement. Across the street from this tenement stood an L-
shaped red sandstone building whose elegant Victorian exterior belied
its dilapidated interior. The long limb of the L fronted on Stockwell
Street and the short limb on the slums of the Briggait (the road to the
bridge) and the malodorous fishmarket. The Briggait, where once the
gentry enjoyed the sweet air of the river, now teemed with the descendants
of the Irish immigrants who settled there when they left their native isle
in the "Hungry Forties". I can recall how, twice a year, we gathered with
the unemployed to watch the minions of the local authority armed with

wooden clubs and iron bars purge the market of its rats. Hundreds of the rodents were slaughtered, and as many escaped into the neighbouring tenements, chased by cheering spectators. In this enclave, a microcosm of the notorious Gorbals south of the river, the newly arrived Russian Jews lived in noisy amity with their neighbours, Protestants and Catholics, Scots and Irish, and even one coloured family that was accepted without question. Some of these Jewish families come to mind.

At number 140, in the black crumbling tenement, lived the Nimans who owned the newsagent's shop where winning tips for the races were sold in little envelopes for three pence. Here too lived the Schneidermans and the Bernsteins. Mrs. S, a First World war widow of iron determination, ran a thriving tailoring business from her home, where she employed two people in a room converted to a workshop. She had three sons and three daughters. Her oldest son had served time in Borstal for some misdemeanour and the lady herself spent a year in prison for resetting cloth. This in no way detracted from her maternal goodness. When Annie, her fourteen-year-old daughter, was run over by a motor-lorry she refused to allow the surgeons to amputate the child's leg. Despite their dire warnings she brought her daughter home, put a room at her disposal, and at great expense had her cared for by a medical practitioner for several months. As a result, Annie was able to walk again on her own two feet, albeit with a slight limp.

Mr. Bernstein, the father of my life-long friend Alec, was a failed drapery peddler and an even less successful entrepreneur. Having abandoned the drapery business, he decided to branch out in another direction. He would buy used and damaged jute sacks – sugar sacks, potato sacks, flour sacks, sacks of any kind as long as they were made of jute. He planned to clean the sacks that were dirty and repair those that needed repairing, to accumulate thousands and then to sell them on a rising consumer market. He was a man before his time. When his cousin, a "millionaire", refused him a loan to buy a horse and cart, Mr. Bernstein was compelled to hire a push-cart on a daily basis. He and Alec, pushing the cart in turn, covered miles of Glasgow streets in search of jute sacks. The more successful they were, the heavier the cart became. In the end, I do not know who gave up first, the Bernsteins or the push-cart.

At number 150, lived the Klaskos and the Sprouts. Old man Klasko was a revolutionary with watery eyes and a pendulous lip. The first demonstration in Scotland of the Communist Party started off from number 150. Barely twenty stalwarts lined up for it and they were led by Klasko and big Peter Kerrigan with a huge red banner held aloft between them. Klasko died shortly afterwards, but not before Peter had married his daughter Rosy.

Robert Sprout was my uncle by marriage. Gittel, Father's sister, had fallen in love with the tall, blond Catholic boy when they lived in Lithuania. Neither family approved of the liaison but there was little they could do about it. It was all rather reminiscent of *Fiddler on the Roof.* When the recruiting party came to the village, looking for sturdy youths to reinforce the Army in the East, my father hid Robert in the synagogue until the military had gone. In retrospect, said Father, it was a dangerous thing to do, because had the Cossacks discovered him they would have put a torch to the *shul.* When our family emigrated Robert went with them. Gittel married him, over her mother's objections, after he had made a token conversion to Judaism. This was not enough for my implacable grandmother and another excommunication followed. It says much for Robert that only after his death did his devout children learn that he was a convert.

My family lived on the third floor of the five-storey red sandstone building with the decorated façade. The flat below us was occupied by the Bostons, the only other Jewish family in the building. The close, the common entrance to number 145, possessed a refinement rarely found in working-class tenements. It was lined with bright green tiles. The tenants in the ground floor responded by keeping the entrance swept, the tiles bright, and woe betide any of us who tried to deface them with graffiti. So imposing was this edifice, our neighbours in the crumbling tenement across the street regarded us who lived in it as being, if not exactly the élite of Stockwell Street, at least one or two rungs up the social ladder. This at a time when my father was earning two pounds and ten shillings for a sixty-five-hour week and our home, like all the others in this elegant Victorian edifice, consisted of a kitchen with a bed-recess where my parents slept behind drawn curtains, a bedroom with a double bed which I shared with Henny and a single bed for Ray, an inside lavatory but no bathroom. In this confined space, by twist and turn, we managed to insert ourselves like pieces in a jigsaw puzzle. As for Boston, a dentist and the only professional man in our tiny ghetto, I never learnt whether, living in Stockwell Street, he was in the process of going up or down the social ladder.

From the time he was sixteen my father worked those sixty-five long hours as a frame-maker in a furniture factory in the heart of the Gorbals. It has been said that a Jewish community could always be relied upon to help the newly-arrived greenhorn. This is probably true but it did not prevent some Jewish employers from exploiting him. My father's boss was such a one. He also bought frames from other makers, mostly Jews, small men struggling in ill-lit workshops under railway arches. He would screw them down to the last penny and pay them with post-dated cheques. Long before the cheques could be cashed a procession of anxious frame-makers could be seen climbing the dingy stairs to his office.

"Abie, listen to me! I need the money to buy timber. I need the money to pay the rent."

Abie would consider their pleas, for he was a considerate man. Then, in a burst of generosity he would say: "All right. I will give you a cheque, payable now, but I'm taking off 5 per cent.'

Father tells me of the time he cut his wrist with a chisel and shows me the ugly scar. It is one of the hazards of the trade. Abie paid him his wages for the two weeks he was off work. When he returned, Abie prepared a claim for the insurance and asked him to sign to the effect that he had been off work for three weeks. What follows, my father tells me with great dramatic effect.

"You make money from my sweat," he cried. "You want to make money from my blood as well?"

"Lazar," said his boss patiently, 'you've been paid, so what difference does it make?"

But Father, with the honesty that kept him a poor man for the rest of his life, refused to sign.

"And then what happened?" I prompt, for I have heard the story before.

"Then," said Father, "Abie changed the date, and I signed." There was a pause. Then, as though to absolve his employer, he added, "But he didn't sack me."

After supper Father would read a Yiddish paper or one of our library books, painstakingly at first and later with ease. It was just as well we were a small family both in size and number because there would not have been room enough for us and the books. The walls bulged with books. There were columns of books on every level surface. When I was learning my alphabet, Henny was already reading *The Children's Newspaper* and saving up for Arthur Mee's *Book of Knowledge*, the earliest children's encyclopaedia. Mother was also an avid reader. From the day she landed in Scotland she had gone to night-school to learn English. If she never learned to write English properly, she mastered the language enough to enjoy its literature. One night Ray was awakened by the sound of someone sobbing quietly. It was Mother sitting at the kitchen table reading *Ivanhoe* by gaslight. While Father slept soundly in the recess bed, she was crying for the sorrows of the beauteous Rebecca and her unfortunate father, Isaac of York.

Once there was a knock on the door. Ever cautious, Mother opened the door a crack. There stood a lady with a brief-case in her hand and a solemn look on her face.

"Mrs. Mair?" she asked.

"Yes," said Mother suspiciously.

"I've come from the Gorbals Library. I'm afraid your children have been taking out more books than they are entitled to, and they are all overdue."

Without a word Mother ushered the lady in, led her into our bedroom, opened a cupboard and out tumbled scores of books that had been held upright by the closed door. The lady looked dumbly at the pile of books, and Mother said, "Lady, do I need your books?"

"No", said the librarian, "but we would like ours back."

Many years later, Hélène and I were attending a family wedding in Glasgow. I introduced her to an old friend. He came to the point right away, as though nursing a grievance he was determined to air.

"Mrs. Mair, your husband was a great reader. He had the finest library in Glasgow – all borrowed books, mine included."

Except for a Catholic family which occupied the flat above us, I have only a vague recollection of the gentiles among whom we lived. After the trauma of the Pale, I think our parents tended to keep to themselves. They lived in amity with their neighbours, but they were not intimate. We were never aware of overt antisemitism. It might appear later in private golf clubs but it was not prevalent among the working-class in Scotland, which seemed to be more occupied with the conflict between Irish Catholics and Protestants. The childhood challenge, "Are you a Billy or a Dan?" became the Orange procession celebrating the victory of King William of Orange over the Catholic forces of James II in 1690 at the River Boyne, a victory which saved the North of Ireland for the Protestant cause and still keeps it under the Crown. The fervour at these marches, which are held on 12th July wherever Irish Protestants are gathered together, must be seen to be believed. There is a story they tell in Glasgow about an American visitor watching his first Orange procession. The fifes were tootling, the drums were beating, the Orange banners and the Union Jacks were flying. Behind the flags marched the members of the Orange Order with their bowler hats and furled umbrellas. The American, turning to a wee man who was cheering himself hoarse, asked what the parade was all about. "We're celebrating King Billy's victory over the papists at the Battle of the Boyne."

"Never heard of it," said the visitor.

"What!" said the disgusted Glaswegian, "Awa man and read your Bible!"

Then, there was the occasion when my wife, Hélène, was taking blood samples from Cistercian monks who had volunteered to take part in an influenza vaccine trial at Mount St. Bernard Abbey in Leicestershire.

An Irish monk, about to be bled, expressed surprise that samples taken from his Brothers appeared dark. He had expected the blood to be bright red. She explained that venous blood, lacking oxygen, was invariably dark. Then she added jokingly, "Perhaps yours will be green." At which he replied in his rich brogue, "That's all right, as long as it isn't orange!"

In this conflict we Jews remained neutral and got on with the business of surviving. The Catholic family who lived above us were also neutral for the same reason. Mr. Forrester earned a pittance as a pawnbroker's clerk. He was a quiet, self-effacing man who rarely raised his voice when his two rumbustious sons, Frank and Tommy, were creating havoc upstairs. In the last year of the War, he and Father got their calling-up papers at the same time and went together for their medical. Father came back all smiles. His hernias, which caused him so much distress, had stood him in good stead. Mr. Forrester was not so lucky and soon he was in khaki. I can remember coming across him sitting on the stairs crying quietly. I rushed down to tell my father, "Mr. Forrester's greetin' on the stairs."

At once, Father went up to see him. I had never seen two men crying together. One, who could hardly keep his wife and children in food and clothing, was promising the other he would look after his family while he was at the Front. In the absence of her husband, Mrs. Forrester went from house to house collecting old clothes, even those discarded by the poor. She took them in bundles to Paddy's Market in the Briggait next to the fishmarket. There were no stalls in this market. Clothes, or whatever was being offered for sale, were laid on newspapers spread out on the ground. Her customers were the lascars who crewed the ships moored at the Broomielaw in the heart of the city. She saved enough pennies to send Tommy to St. Aloysius College, a prestigious Catholic school in Glasgow. Mr. Forrester came back safely from the War. Tommy went to the University and became a teacher. Frank, who had run magic lantern shows for the kids on the landing outside his flat, emigrated to America. I like to think he went West and made his fortune with his magic lantern in Hollywood.

My father's fortunes also changed. Eventually he set himself up in a small way as a frame-maker in the inevitable railway arch off Rutherglen Road in the Gorbals. His old boss also prospered. He became the owner of a large chain of furniture stores, a public benefactor and a knight of the realm.

Chapter 2

Schooldays

I began my formal education at Gorbals Elementary School when I was five. In those days there were no kindergartens or parent-participation pre-schools to ease a child's way into the system, certainly not for the children of the Gorbals. Initiation was swift and painful. Mother or big-sister took you by the hand and led you protesting into the bedlam of the playground, left you with the group of smallest children and then went home, but not before she had waved to you through the iron railings. Once I had accepted my fate, Mother saw me across Stockwell Street and left me, confident that, like my brother and sister before me, I would make my way safely to the school at the other end of the bridge.

Built in 1884, its old registers show the sudden influx of children from Russia at the turn of the century. At one time, nearly three-quarters of the pupils were Jewish. Even without the typically Russian-Jewish names, those first Jewish pupils are identified in the school registers by the "Yes" in the column headed: "Exempted from religious instruction."

One day the teacher gave each of us a paper Union Jack on a stick and told us to wave it because we had won the War. I can remember running all the way home, waving my flag furiously to break the news to my mother, though what it meant I had no clear idea.

I was nine when I came across a floating oracle. From time to time I had noticed a small ship tied up at the wharf near the bridge. Painted on its stern and rusty bow was the word *Luculent*. Only in scholarly Scotland could a dirty little coaster be called *Luculent*, the Latin for "Light". But

13

when I saw it, I only saw the first three letters and for me they read "*Luck*". When the ship was moored at the wharf when I crossed the bridge it meant I had nothing to fear at school. If not, I was in trouble. That little coaster, whose mooring was often vacant, was rarely wrong.

I was hardly an outstanding pupil. Henny was dux of the school before he won a bursary for Allan Glen's. I received the average quota of praise and censure; I had the average number of playground fights, one of which ended in a chipped tooth for my opponent and badly infected knuckles for me, and because the human mouth abounds in potentially pathogenic bacteria it took weeks in those pre-antibiotic days for my hand to heal. If I won no medal, I did at least win a draw in a lottery. One day the teacher brought a man into the classroom. He was tall and thin and his trousers barely covered his knees. He wore what looked like a cowboy hat and a hankie round his neck. You could have mistaken him for a cowboy if it were not for his bare knees. The teacher explained that the gentleman was a scout, in fact, a scoutmaster, and he had come to offer three of us a day with his troop. I drew one of the places. A few days later he collected us and drove us in his car to a park in a more salubrious part of the city. There among the bushes of the park we were shown in single file how to track savages and avoid man-eating tigers. In the late afternoon we adjourned to a hut for a cup of tea and then sat in a circle round an imaginary camp fire while the regulars sang incomprehensible songs. We then sang "God Save the King", which I knew, and went home. It all seemed meshugge to me, and put me off scouts for ever. When I look back on it all, I am sure he was a kind man and his intentions were good. He was giving the slum kids, if not a day in the country, at least an afternoon in the fresh air of the park. But all we wanted when school was finished for the day was to play in our own backyard.

Our backyard, or "back" as we called it, was a small cobble-stoned area about five or six paces wide and a dozen paces long with a midden at one end. In this "back" we played the national game with a staggering ferocity. Our cries of "Shoot! Shoot!" could be heard up and down the street. As often as not the small rubber ball landed on a low roof and to the well-known Glasgow cry of "The ba's up the dyke" we scrambled over the open stinking midden to retrieve it.

As I write this there comes to mind a battle fought between the "big" brothers and the "wee" brothers in the "back". The weapons were catapults and the missiles pellets made from discarded tram tickets that littered the streets in those days, and, lest we ran out of ammunition, old exercise books thrown down to the combatants from a second story window. The battle was fought amid fiendish yells of defiance over twin barricades of foul-smelling fish boxes and I am happy to record that the "wee" brothers gave as good as they got.

We also had our own sports stadium, known as the 'broken building'. Why it was given that name is still a mystery to me because it was a piece of circular waste ground on which some structure had once stood but of which not a remnant remained. A narrow lane barely eight feet wide, the Goosedubs, led from the stadium to Stockwell Street, and was always our path of retreat when harassed by the police. The highlights of our sports meetings were races round the periphery of the waste ground. Henny was always in charge and saw that there were no false starts. The events were treated with great seriousness, especially the relay races. There were cries of encouragement and howls of anguish, depending on which side you were on, and near hysteria if anyone fumbled the baton. From time to time we were chased by the police. All the police had nicknames like Beery, Mars or Big Diddie. The latter was constantly given the raspberry by the corner boys when he walked past without his mate. The police liked to have their fun with us. I recall Beery, who had a nose to match his name, confounding us by coming suddenly from the Briggait while we were playing football at the stadium. There was a panic rush towards the escape route down the Goosedubs, but just as we were within a few feet of Stockwell Street and freedom, another policeman came out of cover and spreading his arms wide blocked our way. With pounding hearts we rushed back up the lane before Beery could close the trap, not that he really tried to. After the escape I dived upstairs and into bed, and every step on the landing was to my guilty mind the police coming to take me away.

One popular pastime I did not indulge in was catching flies and bluebottles. I had a horror of bluebottles. At the end of Stockwell Street was a fishmonger who slung his empty fishboxes into an adjacent backyard. To the children playing there these boxes were a boon for they attracted myriads of bluebottles. It required no expertise to catch them. It took no more than a lazy sweep of the arm to enclose in one's fist a dozen of the beastly things. The art was not in catching them but in opening the hand in such a way that they could be transferred one by one to an empty jar without letting any escape. Some twenty-five years later I found myself playing the same game with a different insect in a distant country.

Like all Jewish children I was expected to attend "cheder" where I would learn Biblical Hebrew and the history of my people. My religious education was intermittent and incomplete, for which I had only myself to blame, though my mother pointed a finger at my father from time to time. She kept a kosher household, lit the candles on Friday evening, observed the Sabbath but not as strictly as her mother, and did her best to send me off after regular school hours to Hebrew School with a good tea inside me. All she wanted from me at that time was to do well in the ordinary school and to become bar mitzvah on my thirteenth birthday. On that day I would sing a portion of the Law and an excerpt from the Prophets in front of the congregation in the synagogue. My brother had done this six years before and I was expected to follow in his footsteps. But even at an early age I had proved recalcitrant. In cheder we were taught to read Biblical Hebrew, the faster the better, irrespective of whether or not we understood what we were reading. True, we were taught key words and phrases, but this was not enough for me. When I complained to my father, who listened with a sympathetic ear, he said, "So, does it matter you don't understand what you're saying – God will understand."

My father had attended a yeshiva in Lithuania and was well-read in Hebrew and Yiddish, but somewhere between Riga and Leith he had shed much of his orthodox Judaism for socialism and the brotherhood of man, and some of this must have rubbed off on me. He went to shul on the high holy days but he looked on these as social rather than religious occasions. There he met family and acquaintances and at frequent intervals in the day-long services he would nip out to the sidewalk for a smoke (but not on Yom Kippur). Between puffs of the cigarettes that ultimately killed him, he would argue fiercely with his fellow members of the Workers' Circle about the future of Palestine and the wonder of the recent Russian revolution. In these heady days Father really believed the millennium had come. When he had finished his last cigarette he would go back to his seat near the exit, drape his prayer-shawl round his shoulders and resume praying as though he had never been away. And I would be plucking at his sleeve, asking, "How many more pages to go?"

Among his heroes, who became my heroes, were Baruch Spinoza, the seventeenth-century Jewish-Dutch philosopher whose *Ethics* made his name anathema to the Jewish community of Amsterdam, the Englishman Tom Payne who espoused the cause of the American Revolution, the Norwegian dramatist Henrik Ibsen who waged an unceasing war against conventional Christianity, and others whose names do not come readily to me, but all "movers and shakers of the world". No wonder when I left, or was asked to leave, my third cheder in as many years, my exasperated mother called me a real "skooder", a word that remained a mystery to me until I learned that my father came from Skuodai, a small town near the Lithuanian-Latvian border.

Finally it was decided I should go to Zoller's cheder if I were ever to become bar mitzvah. In Zoller's cheder, it was said, everyone learned to read. He was meticulous and thorough and brooked no nonsense in his house. When my father took me there for the first time, Zoller, a portly bearded German, wearing a black homburg, was the picture of geniality. Putting his arm round my shoulder, he led me into a large book-lined room in which about two dozen urchins wearing school caps or yarmulkes sat on benches on either side of three long tables. Not one raised his eyes from his book or stopped his sing-song recital of the Torah to look at the newcomer. Two prefects, like capos, walked up and down the passageways alert to detect any misdemeanour, as I learned later. This should have served as a warning but at the time it escaped me.

Within a week or two, Zoller was pouncing on me from behind, twisting my ear if I stopped to whisper to my neighbour, "Where's the place?" which I was constantly losing. He also used the cane freely. Grabbing the tip of the victim's fingers, he would bend them back until the palm was as tight as a drum, and then bring the cane down with a vicious cut.

Since many of his pupils were often delayed at school or at home, Zoller arranged his classes in three overlapping periods each of two hours; from five to seven, five-thirty to seven-thirty and six to eight. In this way he was able to accommodate the maximum number of pupils in the time and space available. In effect he was squeezing a quart into a pint pot. There was always some congestion on the benches between six and seven but on the whole the scheme worked because Zoller insisted on prompt arrival at the beginning of each allotted period. Anyone arriving five minutes late found himself enjoying an extra half hour's tuition. Since the tuition consisted of a continuous reading of the Torah or the Prophets it did not matter when you came in.

Zoller controlled the ebb and flow of pupils by issuing a white cloakroom ticket to those who arrived at five o'clock and a blue ticket to those who came at five-thirty. These tickets were returned by the pupil when he left at the end of the prescribed period. Tickets were not issued after half-past five.

Apart from Zoller the arbiter of our fate was a large wall-clock. On its battered face were the faded words "Maples & Co., London". Never did a clock extend Time like Zoller's clock. The downward progress of the minute hand was reasonable, but the climb upward from VI to XII was agonizing. Who would have imagined that a cloakroom ticket and a Maples' clock would come between me and bar mitzvah?

I must admit I had already had my fill of ear-twisting and caning when I rushed into the room on that bright summer day three months before my thirteenth birthday. I was anxious to get the two hours over with so I could enjoy the rest of that day. The hands of the clock stood at twenty-five past five. Zoller was on a ladder sorting out his books on the topmost shelf. The class was deep in the Torah. He looked down, saw me standing at his desk, and continued with the sorting, pausing to peruse the contents of the books from time to time. Finally he climbed down the ladder and looked at me as if he were seeing me for the first time. It was nearly twenty to six.

"Vot are you standing there for, boy?" he said in his thick German accent. "For my ticket," I replied. "Vot ticket, you stupid boy? It is already twenty to six. I do not give tickets at this time. You should know that." He was enjoying himself. He was telling me I could not leave until eight o'clock, until the day was almost spent. When I still remained standing he pushed me into a seat that had just become vacant, pointed with a thick finger at a book that was still open and said, "Read!"

I may have made a pretence of reading, but I did not read. Instead, I watched the clock as I had never watched it before. At twenty-five minutes past seven, exactly two hours after I had arrived, I got up, closed the book, walked quickly past the astonished Zoller sitting at his desk, hurried down the long lobby, opened the front door, slammed it behind me, and never came back. Thus ended my final attempt to become a "son of the commandment".

But I won a bursary to Allan Glen's School.

". . . and you sat an exam for a bursary for Allan Glen's (wrote my sister in February 1987) and when the results were published we looked at the list and there you were, the very last. And you wouldn't have been even there if it hadn't been for Henny's nagging to get you to do some work."

My brother had entered Allan Glen's with a similar bursary six years earlier and had proved an outstanding pupil. Now he was about to enter the medical school at Glasgow University and I was expected to carry on where he had left off. It was intimidating, to say the least.

To understand what it meant to me (and Henny) to be selected for A.G., as it was affectionately known, it is necessary to know something about its history and its aims.

Allan Glen, born in 1772, was a successful tradesman, a wright by profession, and a capable business man. An active and earnest supporter of the Unitarian Church in Glasgow, he left a considerable portion of his property for the endowment of a school which, in the words of his bequest, "would be free of sectarian trammels". Within three years of his death an advertisement appeared in the *Glasgow Herald* on Friday, 14th January 1853:

Teacher Wanted
for
Allan Glen's School

"The late Mr. ALLAN GLEN, Wright in Glasgow, having by his Deed of Settlement, appointed his Trustees to set aside a certain portion of his Estate for the erection and endowment of a School for giving a good practical education to and for preparing for Trades and Business from Forty to Fifty boys, sons of Tradesmen or Persons in the Industrious Classes of Society; and his Trustees having erected a suitable School House with playground and other conveniences – fronting Cathedral Street and Hanover Street and a commodious dwelling-house for the Teacher above the School and being now about to carry Mr. Glen's wishes into effect, they wish to appoint a Teacher who must be qualified to teach Reading, English Grammar, Geography, Writing and Arithmetic; the lower branches of Mathematics and such other branches as may be necessary for giving a good practical Education to the Boys attending the School. No student who has ulterior views to the Church or any other Profession need apply . . ."

The trustees were obviously not sitting on their hands because applications for the job had to be submitted by 31st January, and those for admission to the school five days later. They soon selected a teacher whom they subsequently found to "give much satisfaction". Fifty boys were selected as pupils and the school was opened in May of the same year.

By the time I became a pupil, the original small, self-contained two-storeyed house had long been replaced by an imposing sandstone building on the same site, and the multi-disciplinary Teacher by more than forty masters, each a specialist in his own field. The pupils were drawn from a wide area round Glasgow. They came each morning by train (Queen Street and Buchanan Street Railway stations were within convenient walking distance of North Hanover Street), by tram from eastern outposts like Airdie and Coatbridge, by bus and cycle. Through the portal of the school came aspiring chemists, physicists, doctors and engineers. Allan Glen's, a pioneer in its field, had become the High School of Science. But in recognition of its motto *"Cum Scientia Humanitas"* the curriculum also included those subjects usually found in secondary schools. We were taught Latin (necessary to enter medical school in those days), but out of respect for our founder, no Greek.

We usually remember our teachers, not so much for their worth as for their eccentricities. Certainly, two or three of them were real "originals". There was Mr. Augustus Hodge. "Gussy" would never go barefoot so long as he taught Latin at Allan Glen's because, on the day of the Oxford-Cambridge boat race, each class that he taught presented him with a pair of light blue socks. Gussy was a Cambridge man. And no Latin would be taught that day because the length of the blackboard was taken up with a chalked outline of the Thames from Putney to Mortlake.

He would explain to us the tactics to be adopted on winning the toss. Depending on the wind and tide prevailing at the time of the race it might be preferable to choose the Middlesex rather than the Surrey side, or vice versa. It was all over our ignorant heads but so long as he went on for the whole period we were satisfied and, of course, we all rooted for Cambridge.

I never did learn much Latin from Gussy. In fact, I had to sit the University Entrance Examination in Latin to get into the Medical School. I managed to pass after studying through a long hot summer. However, I remember to this day one of his pearls of wisdom.

"The word 'city' in Latin is U-R-B-S. But it is pronounced U-R-P-S. The eye –" (with a glint in his own) "catches the B but the ear catches the PEE." And we would hoot with laughter, in which he would join.

Another master, who was known to have a heavy hand with the belt, excelled himself one morning when he took on a whole classful, twenty-five of us in all; one on each hand without pause, for refusing to name the oaf who had scrawled an obscenity on the blackboard. I would be a hypocrite if I said it did us no harm. It hurt and I hated him. But I forgave him when he marked one of my essays, eleven out of ten. A mark I have never exceeded since.

Years after, when I was in my final year in Medicine, I met him in the Picture House Café in Sauchiehall Street, a favourite haunt of students and ladies of the Town. Although, apart from that essay, I had never been in any way distinguished in his class, he at once recognized me and addressed me by name. When I thought of the hundreds of boys who had passed through his class, I felt honoured. He asked me what I had been doing since I left school and, when I told him I was in my final year in Medicine, he asked me if I could advise him about a very good friend of his who had fallen ill with consumption. It tickled my vanity that our roles were now reversed. Drawing on my new-found knowledge, I gave him a lecture on the cause, signs and symptoms, treatment and prognosis of pulmonary tuberculosis. As for the latter I did not paint a very hopeful picture of the outcome. In these days there were no antibiotics, no streptomycin or isoniazid. His friend would have to go into a sanatorium like Ruchill Hospital, where I had just completed part of my training. He might have to lie in bed for weeks or months, often out in the open, in good weather and bad. He could go to Switzerland where the high mountain air was purer than in smoky Maryhill, but that cost money. "Was his friend well off?" "No, he was not well off. In fact, his illness might have been caused by his straitened circumstances." It might be necessary, I continued to tap the fluid that sometimes collected in his lungs, or even to collapse the affected lung itself by instilling air into the pleural cavity. Sometimes the throat was sprayed with a local anaesthetic to allay the pain when the larynx and the pharynx were affected.

I pulled out all the stops so he would know I had not been wasting my time at the University. He listened attentively, asked the occasional question, and then he rose, shook me solemnly by the hand, thanked me and left the restaurant. I never saw him again, but I came across his name in a small paragraph in the inside pages of the Glasgow *Evening Times*

". . . a retired schoolmaster, was found dead on the banks of the Forth and Clyde canal. He had been ill for some time. Foul play is not suspected."

Sport played an important part in school activities.

From the time the first soccer match was played in 1891, the school had a long history of successes, culminating in 1921-1922 when the First Eleven won the Secondary Schools Shield. Over the years many of the masters had been closely associated with the Queen's Park Football Club, the premier amateur club in the country. But rugby was becoming increasingly popular and it became difficult for the school to play both codes.

When I entered Allan Glen's in 1924 I had high hopes of being selected for one of the junior soccer teams. Since the days of the "broken building", I had been playing, summer and winter, for one boys' team or another. But it was not to be. In that year, in keeping with other High Schools, we went over entirely to rugby. New playing fields at Bishopbriggs had been acquired for the purpose.

If those who effected the change had little enthusiasm for soccer (with its proletarian overtones), some of us had less for rugby. I was a head shorter than most of those who played the game, and since I intended to keep mine as long as possible, I did not play rugby. I went out to Bishopbriggs with the rest of the class and jogged round the pitch under the watchful eye of the games master. More than once he pressed me to play but I told him it was not for me. On Saturdays I played soccer on the ash-covered pitches of the Glasgow Green with lads who had never heard of Allan Glen's or been to a grammar school for that matter. In school I dribbled a tennis ball in the playground with one or two subversives until it was confiscated by my friendly enemy, when I would return next day with another ball. I don't think he saw any point in carrying on a feud with a twelve-year-old boy, so we came to an unspoken agreement. I would confine my soccer to Glasgow Green and he would not press me to play rugby at Bishopbriggs.

I was in the third form when I made my first, and what was to prove my last, explosive. I had read, I no longer remember in what book or magazine, that iodine reacts with aqueous ammonia to form a dark-brown solid called nitrogen tri-iodide, with the chemical formula $NI_3.NH_3$. In the dry state this compound is so unstable it will explode with great violence at the slightest touch. What caught my imagination was the claim that brushing it lightly with a feather is sufficient to set it off. I could see possibilities in nitrogen tri-iodide. A few particles on a teacher's desk or on the stairs of a tenement could give rise to interesting secondary reactions. It was not the kind of experiment that one was likely to find in a school text, and this was so. Consequently, my methods could hardly be described as scientific.

While the rest of the class was busy with a textbook experiment, I set up my own at the end of the laboratory as far from the master's desk as possible. I poured a quantity of ammonium hydroxide into a flask, added a handful of iodine crystals, mixed them thoroughly together, and set the flask on a tripod over a Bunsen burner. As the contents of the flask came to the boil, brownish black floccules began to form in the fluid. Was this the nitrogen tri-iodide I was looking for? When I thought the reaction had gone on long enough, I turned the Bunsen off and collect the violet-tinted fluid. I took the precaution of setting up the filter stand in a cupboard under the bench, as much for secrecy as for safety. Next morning, surrounded by a half-circle of awed class-mates who had been let into the secret, I opened the cupboard door and there in the apex of the filter cone was a black deposit about the size of a pea. Warning my audience to stand back, I stroked the surface of the pea with a feather borrowed from my mother's best hat. Nothing happened. I stroked the deposit again, a little more vigorously. Again nothing happened. The awed silence had now turned to jeers. Piqued at the failure of my experiment, I lifted the filter paper out of the glass funnel, and with my hand still in the cupboard, pressed the deposit firmly between my fingers.

There was clap of thunder which must have been heard throughout the school. A stout Winchester quart bottle in the cupboard split from top to bottom, spilling its contents all over the floor. My fingers felt as though they had been struck by a gigantic hammer. I counted them carefully and they were all present.

The chemistry master looked up from the book he was reading and said, "Mair, do be a little more careful", and returned to his book.

I am sure he was aware all the time what I was up to. But a man who, only a few years before, had revealed the wonders of chemistry to Alexander Robertus Todd, later Baron Todd of Trumpington, recipient of nineteen honorary doctorates, member of innumerable learned societies and winner of the Nobel Prize for Chemistry, was unlikely to let the prospect of a violent explosion curb the curiosity of another of his pupils.

The person who made the most lasting impression on me was John Talman, who taught English Literature to the senior boys. He was a fervent advocate of those writers he liked and a vitriolic critic of those he did not. He could be amusingly or bitterly sarcastic as the mood took him.

Once, he gave us an unusual assignment. We were to write a poem, in any form and on any subject. But it had to be finished before the end of the period because he proposed to read our efforts aloud. I cannot speak for my classmates, but I sat staring emptily at the paper in front of me, scratching my brilliantined head from time to time to summon up inspiration.

Before the end of the period, Talman called in the papers and began to read the poems to the class. Most were couplets, others dubious limericks and one brave attempt, a sonnet. Then he picked up one paper, looked at it impassively for a long time, looked at me over his half-moon spectacles, then held the paper aloft for all to see. It was completely blank except for my name and a set of greasy fingerprints.

"Behold!" he said, "the sweat of Mair's brow."

The applause was loud and prolonged.

If he never gave me eleven out of ten for an essay, he did give me the Vth form prize for English, *A Quartet of Comedies* by H. G. Wells.

To Talman, teaching English Literature was a crusade and not a chore, and I believe I might have followed him into that promised land had he not threatened to expel me from the school. I was then in the VIth (and last) form. In three months I would be ready to say goodbye to Allan Glen's.

The school was preparing for a concert and pageant at St. Andrew's Hall. Talman, who was actively engaged in the production, asked those of us who were not taking part in it to stand. He then asked us if we were prepared to act as ushers and programme sellers on the night. Most agreed. I, and two others, did not. We were left standing, isolated, hands behind our backs, like deserters before a firing squad. Only the stakes were missing. But he executed us just the same when he said to the fellow standing next to me, "Maclean, I did not expect to find you among the dregs of the class."

These words are etched in my memory. They were vindictive and uncalled for. But there was worse to come. Outside the classroom I said to MacLean, "Talman had a bloody nerve calling us 'the dregs of the class'."

"Aye," replied MacLean. "That's Talman all over – pays me a compliment and insults me all in the same breath."

MacLean may have treated the insult lightly but I was not satisfied. The words rankled. Next day as the class assembled, I waited outside for Talman and told him I objected to the words he had used to describe me because I had not volunteered to sell his programmes. He did not seem to know what I was talking about. (I saw no need to tell him I had refused because I thought my best and only suit was not up to the occasion.) I repeated what he had said, word for word. He denied using them.

I said, "If you don't believe me, why not ask Maclean? He heard you."

Talman flared up. "Are you calling me a liar? If you do not apologise this instant you will not enter my class or the school again."

Before I could reply, he went on to remind me of the sacrifices my parents had made to put me and my brother through the school and what it would mean to them were I to be expelled.

I went away to think about it. I had not much choice. Next day I told him I was prepared to apologize but it was only because of my parents. He had the grace to accept that. I went back into the class.

At the end of the term he awarded me the prize in English, Galsworthy's *Forsyte Saga*. Was this a peace-offering? I shall never know. I passed the Higher Leaving Certificate examinations and entered Glasgow University Medical School in October 1930. The following year, John Talman departed to become Rector of Glasgow High School.

Chapter 3

The Wheel of Fortune

At the beginning of the twenties the family fortunes took a turn for the better when Father went into partnership with his brother to manufacture sofas, chairs, tables and other sundry furniture. The venture prospered and soon they were employing many workers and supplying stores all over the town.

In 1926 Father decided it was time to leave Stockwell Street and move to Mount Florida, a suburb in the south of the city. Our new home, on a hill, was a detached granite building with a basement, two floors and an attic. Where once, Henny, Ray and I had shared one bedroom, we now had three to choose from. My choice was a small bedroom that looked down on the garden and beyond that to a gravel football pitch which served as a car park for the main stand of Hampden Park, the Mecca of football. At that time it was the largest stadium in the United Kingdom and home of Queen's Park, the premier amateur football club. Once, when a November fog lay heavy on the ground, I stole through the garden gate with a football under my arm, crossed the gravel pitch, slipped through one of the open entrances of the stand and climbed on to the sacred turf. In the impenetrable fog, unseen from the pavilion, I dribbled the ball through the goal posts, time and time again, to the roar of thousands. In the basement of our new home I set up my first laboratory with a bench and shelves made in the workshop. What boy could ask for more ?

Each morning Henny, in a sober suit befitting one who was about to start ward rounds at the Western Infirmary, and I, in my trim blazer, would take the tram to the city centre, where we parted company, Henny to Kelvingrove and the University and I to North Hanover Street and Allan Glen's. Father had already gone to work two hours earlier. At first, Ray stayed at home to help Mother until we acquired a maid-of-all-work, a young girl pink and fresh from an Irish farm. She scrubbed and cleaned and washed the dishes, learning to recognize which were for meat and which for milk. For her services Bridget received a few shillings a week, her keep and a bed in the attic. Ray went off to learn shorthand and typing so she could help Father in the office. In retrospect, I believe she was the cleverest in the family. Later, when I told her our parents had made a mistake in sending their sons to the University instead of their daughter, she replied that Father had offered her the chance but she had declined because she was not clever enough. But I am sure that was not the real reason. She had refused because she believed that putting two through the University was burden enough, without adding a third. Ray was not pretty but she had beautiful eyes and she sang all day in a pure sweet voice as though she hadn't a care in the world. Mother used to call her "Bontche Shweig". This is a classic short story by the great nineteenth-century Yiddish writer Isaac Loeb Perez. It is the tale of Bontche Shweig, who never complains no matter whatever happens to him in life. God and His Angels get to know of his wonderful acceptance of this, the best of all possible worlds, and when he dies bells are rung in heaven. When Bontche comes before the Heavenly Court, God's advocate recites a long list of miseries and indignities suffered in silence, and it takes Bontche a little while to realize they are talking about him. Finally he is told, "Take what you will."

"Taki?" he asks shyly.

"Yes, really!" answers the advocate.

"Taki?" asks Bontche again, still doubtful.

"Taki! Taki! Taki!" comes the answer from all sides.

"Well," says Bontche, "if you don't mind, I would like a hot roll with fresh butter for breakfast every day."

The angels go away laughing.

Our idyllic existence lasted exactly two years, swept away by the Great Depression of the late twenties. 'Mair Brothers', apparently unprepared for the debacle, found itself squeezed between debtors who would or could not pay and creditors who refused to wait. Against the wishes of his younger brother, Father refused to go bankrupt. He paid his creditors twenty shillings in the pound and in the process lost his brother, his factory and his home. The wheel of fortune had turned, so that we, who had been sitting comfortably at the top, were now hanging on by our finger-nails at the bottom. It broke my heart to leave the home in which I had been so happy. I dream about it still, two constantly recurring dreams, or rather the same dream with variations. In one dream I am in a high-ceilinged, wood-panelled room with a long mahogany table in the centre and elaborately carved chairs on either side. On the table is an ornate candelabra. The walls are hung with family portraits. I am evidently in a stately home and the home is mine. But soon cobwebs begin to hang from the branches of the candelabra, the pictures tilt on the wall, the table is covered with dust and I wake with a sense of loss, In the second dream, I am walking along a country road with a companion. I point out to him a ruined ironstone house on a hill, always on a hill. It is vaguely familiar. I say to my companion, "Do you see that house up there? I used to live in it but it's gone to ruin since I left."

Again the feeling of loss when I awake.

We moved to Houston Street in Govan, a distressed area racked by unemployment. Father looked on this as a temporary measure until he had built up his business again. We stayed there for five years.

With one exception, I have little recollection of the life we led in Houston Street. Age, which dims our sight with incipient cataracts, provides us with rose-coloured spectacles to view the past. We remember what we want to remember and forget that which is too painful to recall. I try to take this into account in my writing of this memoir.

According to Ray, the poverty there was no less than it was in Stockwell Street. She tells of the day a neighbour asked Mother to have a look at her little boy who was ill in bed. Entering the flat, she was shocked to see that there was nothing on the kitchen table or on the stove. The floors were only bare boards and the boy was covered with a thin blanket and nothing else. "You could see through it," Mother said. She covered the boy with a blanket from her own bed and told the distraught woman she must call a doctor because the boy was very ill.

"I canna get a doctor. I haven't any money for a doctor."

"Never mind," said Mother. "Get the doctor, you can pay him later."

The doctor came and diagnosed pneumonia. The boy recovered in hospital. Later, when they met on the stairs, the neighbour said to my Mother, "Mrs. Mair, I owe you my son."

I have one pleasant recollection of my life in Houston Street. The apartment we lived in must have been larger than the tiny flat in Stockwell Street, because Bridget came with us. Perhaps she had nowhere else to go, or by this time she had become part of the family. If the latter, then ours was a brief incestuous relationship which occurred a few months before she returned to Ireland. Maybe, she wanted me to keep some remembrance of her. But now, in my old age, in the limbo between sleep and awakening, when I try to bring back her "pale, lost lilies" she eludes me.

We had been living in Houston Street for two years when the Wheel began to turn. Father had re-opened his workshop under the old railway arch. His customers were coming back. He was so busy that from time to time, during the school holidays, I was called upon to trundle a push-cart full of frames to the upholsterers. I was following in Alec Bernstein's footsteps, and he never failed to remind me of it. Then one day, when Henny was about to enter his fifth and final year, the Wheel of Fortune stopped and went into reverse. What began as a common cold became a serious purulent infection of his ears and nasal sinuses. Penicillin as a therapeutic agent was ten years in the future. Both of his mastoids became infected. In great pain, he was admitted to hospital where he underwent several operations. When the surgeons were finished with him, the infection was under control, his life was saved, but he could no longer hear. He spent several months convalescing with relatives in South Africa. He came back brown as a berry, but still deaf as a post.

My desperate parents tried one specialist after another to no avail. Today, with all the aids available to handicapped people, it might have been possible for Henny to complete his final year and find a place as a radiologist or a laboratory worker. But in their absence, and the medical school unwilling to make concessions, Henny decided to join Father in the workshop. Under the sign of "L. Mair & Son" he worked there for more than forty years until he retired in 1970. Like Ray, he never married. When my parents died, he and Ray continued to live in the terrace house in the village of Thornliebank, to which the family had moved for the last time in 1933. At five o'clock each morning he left, at first with Father and later alone, for the long tram journey to the Gorbals. He rose early because he had to melt the cakes of glue to the right consistency and that took a long time, and there was the timber to be cut to the right lengths so that the workers who came in later could start assembling them at once. He chain-smoked at least sixty cigarettes to help him through the day. When he returned in the evening, after supper he read the *Evening Times* and then tended the exotic plants that filled his bedroom and spilled over into the living room. I do not know if he ever looked at a medical text again.

Chapter 4

"Now I sojourn among the wise"

I. Phyllis in verse

My brother had been working at the bench for a year when he gave me his textbooks, signifying his final break with the past. With the help of a Carnegie grant and the support of my family I went up to the University carrying his old leather briefcase containing some of his books and a notebook inscribed with my more profound reflections and a few tentative verses. To commemorate the occasion I wrote on the first page "Scrapbook of a budding genius, 8 October 1930." I had just turned eighteen.

I soon came into conflict with Henny and to a lesser extent with the rest of the family. Henny had been a "slogger", studying every night often for several hours. I was expected to do the same. But at that time I had a photographic memory. I could quickly grasp the content of a page and recall it readily. Anatomy, as it was taught then, was like memorizing a railway timetable.

As for physics and chemistry, I soon realized that what I was being taught was a repetition of what I had already learned at Allan Glen's. In the evening I was able to dispose of my studies quickly, and in the absence of a date, it seemed to me that the only thing to do was to find out what doctoring was all about. At that time, the pre-clinical subjects were taught at the University. The medical student did not enter the teaching hospitals, like the Western Infirmary adjacent to the University or the Royal Infirmary a tram-ride away on the ancient High Street, until his third year. I decided to go to the emergency department of the Royal Infirmary, known to generations of students as "The Gate". For nearly three months, unknown to my family, I went there two or three nights a week and always on a Saturday night.

On a Saturday night, when, in the words of the song, Glasgow belongs to every citizen, the reception-hall of "The Gate" looked like something out of Hogarth. His Rake would have felt at home among the drunken patients and their drunken friends, sprawled on the wooden benches, their raucous laughter mingling with the howls of frightened children. Broken heads and bruises abounded. Occasionally there was the more exotic patient, like the young man who presented himself with the end of his penis resembling a mandarin orange. He swore he had hurt it vaulting on to the seat of his bicycle. Greeted with derision, he confessed he had been, for the first time, with a "hoor", and afterwards, frightened of the consequences, he had poured neat lysol on the endangered part. Another patient seemed to have a similar affliction but on examination the cause was found to be a constricting wedding ring! He was a huge Irish labourer, drunk as a lord, and in great pain. Any attempt to approach him was greeted with angry roars and waving fists. It required five equally brawny medical students to corner him in the dispensary before he was subdued, pinned to the floor and the ring removed with the surgical equivalent of wire-cutting pliers!

Amid all this turmoil, wearing Henny's old white coat, I went round trying to look like a third-year student. I must have succeeded because no-one ever asked me what year I was in. In fact, I became friendly with Mr. Montgomery, a surgeon who sometimes asked me to assist him in the emergency operating theatre. Once, when we were both scrubbed-up and about to amputate a workman's finger badly crushed in an industrial press, the surgeon was called to the ward to deal with an urgent case. As he stripped off his gloves he told me to "carry on". My heart sank when I saw him push through the swing-doors of the theatre. What had I let myself in for? It was one thing to assist the surgeon. It was another thing to perform without his supervision. But I need not have worried. The theatre-sister had seen it all before. I believe she could have operated blindfold. She handed me a scalpel and indicated silently where to make the incisions through skin, muscles and tendons, until I had snipped the last shred of flesh that connected the finger to the hand. I sweated blood trying to tie-off the severed blood vessels, and once again Sister came to the rescue. I closed the wound before Mr. Montgomery returned from the ward. He seemed to be satisfied with what he saw. I had a few sleepless nights and nervous days before the patient came back, also apparently satisfied. At that time the Royal Infirmary, like other teaching hospitals in the country, was a charitable institution, and its patients were grateful for small mercies.

I was just recovering from the effects of that operation when I met Phyllis at a meeting of the Young Zionists. From the moment she sat down beside me it was love at first sight. She had a button of a nose and an oriental cast to her eyes which made her immensely attractive to me. She began by telling me how much she had enjoyed my talk on Tibor Levai, the nineteenth-century Hungarian Jewish poet. Levai was a figment of my imagination. Members of the society were encouraged to read papers on the founders of Zionism like Theodor Herzl and Chaim Weizmann, philosophers like Spinoza, historical heroes like Bar-Kokhba and on the Jewish problem in general. Over time, these lectures tended to be repetitive and, let us be candid, dull. When I was invited to make a contribution I concocted Tibor Levai. It has been said that if a Hungarian enters a revolving door behind you he will be in front of you when you step out. Levai (Mair?) was like that. He was young, handsome, dashing and fearless, victor in countless duels and a reckless horseman who rode from one end of Transylvania to the other, leaving behind him a trail of love poems and broken hearts, Jewish and Gentile. Besides providing him with a life, I had to write his poems. The last poem was about a troubadour (Levai) serenading his love who, unknown to him, is dying in the dark tower above. I had just recited the last verse,

Troubadour, Troubadour, fleet is thy sorrow,
Sunrise will bring what nightfall must borrow,

Sunrise will bring a new love tomorrow,
Troubadour, Troubadour, gone with thy sorrow.

when my friend Morris, sitting at the back of the room, burst out laughing, broke the spell and gave the game away.

So here was this girl who liked my talk, who did not mind being the victim of a hoax; what else could I do but love her? And I was sure the feeling was mutual. When I should have been studying I haunted the street she lived in, in the hope I might meet her accidentally. We went walking over Cathkin Braes and along the stream in Rouken Glen. I wrote her poem after poem and read them to her as we lay close in the high grass. I meant every word when I told her,

> Now I sojourn
> Among the wise.
> New pleasures spurn
> The old despise
> And candles burn
> That truths may rise
> Then I'll return
> And find them in your eyes.

I sent some of my poems to Sir John C. Squire, poet and founder of the *London Mercury*. He sent me a most encouraging letter written in his own hand. The future seemed assured.

Then she met Archie, the furrier. I could not see what she saw in Archie. Admittedly, he was taller and better-looking than I was; he was older and more mature than I was; he was a business-man with more money than I had (I had none). But, could he make her immortal?

Sometimes, I harboured the hope she might tire of Archie and return to me. Then, I wrote, but kept to myself:

> When we meet again
> I shall raise my hat

And say, "Good afternoon!"
And you will smile at that
And say, "Come back so soon?"
Then I will raise my hat
And say, "Good day!"
And you will cry at that
And I shall stay.

When she became engaged to Archie I tried to console myself with the thought that the person who had so enchanted me was not so special after all:

When Love falls out Reason steps in to place
And like a tradesman weighs the loss and gain,
Adds here a joy, subtracts a little pain,
And calculates the beauty of her face.

When Phyllis married Archie, in a bitter moment I wrote an epitaph for a lost love:

She will not be immortal
She will pass
When rime and rain
Have made this stone a glass.

Nevertheless, over the years we could not help but keep in touch with one another. Phyllis died suddenly on 9th October 1987. I sent Archie a letter of condolence and a verse I had written shortly after they were married:

Phyllis won me when she smiled
O'er the hedge aflame with roses
And my twitching heart beguiled
Phyllis won me when she smiled.

Though my suit, last summer filed
With the rest in dust reposes
Phyllis won me when she smiled
O'er the hedge aflame with roses.

II. How Schloss lost his head

Apart from problems of the heart and one or two diversions, most of the second year was taken up with anatomy and physiology. Of the former, Guy de Chauliac, Father of French surgery, wrote at the time of the Black Death, "The surgeon ignorant of anatomy carves the human body as a blind man carves wood" – a lesson I learnt at "The Gate".

How to obtain bodies for dissection was the problem faced by the medical faculties of British universities early in the nineteenth century. So desperate was the shortage that students and surgeons in the colleges sometimes resorted to rifling graves of the newly buried or were prepared to accept corpses from any source and no questions asked. They even imported bodies from Ireland. The body-snatchers or "sack-'em-up boys" as they were called in Glasgow, always took the precaution of carrying the body away unclothed because, in law, abduction of a naked corpse was not an indictable offence. A corpse clothed in even the wispiest of garments was another matter, as the students of Trinity College, Dublin, learned in 1759 from Dr. Robinson, their professor of anatomy. Speaking, I suspect, with tongue in cheek he said,

"Gentlemen, I have been told that some of you in your zeal have contemplated carrying off the body. I most earnestly beg you not to think of such a thing; but if you should be so carried away with your desire for knowledge that thus against my expressed wish you persist in doing so, I would have you to remember that if you take only the body, there is no law whereby you can be touched, but if you take so much as a rag or a stocking with it, it is a hanging matter."

In Edinburgh two Irish labourers, William Burke and William Hare, resorted to murder to meet the demands of the respected Dr. Robert Knox, a leading Scottish surgeon. The two men inveigled obscure migrants, usually women, to Hare's lodging house, made them drunk and then suffocated them. Dr. Knox paid from £8 to £14 for each body, a princely sum in those days when many honest folk were working for only three pence a day. Eventually, after at least fifteen victims had been disposed of, police suspicion was aroused and Burke and Hare were arrested. Hare turned King's evidence and Burke was found guilty and hanged at Edinburgh on 28 January 1829. Hare died in England under an assumed name. Dr. Knox became a corpse himself in 1862 but still lives as the central character of *The Anatomist* by the Scottish playwright James Bridie.

If Glasgow had no murderers to boast of among its body-snatchers, at least it had a *cause célèbre* in the exploits of Dr. Granville Sharp Pattison and his lecturer on surgery, Andrew Russell, with his band of zealous students who were only too happy to compete with the professional body-snatchers. They systematically robbed graves, particularly in Ramshorn Kirk close to their quarters. Angry relatives of the dead took to patrolling the church precincts at night. Heavy stones were put on top of the graves and iron railings erected round them, but this did not deter the thieves. Matters came to a climax in December 1813 when the body of a local beauty, Mrs. McAllister, was "resurrected". Suspicion fell on students of the medical school. An angry mob stoned Dr. Pattison's house and his rooms were searched. In one of them the investigators found what appeared to be portions of the unfortunate lady in a tub of water. The doctor, his lecturer and two students who were on the premises were arrested and hurriedly jailed to protect them from the angry crowd who threatened to lynch them.

The trial took place in Edinburgh in June 1814. Fortunately for Dr. Pattison and his colleagues, the defence was able to prove that the contents of the tub belonged to a woman who had never had a child, whereas Mrs. McAllister had had several children. All four were set free. Public resentment was so great against Dr. Pattison he soon left

Glasgow and emigrated to America, where he became an eminent surgeon and physician. He never forgave the citizens of Glasgow for behaving like savages towards one whose sole aim was the advancement of knowledge.

I have always been intrigued by the story of Dr. Pattison and his body-snatchers because when I was a medical student I indulged in a little bit of it myself. To understand how I came to possess half a human head, I must go back to the first day of the anatomy class. On that day, 161 medical students (150 men and 11 women, to be precise) descended on the dissection room of the anatomy department, some with trepidation, some with enthusiasm, most like me with studied indifference as though anatomy was just another hurdle to get over. The air stank of formalin. It impregnated our coats and our skin. Anyone with a normal sense of smell could tell we were second-year medical students. In our white coats some of us were as pale as the cadavers that lay, strangely sexless, on the metal tables.

We were herded into groups of four. At each table one group was allocated the right side of the head and neck and the right upper limb, another the left side and so on until each group had staked a claim to some part of that vulnerable body. There might be as many as sixteen students at one table. When we had been sorted out, the senior lecturer went round with a register noting down the name of each student and where he had come from. At my table most of us came from the West of Scotland, one tall black man was the son of a Nigerian chieftain and the last, a small man with a pencil-thin black moustache, said in an unmistakeable American twang that he was "Cohen – New York." "Ah! C-o-h-e-n," said the lecturer, prolonging and savouring the name, "One of the Four Hundred, I presume." Back came the answer in a flash, "No Sir! More exclusive, one of the Twelve." It was one of those wisecracks you never forget.

The dissections would begin with one member of the group reciting from the appropriate part of Cunningham's *Practical Anatomy* while his mates took turns at dissecting the stringy nerves and the bloodless veins and arteries. The emaciated muscles were carefully isolated at their origin in one bone and followed to their insertion in another. (One of our favourite quizzes, hallowed by antiquity, was "What is the longest muscle in the body?" Answer: "The penile muscle – it rises in Sauchiehall Street and is inserted in Kelvingrove Park.")

Soon the low-roofed room resounded with a cacophony of voices, muted at first, then becoming more ribald and raucous as the days went by. Behind us were our first-year studies – chemistry, physics, zoology and anaemic botany. Now we were getting down to what really mattered, we were on the way to becoming doctors.

I cannot recall exactly how the different teams rotated but, of course, it involved for each group the dissection of more than one cadaver. Finally, as the months went by, my three classmates and I had reached the last phase of our investigation of the human body. A severed head lay before us on the table. Our task was to dissect the right side of this head. The group allocated the left half had been delayed and would not start on it for another week or more.

Then Schloss appeared. Like Cohen, he was a New York Jew. And again like Cohen, although properly qualified to enter an American medical school, he had found none prepared to accept him. In all, there were eleven such students in my year. Most of them felt they were victims of religious discrimination. It was not possible to confirm this, but it is worth mentioning that the only student of our year to graduate with honours was one of them, Isidore Zerlin, of whom it was written in our Final Year Dinner Book:

"The stone which the builders rejected is become the head of the corner." – Holy Writ

Schloss was fat, lugubrious , balding and looked older than his years. Unlike his compatriots he found it difficult to adapt to our barbarous ways. He came with a tale of having been with two or three groups which apparently he found wanting. The senior lecturer had finally sent him to us. He was really scraping the barrel. My friends, as a courtesy to me, were prepared to accept Schloss provided he fell into our routine.

We explained to him that after lunch we played a frame of snooker in the students' union. Since the game was always played to a finish we were liable to be a little late returning to the anatomy department. We expected him to wait until we returned before continuing the dissection. He agreed. But the next day after an exceedingly suspenseful game we found him busily exposing the trigeminal nerve. I remonstrated with him to no avail. If we were not present at 1.30 p.m. he began dissecting. It was the last two weeks of the term. By this time my colleagues were no longer enamoured of anatomy and preferred to take their books into the warm sunshine of Kelvingrove Park to do a bit of swotting and watch the girls go by. But I remained incensed with Schloss. We had taken him to our bosom and he had stuck a scalpel into it. He was one stubborn Jew, but I also was one stubborn Jew. In retrospect, I wonder if Schloss understood half of what we told him. The Glasgow patois with its abundance of gutturals is understood only by Glaswegians, and is barely intelligible to others. Perhaps it was asking too much from this sad man from the Bronx. But this is now and that was then.

Then, I waited until the next afternoon when everyone including the attendants had gone for lunch. I went into the deserted dissecting room, sawed the head down the middle from back to front, wrapped our half in brown paper, took it home and dissected it on the kitchen table. Mother did not like me to dissect on the kitchen table. She had made that clear earlier, when I had brought home a surplus brain in a biscuit tin for the same purpose. But after what happened to Henny she could not refuse me. I could not be allowed to fail. But I did. In my final year. But that is another story.

Two days later I brought back the dissected half-skull and put it back on the table with what was left of the corpse. In the meantime, I learned that Schloss, to a chorus of "Scram!" and "Beat it!", had gone from table to table, scrabbling among the entrails, crying, "Where's my head? Where's my head?"

But as they say, all's well that ends well. Schloss, like his erstwhile colleagues, passed his anatomy examination, and went on to become a respected physician in the Bronx.

My action did not trouble me at the time, but since then I have often wondered whether, in removing even that small portion of the corpse from the dissecting room, I might have broken the law. After all, society had become more enlightened and more fastidious about these matters since Dr. Robinson assured his students they were safe provided they did not take "a rag or stocking" with the corpse. Recently, I came across the answer in the *London Observer* of 28th August 1988.

> "Two men appeared in a Barnsley court yesterday after the theft of a body from a morgue. They were arrested after the corpse of a 61-year-old man was stolen from Barnsley District Hospital. His body was found 36 hours later in a car park . . . they were charged with breaking into the mortuary and stealing a shroud and sheet. The prosecutor said there was no charge of theft of a body on the statute books."

During the long, summer vacation, in August I think it was, after the anatomy and physiology exams, I went berry-picking in Blairgowrie with my three snooker-playing companions. We were put up in a long wooden shed with whole families, transients and gypsies. We slept in bunks one above the other like inmates of a concentration camp. Once I slept in, for we were worked from dawn to sunset, and the next thing I knew was the foreman shaking me by the shoulder and saying, "Come on, Curly! This isn't a convalescent home."

I was the only occupant of the hut.

We got three farthings for every pound of raspberries we picked and an extra farthing for strawberries, as these were picked with more care. The raspberries were used to make jam and the strawberries were sold by the punnet. The fruit was never picked immediately after the rain because part of the weight would be water. I was told that the gypsies peed in the bucket of raspberries to make them heavier, though I never saw any of them do that. Saturday nights we went pub-crawling in Blairgowrie and on the Scottish Sabbath made decorous excursions round the lovely countryside.

When the berry-picking season was over, my friends stayed on to get work as beaters for the grouse-shooting. I did not fancy being shot at, so I left and made my way westward across beautiful country to Crieff and then to Oban, hitching lifts most of the way, until I came to the western end of the Crinan Canal. Ten miles south of Crinan, lay Tayvallich, a delightful village on Loch Sween, where I found accommodation in a farm near the sea.

Much of the countryside round Tayvallich was bleak moorland. About a mile from the farm I came across a track which led through the bracken and the heather to a narrow promontory jutting for a hundred yards into the sea. On one side of the headland a twisting path ran steeply down to the sea and on the other, halfway down the sheer cliff, lay the decomposing carcase of a sheep. It was a desolate and sad place, its silence broken only by the strident calls of the scavenging gulls and the plaintive baa-ing of lonely sheep. At the very tip of the promontory stood four crumbling stone walls enclosing three tombstones, horizontal moss-covered slabs, the names of the dead obliterated. One stone, larger than the others, had a hole the size of a head at one end and what looked like a muddy stick protruding from its side at the other. It was getting dark so I returned to the farm. When I told the farmer where I had been he raised his hands in horror. He said that most of the locals kept away from the headland because it was haunted by the spirit of a dead shepherd. At the bottom of the cliff, he went on, there was a cave which ran right through the headland from one side to the other. One day, in search of a missing sheep, the shepherd and his collie entered the cave, but only the dog emerged on the other side and its coat had turned white! I asked him if he had ever been down there. "Never!" he said, "I heard it from my father, and he never went down there either."

When I asked him about the tombstone with the hole in it, he didn't disappoint me. Beneath it, he said, lay the corpse of an ancient chieftain who asked for the hole so that he could see the sun set every evening behind the Paps of Jura, which lay on the other side of the Sound.

The next day, in a spirit of bravado, I took a torch and went down the twisting path to the bottom of the cliff. Sure enough, after struggling through a wall of thorns I found the entrance to a cave. High at the entrance, the roof of the cave came to ground within a few yards. I sprayed the light round the empty cave but could not find a crevice large enough for a dog to squeeze through, let alone a shepherd. Either I had been told an old wives' tale or the cave had suffered a subsidence since the shepherd entered with his dog.

But I was not finished with the haunted headland. I went back to the graves. Black clouds were racing in from the Atlantic and a light rain began to fall. I knelt down beside the chieftain's grave and pulled the stick away from the side of the slab. When I had cleaned the mud from it, I saw, from my newly acquired knowledge, that it was part of a human shinbone probably brought to the surface by some animal. I leaned on the tombstone and it rocked!

I can offer no excuse for what happened next. I was seized with an insatiable urge to see what lay beneath the slab. I visualized the dead man laid to rest with his dirk and other war-like accoutrements. I got my hands under the edge of the stone and with a mighty heave propped it up against the stone next to it. There were some small foot bones on the surface, which I placed on a handkerchief. I think the grave must have been disturbed before because I thought I saw a human skull covered by a thin layer of earth. I was about to brush the earth away when I heard a Voice that seemed to come from out of the clouds. Startled, I looked up instinctively. The enormity of what I was doing came home to me. I was desecrating a grave even if only at second-hand. I was no better than Burke and Hare. Then I heard the Voice again, and this time I was relieved because it had an American accent, and I knew whoever God was, he was not an American. When the Voice was answered by a Scottish voice I poured the small bones back into the grave and rolled the stone back into place. A moment later the tourist and his driver entered the graveyard.

The American, an elderly man whose voice I can recall but whose appearance escapes me, explained that he had come to Scotland to look for his roots, a practice that was less fashionable then than it is now. His search for his forebears who had fled from Scotland after the defeat of

Bonnie Prince Charlie's rebellion in 1745 (a story familiar to every Scottish schoolboy) had led him to Lochgilphead, only ten miles from Tayvallich as the crow flies. There he had learned about the graveyard on the headland. Now, he was disappointed to find that the graves could not be identified but he was delighted when I told him the story of the highland chieftain. He would have something to tell the folks back home.

After they had gone, I made my way back to the farm. Two days later, I was in Cleland Lane ready to do my stint in the workshop.

Chapter 5

Cupid and the "Apikornik"

As I write this chapter, I have before me a sixteen-page booklet entitled *Curriculum Book for Faculty of Medicine*. My name, in pale blue ink at the top of its soft cover, is barely decipherable. At the bottom of the cover is printed, "Students are warned that they must take every care to preserve this book."

I have done so for nearly sixty years.

The book records, for better or for worse, my progress through the five years of the course that finally ends with my graduation. In the *Curriculum Book*, honours in the different subjects are recorded as First or Second Class. In my first two years I count several Firsts and two Seconds. In open competition, I also won the Arnott Prize in Medical Physics, for which I received £25, a lot of money in those days. (I should point out that in my family there were no hosannas when I came in first - it was expected of me – and when I did not, someone wanted to know the reason why.)

It is therefore surprising that, when I turn the page, I find quite a different picture. The subjects in the third year are pathology and bacteriology, materia medica and therapeutics, and honours are conspicuous by their absence. The third year, I recall, is the year I went dancing.

I had become friendly with Leon Cohen, the American who had answered the anatomy lecturer so wittily. Leon, in the North American tradition, was working his way through college with his students' jazz

49

band. By the simple reversal of his first name and the perusal of the Glasgow telephone directory, Leon became Noel MacKenzie, the leader of the band. Since I knew little about music and less about jazz, he appointed me unpaid manager at the beginning of my third year. (I may have been unpaid, but there were many benefits on the side.) The band was very popular at student dances and soon I began to come home in the small hours, which did not please my mother. She took to calling me an "Apikornik", a word which puzzled me considerably. I was then, and still am, obsessed with words. When I come across a word new to me, I worry it like a dog with a bone. I chew over the two Oxfords, the *English Dictionary* and the *Dictionary of English Etymology* to learn its many meanings and its origins. Neither was available then. The *English Dictionary* was about to be published for the first time and the *Etymology* did not appear until 1966. Had they been available, I am not sure I would have found the answer, although the answer is there.

The word, as my mother pronounced it, seemed to be a combination of Yiddish and Russian, which she brought over from Lithuania. I knew from her manner and her tone of voice that, if I was not a rake, I was akin to one. And the sooner I stopped being one, the better it would be for everybody. Many years were to pass before I discovered the origin of "Apikornik". "Apikoros", derived from the Greek *"Epikouros"*, was the curse the Hassidim (the Pious Ones) laid on those Jews seduced by Hellenism and the philosophy of Epicurus. The word had indeed come a long way in the last 2,000 years from *"Epikouros"* in ancient Greece, *"Apikoros"* in Biblical Palestine, "Epicure" in sixteenth-century England and finally to "Apikornik" in the Russian Pale and Scotland!

At the beginning of May it suddenly dawned on both of us that the professional examinations would be upon us in less than six weeks. These examinations were held at the end of each academic year and determined one's progress into the next. There was a lot of leeway to make up. The band went by the board. We attended classes during the day and studied long into the night. Leon found what he claimed was the answer to our problem – a handful of pink pills that had just come on the market. They would, he said, keep us awake, alert, bright and confident.

There would be no difficulty in catching up on what we had neglected. Much of our revision was carried out on the street. We must have looked a very odd couple to the policemen walking the night-beat, arguing at the top of our voices with our hands full of texts and notebooks. Sober as judges, except for the amphetamine coursing through our veins, we recited Materia Medica and Pathology like Holy Writ. For the former we memorized the names of drugs and exotic medicinal plants and hoped they would stay with us until after the examination. We ran off lists of pathogenic bacteria for which, at that time, there were few if any remedies. We slogged away for six hard weeks, and at the end we sat the examinations. On the afternoon following the last viva voce, I staggered into a cinema to let the tremors subside. I had been staring for ten minutes at the moving shadows on the screen when I realized that I had been in the same cinema watching the same film only three days before. I left the cinema there and then, resolved from that moment that my days as an Apikornik were over for good – or at least until I graduated. The results came out two days later – we had passed. I cannot recall if Leon ever resuscitated his band. If he did, he must have got a new manager.

I was at a loose end after the exams when my father invited me to play the role of reluctant Cupid, or rather reluctant Eros for the latter was the son of Chaos and much of what I am about to relate can be attributed to that primeval god.

Many years ago, in the City of London, a young apprentice furrier fell in love with his master's daughter. Mr. Pomerantz, a widower, approved of the alliance, but the boy's parents, believing he could get a better dowry than the promise of a future partnership in a precarious business, refused their consent. At that time no one under twenty-one could marry without parental approval. That was the law in England. In Scotland, where the law was different and more enlightened, no parental consent was required after the age of eighteen, provided the groom, in this instance, had been resident in the country for at least three weeks. So, Mr. Pomerantz, who formerly had lived in Glasgow, appealed to my father to help him in his predicament. What he had in mind, he assured his old friend, was very simple. All my father had to do was find the bridegroom accommodation, either at our home or in a modest hotel, for as long as it took to establish Scottish residence. On the day that condition was met, there would be two ceremonies, which my father would also arrange; a civil marriage at a registry office, followed by a religious ceremony and perhaps a small reception afterwards. Forewarned, the furrier and his daughter would arrive in Glasgow for both ceremonies, after which they and the groom would return to London the same evening. Pomerantz did not want to spend more time away from his business than was necessary.

Never averse to taking on more than he could cope with, Father agreed to help his old comrade of the Workers' Circle. He asked me to make the necessary arrangements. In turn, I recruited big Alex MacGregor, a law-student from Inverness, to handle all legal matters. Alex had just failed his final examination and needed money for a second attempt, money we hoped to extort from Mr. Pomerantz for our services.

In due course, Sammy Hertz, for that was the young man's name, stepped off the train at Central Station carrying a suitcase containing, among other things, his tallis and tephillin. He came from an orthodox family, and under normal circumstances it is unlikely he would have disobeyed his parents, but he was in love and that was a different matter.

I found a room for him in Mrs. Geneen's hotel in Abbotsford Place. In retrospect, I don't know if this was the best place to hide a Jewish fugitive, since Geneen's was the only Kosher hotel in Glasgow. But it was near the Great Synagogue in South Portland Street, the adjacent Jewish Institute and the Coliseum Cinema. He could pray, dance and enjoy the vicarious romances of the screen without going far from Abbotsford Place. With all these diversions, time would pass quickly. Mrs. Geneen was also prepared to make her reception room available for the religious ceremony and even provide a rabbi to conduct it.

While I was completing arrangements for the Jewish ceremony, Alex was doing his part too. Sheriff Mackay would hear Sammy's application for Scottish residence three weeks hence in the imposing Justiciary Building opposite the Glasgow Green. Immediately this was granted, the civil marriage would take place in the Registry Office across the Clyde in Crown Street.

The afternoon finally arrived when all the parties involved, Father, Alex and I on one side, and Pomerantz and the young couple on the other, gathered in the corridor outside the court-room where Sammy's application was to be heard. We were surprised to see several constables and other uniformed men, who we learned later were prison warders, passing in and out of the courtroom. I could only conclude that we had come to the wrong place, or something unexpectedly sinister had arisen with regard to the application. But all was made clear to us by a court official who explained that there had been a fracas at Barlinnie Prison and some of the prisoners were up before the Sheriff. There would be a delay, but eventually the application would be heard.

It was late in the afternoon when we entered the courtroom where the Sheriff sat on a high dais. Sammy was called first, and identified as the applicant. Then Father entered the witness box. The judge looked at him over his half-moon glasses and in a solemn tone asked, "How long have you known the accused – I beg your pardon, the petitioner?"

Laughter in court. I wondered how often the Sheriff allowed himself this little joke. After that, it was all plain sailing. Sammy became a temporary Scotsman. But there was no time for congratulations. We rushed out into the street and boarded a tram to the registry office. But, alas! the Registrar had gone home and the office was about to close. We had to be satisfied with an appointment for the following morning.

Disappointed, we made our way to Geneen's hotel. In the reception room the huppah, the wedding canopy, had been erected. A number of guests were already present, including partisans from the Workers' Circle come to meet their old comrade, and a few curious hotel guests who were apparently co-opted to make the wedding look more like a typical Yiddish wedding and less like an elopement to Gretna Green.

The rabbi had not yet arrived. I was tired. I decided to miss the ceremony and return for the three-course meal Mrs. Geneen had promised. I went to the Coliseum to see Charlie Chaplin in *City Lights*.

Two hours later I returned to Geneen's to find the wedding party in turmoil. Everyone was shouting and no one was listening, least of all the rabbi, a very old man with a white frayed beard, a wide-brimmed black hat and a long, black coat, who sat quite oblivious of the storm that raged around him. From time to time, Pomerantz would come up to him, shouting and shaking a fist in his face, while the rabbi would shake his head in return. Even the co-opted guests put in their pennyworth, all to no avail. Poor MacGregor, lost in the storm of Yiddish, stood dumb-struck in a corner, completely at a loss. The two people most concerned sat disconsolately near the canopy; so near and yet so far, because the rabbi refused to marry them.

Finally, I found my father and asked him what this was all about. In a voice choked with indignation, he told me that not only had the rabbi arrived late, but he would not marry them because they did not have a civil marriage certificate.

"But did you explain the circumstances to him, the delay at the Justiciary building, the absent registrar, the appointment for the following day?"

Father insisted he had explained all this to the rabbi. Pomerantz had also explained it. It seemed everyone had explained it. But the old man was adamant. He had never conducted a marriage before without a registrar's certificate and he had no intention of starting now. He wanted no trouble with the Law.

Desperate circumstances call for desperate remedies. I went up to the old man and asked him, "If I get Sheriff Mackay on the phone will you speak to him?"

No sooner had I made the suggestion, than I realized that the judge, who had more important things to think about, like prison mutinies, was unlikely to lend an ear to Sammy's plight. But the rabbi seemed pleased to have the opportunity to talk to a judge about the legality of conducting a Jewish religious ceremony in the absence of a civil marriage certificate. Not surprisingly I was unable to find the Sheriff's name in the telephone directory. Judges need protection from fools like me.

But, as they say, one thing leads to another. I thought of Philip ("Feeshy") Jacobson, a law student and also a good friend. Fortunately, he was at home when I phoned. I explained the situation to him – "Would he play Sheriff Mackay for me?"

He agreed. I called the rabbi to the phone. A few minutes later he returned, beaming. He took off his hat and coat, put on his tallis and yarmulke, and beckoned Sammy and his bride to join him under the canopy.

In normal circumstances it was customary for the groom to be led to the huppah by his and the bride's father. On this occasion Sammy walked between Pomerantz and my father. In the absence of female relatives, Mrs. Geneen and another lady led the bride seven times round the groom to ward off evil spirits. From then on the ceremony proceeded without interruption.

Towards the end, when the bridegroom shattered the wine glass under his heel, reminding us of the destruction of the Temple, that in the midst of joy the miseries of the world are still with us, there rose a great sigh of relief like a hosanna to Heaven. The much-delayed wedding feast was eaten. Pomerantz paid his debts, gathered up his children, and hurried off to catch the train to London.

Some days later "Feeshy" told me he had taken my call in the living room where his parents were sitting. They looked at him in astonishment when he declared he was indeed Sheriff Mackay, that he did indeed grant Scottish residence to a fine young man that morning. He understood the young man was desirous of having both a civil and religious marriage, but owing to a delay in court, the civil marriage had to be postponed. It was most gratifying that in this day and age, when most young people were satisfied with marriage in a registry office, there were a few like this young man who wished to sanctify their marriage with a religious ceremony. It should be encouraged . . . and so on.

"Feeshy" would have made a splendid lawyer. Instead, after he qualified, he went into his father's business, transmuting mountains of old rubber tyres into gold, and using part of the proceeds to expedite the illegal entry of survivors from the Holocaust into Palestine, at great risk to himself.

Did the newly weds repeat their vows in the dusty precincts of a registry office and live happily ever after? I shall never know, because Pomerantz never got in touch with my father again.

Chapter 6

The Final Years

"Missus Rafferty," I said, "this is your sixth baby and you're still a young woman. Don't you think you should do something about it?" She laughed between her grunts and groans, "Och, lad, don't tell me. It's Father O'Donell you should be telling."

It was ten o'clock of a cold, dreary, December night. One hour earlier Mister Rafferty had called at the reception desk in the Rottenrow Maternity Hospital to report that his wife's waters had broken and she needed a midwife right away. So Max Freedman and I collected a black maternity bag containing sterile surgical gloves and dressings, a stethoscope, a bottle of strong potassium permanganate solution, and Munro Kerr's *Obstetrics*. We left the hospital with Rafferty who did not seem unduly disturbed to find himself accompanied by two medical students instead of a qualified midwife. He had seen it all before.

As part of our training we delivered babies at the hospital under supervision. When we were considered reasonably proficient we were expected to repeat the procedure unaided outside the hospital. Our clients were drawn from the densely populated slums surrounding Rottenrow. We worked in pairs, taking all calls between 6.00 p.m. and 6.00 a.m., while the pupil midwives went out in the safer daylight hours. I cannot recall exactly what our quota was, but it certainly was not less than ten deliveries. The students working on "the district" occupied a hostel attached to the hospital. When the hostel was full there might be as many as twelve couples on the continually rotating roster. Those near the bottom of the roster, who had recently delivered a baby, could be assured of an undisturbed night or nights, before they reached the top of the list again. In these circumstances it might take two weeks or more to fill the quota. It was evident to both of us that, although the charge for our accommodation was nominal, it would still be asking much of our parents. If we could fill our quota quickly it would be a help. We decided to go into residence two or three weeks before the end-of-term class examinations, when most of our colleagues would be busy at their books, and there would be few in the hostel. (I had kept strictly to my resolve and had been studying steadily throughout the term so that there was no need for a "last minute" revision.) There was one snag. We were also expected to attend our other classes during the day and visit the mothers we had delivered before going back to the hostel, hardly a hardship if one were called every second or third night. We had no idea how often we would be called, and that nearly proved my undoing.

On our first night at the hostel there was only one couple in residence and they were waiting for their last call, which came shortly after we arrived. I had drowsed off in an armchair when I was roused by the sound of two strident Glasgow voices coming from the Night-Sister's office down the corridor. I went along to see what was the matter. One of the students I had seen earlier was leaning over the Sister's table waving what appeared to be a small flounder. His unshaven face flushed with anger, he slammed the flounder on the table shouting, "Is it or is it NO?"

Equally emphatically, and also flushed with anger, the Sister who was the arbiter in these matters, replied, "It's NO!"

Evidently an early miscarriage did not count as a goal in this league. Later that evening they managed to complete their quota. It was just after they had gone that Mr. Rafferty had arrived to report that his wife was about to go into labour. The Raffertys lived on the ground floor of a condemned tenement, the kitchen door opening directly on the close a few yards from the midden. In a small box-like room the five children were asleep. From the darkness of the recess bed, where Mrs. R. lay under a mound of coats and blankets, came some preliminary rumblings.

On the worn kitchen linoleum stood a table, two chairs and a stool on which sat a stout, cheerful next-door neighbour who had been keeping watch while Rafferty was away. She greeted us with the usual Glasgow welcome – "Would you like a cuppa tea?"

While we drank the hot, sweet tea, by the feeble light of a gas-mantle she told us she had got everything ready for the confinement – a saucepan of water simmering on the single gas ring, clean towels, one of her own sheets she was able to spare, and a bucketful of coal should it turn out to be a long night, which it proved to be. Despite our urgent pleas to "Bear down, Mrs. Rafferty, bear down", our patient seemed to have withdrawn from the contest. I have an imprecise memory of crouching on the stool, half asleep, trying to coax some heat from the smouldering fire in the grate, my gloved sterile hands raised before me as though in prayer. From time to time, when the fire showed signs of dying, I would pick up a lump of coal from the bucket with my gloved hand and drop it in the embers. Then a quick rinse of the contaminated glove under the tap, a dip in the permanganate solution and asepsis was restored. I would then resume my vigil, till Max took over.

In due course, Mrs. Rafferty's sixth provided us with our first birth on the district. For the next five nights babies seemed to tumble out, helter skelter, from all points of the compass, for we were the only medical students in the hostel. One night we were called out three times, and each time, like Indian scalp-hunters, we were able to present Sister with an after-birth, the evidence that our mission had been successfully accomplished. I cannot speak for Max but in that eventful week I was sound asleep in the hostel when I should have been attending the morning classes at the Hospital for Sick Children, affectionately known as "The Sick Kids", and I barely managed token appearances at other classes in the afternoon. I developed a painful rash on my hands from the permanganate solution, which made writing difficult. For the remaining two or three weeks of the term, my attendance at the "Sick Kids" was sporadic at best. I kept up with the work to a certain extent by borrowing notes. I sat the examination in paediatrics and the result had yet to be announced when I was told the professor wanted to see me. I feared the worst. My abysmal attendance record had caught up with me. I might be compelled to repeat the course. The professor was unexpectedly benign. He said he was surprised I had done so well in the examination because he could not recollect seeing me at his lectures or on his ward rounds. My name was in the register, but was I really one of his students?

I told him everything – my successful attempt to reduce the cost of my stay at the hostel and its disastrous sequel. He listened attentively, then he got up and put his arm round my shoulder, and said, "I think we can comply with the regulations if you attend my ward rounds during the Christmas vacation."

It was an unique experience. I was the only undergraduate there. Hitherto, under the conditions of teaching that existed then, I was accustomed to being one of a large group of students jostling to get near the patient being examined by the professor. Now I was in the front row of the professor's entourage of residents, sisters and nurses which made its way leisurely from ward to ward. I saw how he dealt with his small patients. How he allayed their fears with a few quietly spoken words and the gentle laying on of hands. Once, he asked me if I knew the cause of a certain illness. Perhaps I should have known the answer but I did not. Perhaps I could have tried to bluff it out but I did not. I said, "I don't know."

He turned to the doctors and nurses around him and said, "That is the beginning of knowledge."

I learned more paediatrics than I would have done in the normal course of events and it stood me in good stead in the years to come.

My last year as a medical student passed quickly. On Thursday, 14th February 1935, the class of 1930 sat down to its Final Year Dinner in the Students' Union. I was at the head of one of the long tables that filled the dining hall. On either side of me sat two lecturers, Hector MacLennan and Dugald Baird, each destined to become a professor of obstetrics and gynaecology, a physician to the Queen and a Knight Bachelor. Ten years later when I was serving in the Arctic I wrote to Dr. MacLennan, asking if he would kindly look after my wife who was pregnant with our first child and he did so.

On that evening, Dugald Baird picked up the menu with its black and gold cover. He turned over the pages containing thumb-nail photographs of all those present, both students and teachers. Beside each portrait was a quotation traditionally ribald, rude and rarely kind, contributed by colleagues. Baird, evidently found them amusing because he kept chuckling until he came to one page. He looked at me and said, "Have you seen what they say about you?"

I was busy talking to MacLennan and hadn't opened my menu. Fearing the worst, I turned to the Ms and looked at the picture of a not unhandsome, bespectacled young man with a pencil-thin moustache, his head tilted enquiringly to one side, and beside him the words:

> "I have wisdom from the East and from the West,
> That's subject to no academic rule." – Gilbert

That night I became drunk for the first and last time in my life and ended up asleep on one of the delivery tables at the Rottenrow Maternity Hospital.

If my colleagues believed I was not subject to any academic rule, it was not the view of Archie Young, professor of surgery at the Western Infirmary. Early in his career, Archie had been a pioneer in the clinical application of X-rays and as a result his fingers were scarred with painful radiation burns. His tetchiness was notorious and understandable. I should have remembered this when, in my arrogance or stupidity, I argued with him in the viva of my final surgery examination. He was not satisfied with my presentation of the clinical case, an elderly man with a swollen scrotum. I must admit it was not one of my better efforts. But when he took me up on my failure to mention an infected testicle as an obvious cause of the swelling, I protested fiercely. I pointed out that if I had not referred to the testicle by name, I had gone a step further and localised the infection to an important part of it, the "globus major". I had named part of the whole, without naming the whole itself. In retrospect, I was being too clever by half. I believe Archie missed it but was not prepared to admit it. He riffled through my papers then told me to go. I thought I had had the last word, but I was mistaken. Archie, who had deemed me worthy of first class certificates in his last two examinations, ploughed me and I had to sit the test all over again a few months later. This time I kept my mouth shut, and passed "with commendation". I was a doctor at last.

Two lecturers

I have written earlier that we remember our teachers not by their excellencies but by their eccentricities. If I were told, "You are allowed only two recollections of your teachers at Gilmorehill, who would you choose?" without hesitation I would say, "The lecturer with the button-hole, whose name I cannot remember, and Frank Martin whose name I cannot forget."

The former lectures in an auditorium packed from floor to ceiling with second-year medical students, sitting surprisingly mute, as though waiting for something special to happen. As he does every morning of that term, the lecturer enters, his head bowed, his hands behind his back. He carries no notes, because his lecture, like all his lectures, is in his head. In his button-hole is a flower, which he renews every morning summer and winter. He steps on the rostrum and when he lifts his head he sees that his students have disappeared behind waving, leafy branches, as though Birnam Wood, or rather Kelvingrove Park, has marched on Gilmorehill. Here and there button-holes and lapels sport bouquets of dandelions, button-mushrooms, stalks of asparagus and leeks, and even leaves of wild garlic. Some of the vegetables are past their peak, but they serve their purpose. He takes it all in his stride.

"Gentlemen," he says, ignoring the few ladies in the first row, "shall we begin?"

There is an explosion of laughter and cheers. The greenery is abandoned and the notebooks come out.

Years later, when I told this story to my continental colleagues, they were astonished. When they were students they would never have dared to behave in such a fashion. It would have been taken as an affront to their teachers. I have read somewhere that the students of Bologna University (founded in the eleventh century) were known in olden times for their arrogance and pride. The Italians might have looked upon the students of Glasgow University (founded in the fifteenth century) as upstarts, but we felt we had a tradition to maintain. We were all Glasgow "keelies", which in the local patois means vulgar, rowdy fellows or the salt of the earth, depending on whether one spoke for the town or the gown.

Dr. Frank Martin also lectures in a large auditorium, but this time his audience consists not only of fourth-year medical students but also students from arts, science, law and even theology who have come, out of morbid curiosity, to hear him give one of his scatological lectures on forensic medicine or medical jurisprudence, as it was called in Glasgow.

For many of those present, used to more sober, academic presentations, this is an unique occasion. Fifty years ago Hollywood showed only sanitized versions of sex, violence and death. What they are about to see is the real thing. The lecture today, profusely illustrated with slides, is about identification of dismembered human remains. As the pictures of decapitated bodies and scattered limbs flash on the screen, his coarse remarks on many of the slides are greeted with nervous laughter. In retrospect, I suppose his crudities served the purpose of relieving the stress of seeing death at less than arm's length.

On the next day, he talks about infanticide by burning, by cold and exposure, by beating, by drowning, by strangulation and suffocation. The illustrations are disturbing and some of the "guests" leave hurriedly. Martin, oblivious of the interruptions, goes on and on. As to be expected, there is a full-house when he discusses indecent and lewd practices, and he does not disappoint his audience.

We shall never see his like again. We commemorate him in the dinner menu from which I have quoted earlier. The words are attributed to the English essayist and critic, Charles Lamb (1775-1834): "Martin, if dirt were trumps, what hands you would hold!"

Chapter 7

Shangri La

With the letters M.B., Ch.B. (Bachelor both of Medicine and Chirurgery) after my name, all I wanted to do was get away from Glasgow. Mr. Peter Paterson, a tall, thin, austere and kindly man, Professor of Surgery at the Royal Infirmary, offered me the privilege of working in his department at a salary of £50 a year. A privilege I could not afford. I did not love my family the less, but I was twenty-four and had never crossed the border. England was a foreign country to me. I answered an advertisement in *The Lancet* for a house surgeon in the casualty department of the Royal Devon and Exeter Hospital at a salary of £250 a year and was offered the job. I got out a map of England. Exeter was fifteen miles from the English Channel. I could hardly go further south than that.

Exeter is the county town of Devonshire. The Romans called it Isca Dumnoniorum after an early British tribe, the Dumnoni. It sustained a number of sieges because of its position as the chief town in the southwest of England. It was invested by the Danes in 877, by the Saxons 100 years later, and in 1068 by William the Conqueror who built a castle there, called Rougemont from the colour of the rock on which it stood. Kings came and went. Sometimes the town held out successfully, sometimes it surrendered for lack of water.

When I saw Exeter for the first time in 1936, I was enchanted. Timbered, medieval houses leaned over the cobble-stoned streets. Ancient churches held a peacefulness unaffected by the twentieth century. The great Decorated Cathedral of St. Peter, begun about 1275 and finished about ninety years later, dominated the town. But what I saw then, you will not see now. In 1942, the narrow streets and alleys with their ancient houses and churches were destroyed, and the cathedral severely damaged by German air raids. I never learned the fate of the hospital but it must have suffered also from the bombing because of its proximity to the cathedral. It has since been replaced by a new building.

The front of the hospital was on Southernhay where the senior members of the staff had their consulting rooms. It was not unusual for one particular consultant, having completed his ward rounds, to walk nonchalantly along Southernhay to his rooms, with his stethoscope dangling from his neck. It always went down well with the tourists.

The casualty department could never be mistaken for "The Gate". There was little heavy industry in Devon, and carnage on the road had hardly begun. Nevertheless, I was fully occupied because I had to stand in for residents on holiday or on courses. Sometimes I found myself working eighteen hours a day.

I also doubled as a houseman to Mr. Worthington, an ear, nose and throat surgeon. He was a most irascible man in his sixties, whose temper was not improved by his terrible stutter. One day he took a biopsy specimen, a small piece of tissue from a harmless growth in a patient's throat, and asked me to send it to the pathologist for confirmation of its benign nature. I made out the request form. Instead of writing "?benign", in my wisdom I wrote "?malignant". When Mr. W. saw the pathologist's report that the growth was benign and not malignant, he exploded.

"Damn you! Who the Hell told you to write query malignant?" The words came out fluently and without any hesitation. The patients in the crowded waiting room could hear every word. Then he began to stutter – "You m-m-m-make me out a b-b-b-bloody f-f-f-fool, when you're the b-b-b-bloody f-f-f-fool!"

I thought the last sentence would never end. The nurses looked everywhere except at me, while I looked everywhere except at Mr. Worthington. That episode taught me a lesson I never forgot. From that time on, whenever I was at the giving end I said my piece in the privacy of my office.

We were a pretty cheerful and rowdy lot in the doctors' quarters. A long-dead benefactor had endowed the mess with a beer cask to be filled and refilled in perpetuity with the local brew. The intake of the present incumbents was apparently straining the finances of the charity, and we were offered a rise in salary provided we agreed to one full cask a month. Our ring-leader was "The Major", so called, because he intended to enter the Army when he had finished his house jobs. He had us in stitches as he marched up and down the mess, barking,"At the double!", "Tenshun!", "Stand at ease!", all the while twirling his handle-bar moustache. Little did any of us know that three years later he would be doing all this in earnest. His foolishness extended beyond the mess. One night, an unpopular assistant-matron making her rounds came across, in an ill-lit corridor, a nurse in the lascivious embrace of an ardent house-surgeon. At her indignant cry of "Nurse!", the guilty couple broke apart. The look on the matron's face when she saw that the nurse wore a handle-bar moustache kept us happy for a week.

But it wasn't all fun and games. I had been in the hospital barely a month when I learned how some doctors handled euthanasia. I was standing-in for the resident in the general surgery ward. I used to stop and speak to an old farmer dying of inoperable cancer of the prostate, his pain alleviated only by large doses of morphine. He had only one visitor, his middle-aged son, who would sit silently by his bed holding his worn hand. Then after a short stay the son would get up, and if I was there, he would say, apologetically, "Got the cows to milk and I've a long way to go."

One night I was awakened by the Night-Sister. The old farmer had complete retention of urine and was in great distress. I hurried to the ward and with the assistance of the Sister managed to pass a catheter. It was not the first time this had happened. As he lay, relieved, the old man said, "I wish you could put a stop to this. I wouldn't let an animal of mine suffer like I'm suffering. It would have been put down long ago. Can't you do something about it?"

As an agnostic, I had no religious scruples that would deter me from helping him but that decision lay with the surgeon. The next morning the surgeon made that decision. Looking at the old man, he said, "Is he still here?", leaving unsaid, "What are you going to do about it?"

As it happened I did not have to do anything about it as the resident returned the same day. I went back to the ward two days later and the old man's bed was empty.

There was one resident who took this matter of life and death to an unusual extreme. Only when a patient complained was it discovered that this man was visiting patients the night before their operations, and asking them if they were prepared to meet their God.

It was during that year in Exeter, I found to my delight that I had a flair for handling young children. It was not quite a laying on of hands, but a matter of a quiet voice, a gentle manner and infinite patience, learned at the "Sick Kids". There was one technique I devised for examining a child's throat with a tongue depressor. A child asked to open its mouth usually responds by gritting its teeth to ensure that no way will the depressor find its way into the mouth. In such a case I would say with a shrug, "All right, if you want to keep your mouth shut, keep it shut, but say AH-AH . . ." It worked every time.

When the day's work was done, those of us off duty would gather in the Clarence Hotel near the hospital. There we had the privilege of sharing a private lounge with the worthies of the town. In the dining-room, the portly Italian head-waiter – a grateful patient pulled through a stormy appendicitis – was not averse to playing Cupid on my behalf. To impress the probationer nurse with my sophistication, he would present us with a wine I had never heard of, remark on the excellence of the year I had chosen, and with the utmost tact, forget to put it on the bill.

In contrast to the Clarence, we frequented a pub where you could get a pint of rough cider for a penny. One old man sitting by the fire, when he learned I was a doctor, told me a certain cure for corns. On Midsummer Day you put on a pair of woollen stockings and did not take them off until Christmas Eve. Having delivered himself of this homespun therapy, he plucked a red-hot poker from the fire and plunged it into his tankard of cider which had cooled in the telling.

When I had saved enough money I bought my first car for £25 from a farmer at a horse-fair. Originally, it had been a convertible but it could no longer be converted because the metal skeleton which kept the canvas roof extended had rusted in the upright position. It had two seats in front and a dickey at the back large enough for a child or two suitcases, a starting handle at the front and a spare wheel at the back. The tyres were smooth but intact. Because it wheezed so much I called it *Emphysema*. *Emphysema* ran reasonably well on level ground, but confronted with a hill she complained bitterly. I soon became an expert on the topography of Devon and Somerset where my girl-friend, a nurse, took me at the weekends. On a straight, undulating road I could roller-coast with ease. The problem arose when I slowed down at a corner only to be faced with a steep hill. In these circumstances *Emphysema* rarely reached the summit with a passenger on board. When the wheezing became critical I would give the order, "Out with the cases!" and when we were almost at a standstill, "Jump!". When we still failed to reach the top, I would let the car run backwards to the bottom of the hill, and with much of the load removed, attempt another assault. Meanwhile my passenger, who outweighed me by at least a stone, would retrieve the suitcases with ease from the hedgerows.

One night I was returning from Williton in Somerset where I had left my companion at her brother's farm. Fifteen miles from Exeter a tyre punctured. After a struggle in the darkness I managed to replace the wheel with the spare. As I entered Exeter the spare punctured. It was two o'clock in the morning. There was nothing I could do, except drive on. The noise of the iron rim of the wheel banging on the cobbles like an anvil chorus must have been heard from one end of the town to the other. Just before I reached the hospital *Emphysema* finally gave up – a few yards from a corner where a police sergeant was taking reports from three constables. He broke away from them and came striding up to me, obviously outraged at this blatant disturbance of the peace. At that moment I realized my road-fund licence was more than a month overdue. I was shrinking back in my seat when we recognized one another at the same time. We often had a chat together when he brought casualties to the hospital. Shaking his head, he said, "Doctor! What are you up to?"

"Two punctures, Sergeant, and now the engine's gone dead."

He called to the three constables, "Come on, lads, let's give the Doctor a hand."

So they got behind *Emphysema* and pushed her all the way to the hospital. That was her last journey. A month later she was taken away for scrap, and a month after that I said goodbye to Shangri La and took my first step out of Britain. I signed on as ship's surgeon on the "*Glenaffaric*", out of Liverpool bound for the Straits Settlements and China.

Chapter 8

At Sea

Born and brought up a stone's throw from the Clyde, I was never far from the river, the ships and the sea. Every summer Father took the family "doon the watter" to Millport, Rothesay or Dunoon on the little paddle-steamers that plied the Firth. I shall never forget the excitement of going down below to "see the engines", the spinning wheels and the shining pistons tended by demigods in overalls. When I was a student, a friend often asked me to join him on the bridge of ocean-going vessels that his father, a pilot, was taking down the river. Although the Port of Glasgow was beginning its long decline, ships of all kinds still thronged the River Clyde. Ships from the rest of the United Kingdom and further afield discharged and loaded goods at the Broomielaw. I can remember the awe with which we regarded the unfinished Cunard luxury liner *Queen Mary* standing forlorn in John Brown's shipyard in Clydebank. This was the yard that claimed to turn out the best and biggest ships in the world. But on that day the *Queen* stood, a monument to the worldwide economic depression. Started in 1930, work was suspended in 1931 and not until 1934 did work begin again. The ship was finally launched in the same year, and two years later the keel of *Queen Elizabeth I* was laid down in the same yard.

On many a Saturday we made the run down to the "Tail o' the Bank" where the river widened into an estuary. There, the pilot handed the ship over to the Master, and we would shin down the rope-ladder into the pilot boat, which took us across to Greenock where we caught a train back to Glasgow. So it was, when I boarded the *Glenaffaric* on 20th March 1937, I knew enough not to talk about "upstairs" or "downstairs" or "left" and "right", but about life at sea I was completely ignorant. I have a sepia photograph of the reception committee that greeted me on my first day aboard. I am in the foreground. Wearing a three-piece suit, white shirt and tie, and a nautical cap I had just bought at a ship's chandler, I cannot be taken for anyone other than a landlubber. Beside me the plump Chief Steward, wearing a dark uniform with shining brass buttons, waves an order-book he is about to cook. Next to him is a wooden crate stencilled with the letters TIENTSIN. Behind us the Second Engineer threatens me with a spanner and the first mate is smiling at him. We are all smiling, but the widest smile belongs to the Chief Steward and he is a villain. We stand there like the dramatis personae of a play that is to last more than three months.

The *Glenaffaric*, a cargo vessel of about 5,000 tons, belonged to the Glen Line, a subsidiary of the Alfred Holt group, generally known as the "Blue Funnel Line". The Glen ships maintained the far eastern service of the group. They provided accommodation for about a dozen passengers but we had none outward bound and only three on the voyage home. The officers were predominantly Welsh and the crew Chinese.

Next to my cabin was a small sick bay where I held my morning surgery, which consisted of dispensing medicine from large bottles labelled "Cough Medicine" and "Stomach Medicine". A locked cupboard contained surgical instruments and several blue-tinted bottles whose contents now escape me, except for one labelled "Novocaine". We remained singularly free of serious injuries despite the hazards of slippery wet decks and the loading and discharging of cargo.

Passage down the Irish Sea and across the Channel was uneventful. I soon learned I was going to be the butt of in-house jokes. When we ran into a fierce storm in the Bay of Biscay I lost my new cap, which went over the side and disappeared in the ship's wake. The First Mate told me not to worry – he had made a mark on the ship's rail where it had gone over. I also discovered that even in the roughest sea I was never sick, which disappointed my shipmates, deprived of a ritual source of amusement.

I was in the surgery reading Tolstoy's *War and Peace*, which together with Thomas Mann's *Magic Mountains* is about the right length for a three-month voyage, when a Chinese member of the crew came in, pointed at his open mouth and indicated that he wanted a carious molar removed. In a few minutes I had him seated in the barber-style chair I used for reading, unlocked the cupboard and withdrew the bottle of novocaine and a pair of dental forceps. I had never removed a tooth before – tooth extraction is not in the medical curriculum. No sooner had I injected an unspecified amount of the anaesthetic in the patient's gum, than he fell off the chair in a dead faint. Two of his comrades helped him to his bunk where he soon recovered. It looked as though my career as a dentist was over before it had started. But to my surprise, next morning there was a queue of orientals, including my former patient, waiting outside the surgery to have teeth extracted. I explained through an interpreter that I did not intend to use an anaesthetic, but this did not discourage them. Carious teeth fell before my forceps with hardly a murmur crossing their lips. The fortitude they showed made me wonder whether they had dosed themselves with their own opiates before they came to the surgery.

When the Captain, who was an economical man, heard about the mass extraction, he suggested that I might like to remove a tooth that was troubling him. I felt flattered until I heard what had happened to my predecessor, who had accepted a similar invitation. The operation had been a disaster. The Captain was left with a broken tooth and a jaw the size of a cricket ball. The poor doctor sat at the Captain's table watching him eat slops for 3,000 miles till they reached Colombo, their next port of call. There the Captain had found a dentist who charged more to remove a broken tooth than a whole one. Having been warned, I told the Captain I was unhappy about the purity of the novocaine. I did not hear from him again.

Twelve days after leaving Liverpool we arrived at Port Said. We had no sooner entered the roadstead than a coal lighter came alongside. Coaling is a messy business, and so it proved at Port Said, at that time the biggest coaling station in the world. As I recall it, large baskets filled with coal were hoisted up four or five at a time from the lighter and dumped on the deck in an ever-increasing cloud of coal dust. Egyptian labourers then emptied the baskets into barrows which they wheeled to the ship's bunker. When the chief steward generously offered to show me the sights of Port Said, I accepted gladly, anything to escape the black grit that was spreading everywhere. We went ashore in a bumboat with Jock, a young trainee engineer, who was making his first trip abroad. The Chief Steward had taken a liking to the boy and had apparently decided to take him under his wing for the duration of the voyage. There were few buildings of note, apart from the offices of the Suez Canal Company and the British barracks built by Prince Henry of the Netherlands as a depot for the Dutch trade. But the Chief Steward had not come ashore to admire the local architecture. He led his fledglings from bar to bar, and from one dingy night club to another. He was loquacious and amusing as only a London Cockney can be. He told us what attributes to look for in the belly-dancers, though these seemed obvious to me. He drank generously of the beer we bought him, and if sometimes he forgot to reciprocate that did not matter. We were enjoying every minute of our first Arabian Night. Towards the end of the evening, we were accosted at one club by a dark-skinned man wearing a suit several sizes too big for him. He kept looking over his shoulder as though expecting a large hand to descend upon it. It transpired he had something unique to show us. He put his hand inside his jacket and drew out a pack of playing cards still in its original cardboard container. The back of the cards had a nondescript floral design. He crouched over his prize as though to shield it from prying eyes. We only were the favoured ones. Was he trying to tempt us with a pack of marked cards, promising us the prospect of a fortune as we sailed up the China coast? He dipped his finger in the glass of beer he had brought with him to our table and rubbed it several times over the back of a card picked at random until its flowers were thoroughly soaked. Then he inserted a long dirty finger nail into one corner of the card and peeled off the floral design to reveal a man and woman in the Greek position! The Chief Steward said he had never seen anything like it. Jock and I were awe-struck. In our present permissive age this sort of thing is commonplace, but then it was exciting and forbidden. The card, like those portrayed, lay naked in the centre of the table. The Egyptian waited. The Chief Steward was the first to speak.

"Jock, you must buy them. You'll never find anything like these in Broughty Ferry. Just think, fifty-two positions, fifty-three with the Joker!"

From the look on Jock's face, I could see that John Knox was fighting a losing battle with the De'il. Victory for the latter was assured when the Chief Steward said, "If you don't want to take them home, you can sell them to the compradore in Singapore. He'll give you a good price. Puts them in an album."

The prospect of combining business with pleasure was sufficient for Jock to make up his mind. "How much?" he said to the Egyptian who was gathering up the cards and putting them back in the cardboard container.

"Three English pounds."

Jock looked at the Chief Steward, who nodded. The exchange was made. The cards were burning a hole in Jock's pocket and he could not get back quickly enough to the *Glenaffaric*. An hour later I looked in on him to see how the transformations were progressing. Alas! the erotic couple had become surprisingly modest. They simply refused to reveal themselves.

Jock sat at a tiny table in his cabin, a shallow dish filled with water in front of him. He dipped a rag in the water and rubbed it with increasing desperation over the back of a card. The floral design did not budge. Even the Joker refused to change as he does in most games. Dozens of mutilated cards lay scattered on the floor, some with the flowers ripped and scratched, others obviously torn across in anger. Between gritted teeth he kept muttering, "The sod! The bloody sod!"

It was beginning to dawn on Jock that he had been taken for a ride by the Egyptian with the connivance of the Chief Steward.

It was still dark, but dawn was not far off, when the *Glenaffaric* entered the Canal. A great lantern blazing at her bow illumined the banks and pushed the darkness a ship's length away. I had got up early to see this Canal about which I had read and heard so much. When I was a boy I was taught that Benjamin Disraeli, that far-sighted, baptized Jew, when he was Prime Minister, had borrowed four million pounds from the Rothschilds without the sanction of Parliament and bought a controlling share in the Canal from the Khedive of Egypt, who was heavily in debt. By this audacious stroke, Britain had gained possession of one of the chief doorways to the Orient, and Disraeli had rendered to his country the greatest service of his long career.

On the previous night, between visits to bar and night club, I had bought a pamphlet entitled, "The Suez Canal – Map and notes of the world's most important waterway, in English, French, German and Italian." The publisher was one August Rusenberg. This pamphlet, part of my memorabilia, has lain for more than fifty years in the drawers of the bureau my father made for me. If a memoir is an archaeological expedition into one's life, then the contents of these drawers are the artefacts from which I reconstruct it. Hard as I tried, I could never keep a diary. But I kept many letters written by my brother and sister, by my wife and daughters, by friends who shared my youth and now are old men. There are letters and reports from the six years of my life that belonged to the Army and the forty years of it devoted to medicine and microbiology. In these drawers I kept my degrees, diplomas and citations rolled up in the cardboard tubes in which I received them, the Army newspapers printed in the Arctic, the burnt shards dug up at Masada, and guide books like the one I picked up in Port Said.

It is a curious pamphlet, only four inches wide with only two pages of text for each language, but it has a marvellous map which, when opened, keeps unfolding until it is more than thirty inches wide and four inches high – a narrow strip of a map. The Canal has been turned on its side so that it appears to run from west to east instead of from north to south. The sands on either side of the Canal are appropriately bright yellow and the waterway and lakes pale blue. It reminds me of a medieval map. All over the desert areas are beautifully painted cameos of ships entering the canal, convoys moored in passing-bays, sail boats and a passenger ship with two tall blue funnels. Instead of whales spouting and monsters rising from the deep, there is a great obelisk near Ismailia in memory of those who fell defending the Canal from the Turks in World War I and at Port Tewfik a pharaonic war memorial to the honour of the Indian Army. If Biblical scholars are uncertain where the hand of the Lord saved Israel from Pharaoh's chariots, the cartographer knows where it all took place. On the northwest shore of the Great Bitter Lake he has drawn a small cluster of tents purporting to be "Moses' camp before crossing the Red Sea". A red line runs from the camp diagonally across the lake to show the route the Israelites took when the waters parted and they walked upon the dry ground into the wilderness of Ethan in the land of Goshen.

Armed with Mr. Rusenberg's publication, I took up my position below the bridge where the Captain and the pilot were deep in conversation. We had left Port Said and were making a steady eight knots to El Kantara some thirty miles to the south. By this time the lantern had been extinguished and the sun was rising rapidly over the desert. To the right, according to my map, lay Lake Menzelah and to the left swampy land and the country of mirages. I looked for the Fata Morgana but I could not see any wondrous castle half up in the air, half down in the desert, or the shimmering body of water that ebbs away as the traveller approaches it. But I saw a long line of camels plodding slowly across the desert, and it was then I felt I was truly in the Orient. At Ismailia, the halfway point of the Canal, we changed pilots. The rest of the journey through the Bitter Lakes was uneventful and thirteen hours after leaving Port Said we entered the Red Sea.

When the Canal was nationalized by the Egyptians, the old European hands declared the "wogs" would never be able to run it – just as I heard the "old coasters", over their pink gins at the club in Kumasi, swear that the Gold Coast and Britain's other West African colonies would go to pot if ever they had to leave. Their fears were groundless. In the 1960s under Egyptian administration, the Canal was handling fifteen per cent of the world's sea trade and employing more than 300 pilots belonging to twenty nationalities. The Canal was blocked by sunken ships during the Arab-Israeli war in June 1967. It was not reopened until eight years later. At the present time, the countries around the Canal are in turmoil. How long it will remain undisturbed is in the laps of the various gods who claim celestial hegemony over the region.

Three days out of Suez, the *Glenaffaric* came to a standstill, or rather the engines came to a standstill and the ship wallowed helplessly in the long swells of the Indian Ocean. I could see the Captain pacing the bridge angrily. The engineers kept going below and coming up with reports that seemed to increase the Captain's fury. As far as I could gather from the First Mate, a bearing on the propeller shaft had overheated and seized up. The unfortunate officer on watch in the engine room at the time was the Second Engineer who had "threatened" me with a spanner when I first came aboard. He was slaving down below, as far from the bridge as he could get.

The Captain did not radio his plight, to avoid alerting ships that might offer to help and claim salvage. At night, all lights were switched off and two red lamps that could be seen all round from a long distance were hoisted one above the other. To add to the funereal atmosphere, the ship's siren sounded one long blast followed by two short blasts at frequent intervals all through the night. During the two days and nights it took to effect partial repairs I shared his watches on the bridge with the First Mate, who had become my friend and mentor. Ivor Thomas came from a mining village in the Valleys. His father and brothers had gone into the mines like their grandfathers before them, but at the age of fourteen he had opted for the sea. He had a master's ticket but he was glad to have his present job – there were plenty master mariners walking the streets of Cardiff looking for a ship. His greatest joy, when he was not ashore playing rugby, was reading. He borrowed my half-read *War and Peace* and never returned it – a taste of my own medicine. On the second night, when the wind was rising and the ship began to roll, he showed me how to find the constellation Castor and Pollux.

"Draw a line from the heel of Orion on your right, to the middle of his belt, and from there to the bright star on his shoulder, then tilt the line a little to your left and you will arrive at Cast-iron Bollocks!"

Cast-iron Bollocks are the Heavenly Twins who send St. Elmo's Fire to protect poor sailors from the perils of the sea. I often wonder why he chose to recount the myth when the *Glenaffaric* lay dead in the water at the mercy of the elements.

Before the storm broke, the engineers declared the seized bearing sufficiently restored for the ship to proceed at three-quarter speed. A new bearing would be installed in Hong Kong.The Captain, chafing at the time lost, turned his ship round at the intervening ports in a matter of hours so that I saw little of Colombo, Penang and Singapore. However, I still treasure one memory of Penang. On that beautiful island on the northwest coast of Malaya I had the opportunity to see the colonial spirit at its best. I had just turned in for an early night when I was roused by the Chief Steward and the First Mate, "Come on, Doc, we are going to see *On the Road to Singapore*."

Although the grubby cinema was crowded from floor to ceiling, the performance did not begin until several gentlemen, immaculate in cummerbunds and dinner jackets, and their ladies in long evening dresses, having partaken of dinner, strolled nonchalantly, oblivious of the rest of us, to their reserved seats in the centre of the stalls. Were it not for the chatter of excited natives in the balcony, and the rowdy sailors in the stalls all agog to see Dorothy Lamour in a sarong, these ladies and gentlemen might well have been attending a performance at the Royal Opera House in Covent Garden, more than 9,000 miles away.

About seven days after leaving Malaya, the *Glenaffaric* arrived in Hong Kong without further mishap. Cargo was discharged and we prepared for a stay of two or three days while the propeller-shaft was repaired. After the hurried departures from the last three ports of call, I was glad to seize the opportunity of seeing Hong Kong and its twin city Kowloon, half a mile across the harbour on the Chinese mainland. The Chief Steward could not accompany me – he was too busy loading stores – but by a stroke of good fortune I came across a perfect guide in a most unexpected way.

On the evening of our arrival I had just finished dinner at a hotel in Kowloon. I was standing at the top of the broad stone stairway at the entrance to the hotel, lighting a cigarette (how archaic that sounds now!), when a lady in a crimson gown walked slowly past me down the steps, crossed the pavement and entered a limousine parked at the kerb. I could not take my eyes from her and she knew she was being observed because, a moment later, a window slid down and an imperious finger beckoned me to the car. Unlike Phyllis, this lady was a real oriental but, like Phyllis, she spoke fluent English. She said, "You are a nice English gentleman."

Gallantly, I replied, "And you are a pretty Chinese lady."

The conversation could hardly be described as scintillating but it served its purpose. She said, "Where are you going?" and I replied, "I was going to join my ship, but if you have a better idea, I'll go along with it."

So she moved aside and I got into the car. I do not remember if she told the chauffeur where to go, but he started off at once. Close to her, I could see she was not a girl but a beautiful woman, and from her jewellery and the clothes she wore, a woman of substance. It seemed to me we drove for miles and miles, through the dark streets of Kowloon, further and further away from the waterfront and the *Glenaffaric*. I began to ask myself, who was the hunter and who the hunted? At last the car stopped in front of a block of flats, the chauffeur opened the door and his passengers got out. A few words from his mistress and he drove off. It was a very ordinary block of flats, no canopy at the entrance, no commissionaire. We got off at the tenth floor. Inside the flat, in the vestibule, is a group of Chinese gods to guard it while she is away. The living room is spacious and opens out on to a balcony. She pours us both a drink and tells me, spelling it carefully, that her name is Lai Yuk which means Pretty Jade.

This was the prelude to a memorable night in more senses than one. Pretty Jade was a passionate woman and I had been at sea for nearly two months. All passion spent, I was suddenly overcome by an irrational fear, a grim foreboding. The night was hot and humid. There was not a breath of wind. I lay in my own sweat and asked myself, what was I doing, in a strange house, in a strange city, in a strange country, miles from my ship; and I was afraid. (One need not be brave to be foolhardy.)

I conjured up monsters. I knew that behind the closed door, pyjama-clad assassins, perhaps the faceless chauffeur who had received his instructions just before he left, waited for me to fall asleep, and if I did I would wake up in the morning with my throat cut. So, as Lai Yuk slept soundly beside me, I struggled to keep awake. Sleep lay on my eyelids like brass weights that grew heavier with every passing hour. I must have dropped off from time to time, because as the room cooled and the furniture creaked, I would wake with a start and the struggle would start all over again.

I awoke out of a dreamless sleep to find her standing by the bed with a tray, on which stood two cups of pale, fragrant China tea. I had slept well into the morning. Over breakfast she told me that she was the owner of a large store in Hong Kong left to her by her late husband. Her home was on the island. This flat was her *pied-à-terre*. The chauffeur would be coming shortly with the car. He could take me back to the ship or we could cross on the ferry and explore Hong Kong together. So I saw Hong Kong with the best guide anyone could want.

I saw the great floating villages of the Water People in Hong Kong harbour where a man could be born, live and raise a family without once putting his foot on earth, which received him only when he died. Away from the waterfront, the modern banks, stores, hotels and towers that housed the offices of the great trading concerns seemed to be another world, where the business man rubbed shoulders with the ubiquitous coolie, barefooted and stripped to the waist, as he threaded his way through the traffic, the bamboo pole on his shoulder swaying with the huge weights it carried. We stopped for chow at a restaurant offering cooked duck-bills, shark's fins and birds' nest soup. We swam in Repulse Bay, the colony's most popular resort, and took a ride in the Peak Train to the colony's highest point.

It was evening when I took leave of Lai Yuk. After a farewell kiss and an evanescent promise to write, I boarded the ferry back to Kowloon and the *Glenaffaric*.

I always wanted to buy a gold watch for my father, and Hong Kong, a duty-free port, was the ideal place to buy it. Father had got along for years with his battered Ingersoll. Now I had the opportunity to show him how much I appreciated all he had done for me. When I think about it now, it never entered my head to buy a gift for my mother. After all, who would think of schlepping an electric toaster all the way back from Hong Kong?

I told the Chief Steward of my intention. He said there was no need for me to go to an expensive store like Lane Crawford's, which called itself the "Finest Store in the East". A Chinese gentleman of his acquaintance, a regular visitor to the ship whenever it was in Hong Kong, given enough notice, would find the kind of watch I wanted. He could guarantee me a genuine gold watch at a ridiculous price, provided I did not ask any questions. I had heard of Thief Street in Hong Kong, notorious for its thieves and pickpockets, where, it was said, you could buy almost anything at one end of the street, and find the object you had just purchased being offered for sale before you reached the other end. I had no intention of asking any questions, particularly after I had met the old pirate in person. He assured me he would be back on board the *Glenaffaric* as soon as we returned to Hong Kong.

We left the next day for Shanghai. The great sea-port lies in the estuary of the Yangtze and I can remember the distinct demarcation line where the brown silt of the river met the deep blue of the sea. The Japanese had occupied Manchuria and there was a great deal of unrest in Shanghai. I was not anxious to wander too far from the ship. One evening the Chief Steward came up with the suggestion, "Let's go and view the cattle."

I knew he was not talking about an agricultural show. I declined with the excuse I had letters to write. I learned later from Jock what happened. Travelling by rickshaw, they went from one brothel to another. It was definitely a "see – don't touch" occasion. The Chief Steward seemed to be on familiar terms with the madames and Jock had the privilege of buying them drinks. They must have visited a half-dozen houses, the last one being a stone's throw from the docks. When it was time to go, Jock was about to leave by the front door when the Chief Steward called him back, hustled him down a narrow passage to a lane at the back of the house and started running. While the rickshaw driver, who had pulled them all evening from one brothel to another, waited for his passengers, they were laughing all the way back to the ship. For me, that was the last straw. In so far as the confines of the ship permitted, I would have nothing further to do with the Chief Steward.

From Shanghai we sailed north to the Japanese-occupied port of Dairen in southern Manchuria, where we discharged the crate marked "TIENTSIN" and other cargo, picked up a load of soybeans and returned to Hong Kong.

True to his promise, the pirate came aboard as soon as we had dropped anchor. In the Chief Steward's cabin he undid the strings of a leather pouch and poured the gold watches on to a table. One watch had a white enamel face within which there were five subsidiary dials indicating the time in Bombay, Singapore, Shanghai, Peking and Tientsin. Just the kind of watch my father would need if he decided to become an investment broker in Hong Kong. There were hunters and half-hunters and a watch with a twenty-four hour dial. There was even a Patek Philippe but I wasn't sure it was authentic. I finally settled on the twenty-four-hour watch. For my father, who started work so early and finished so late, it would be just the thing. A thin gold chain was thrown in to clinch the deal. While I was bargaining with the fence, for that is what he was, the Chief Steward examined the watch carefully, looked at the works, listened to the tick and declared I had a good bargain. I went away to find a box in which to put the watch and laid it on a bed of cotton wool taken from the dispensary.

We took on our first two passengers. One was a prosperous Dutch business man bound for Batavia via Singapore. The other was a D.B.S., a distressed British seaman, a scrawny London Cockney who came on board with a bandage round his head and kit-bag over his shoulder. He had been admitted to hospital with a split scalp and severe concussion as the result of a brawl with sailors from an American destroyer. His ship had sailed for England before he was discharged from hospital. He was embarrassingly grateful for my ministrations.

"Mind you," he said, "I haven't much time for ship's doctors. I've met plenty in my time. If they aren't boozing, they're sitting with their feet up sleeping it off. But you're different."

I enjoyed talking with the Dutchman. He had so many stories to tell about life in China, and especially about Hong Kong where he had lived for many years. I don't know what made me show him the watch. He looked at it politely, and then with a puzzled expression. When he opened the back of the watch he became plainly agitated.

"Please wait here," he said, handing me the watch, "I will return in a moment."

He came back with what looked like a small pocket diary. He opened it and showed me a page which, he said, contained a list of valuables and their identifying marks or numbers. He asked me to open the back of the watch. No wonder he was surprised. Eight tiny numbers engraved on it were identical with eight numbers in the diary! He explained that it was necessary, under conditions existing in Hong Kong, to be able to identify valuables, especially for insurance purposes. And this watch was a perfect example, because his home had been burgled only a week ago and many valuables, including this watch, had been stolen. He could hardly believe that it had turned up so providentially. Did I think I would be able to identify the man who had sold it to me? I told him it was unlikely since most Chinese looked the same to me. I left him holding the watch and returned to my cabin cursing my luck.

Before long my misfortune had made the round of the ship's officers. There were two factions. The younger men and the D.B.S. argued that the watch should be returned to the "Doc.". After all the Dutchman could buy dozens of these watches without turning a hair. Besides, he would receive money from the insurance. The more senior officers, including the Chief Steward, with a righteousness which must have surprised even themselves, were on the side of the law. The watch was stolen property and it had come back into the hands of the rightful owner. It was my bad luck to have found him myself. There was an unpleasant atmosphere in what had been a cheerful mess-deck. I wanted to be finished with the whole business. The evening before we arrived in Singapore the Dutchman came to see me in my cabin. He offered me the watch. I refused.

"Take it, take it," he said, "it is yours."

"I don't want charity," I replied.

"No! No! It is yours," he said again. "It is not mine. It once belonged to someone else, but now it is yours."

Then he told me everything from the time I left the Chief Steward's cabin to find a box in which to put my father's watch. The Chief Steward, pretending to examine the watch, had noted the eight identifying numbers and had then persuaded the Dutchman to put them in his diary among a genuine list of valuables. The numbers on a fresh page might arouse suspicions. The Dutchman apologized for his part in the hoax, saying he had not expected the animosities it had created among the officers. As for my *bête noir*, he made himself scarce until everything had blown over.

In Singapore we picked up a remittance man who was escorted on board by two policemen. He was a blond, handsome young man with meagre baggage. Apparently, his behaviour and drinking was considered excessive, even by colonial standards, and he was being shipped back to England. He never stopped drinking and effing all the way back to the Thames. I found his company so wearisome I avoided him whenever I could. Finally I told him, perhaps somewhat priggishly, if he could not curb his foul language, I preferred him not to speak to me at all. My friend, the First Mate, chided me, reminding me gently that I was employed by the company to care for him. I could only reply that my experience was limited. I had no remedies for a constant hangover or a wasted life.

On the 5th of July, 107 days after we had set out, we arrived at the Victoria Docks in London. As we sailed up the Thames, I was already planning what I should do next. I had travelled halfway round the world, the other half could wait for later. I had seen and learned many things. Now I must concentrate on my trade. I would see my family, give my father the watch, stay with them until I had found a job, preferably in England.

The remittance man paced the deck, watching the riverside pubs approach and recede. The ship's bar had closed as soon as we entered the three-mile limit and he had developed a terrible thirst. In his frustration he kept punching the open palm of his left hand, effing with every blow. When we finally docked, and formalities were completed, he rushed down the gangway and that was the last I saw of him. It was also the last I saw of the distressed British seaman to whom I had entrusted six silk shirts, made to measure in Hong Kong, which he had promised to ease through the customs on my behalf.

I received my Certificate of Discharge signed by the Captain and First Mate. Of all my certificates, diplomas and degrees it is the only one that refers to my general conduct. Under that heading the Captain had stamped "VERY GOOD", which pleased my mother when she read it. Father was delighted with his gift. Of course, he still kept the Ingersoll for the workshop, but he wore his gold watch at bar mitzvahs, weddings and on High Holy Days when he went to shul.

Chapter 9

Rita in Residence

My wanderlust appeased for the time being, I decided to look for hospital jobs that would lead to a more permanent appointment in the field of public health.

When I was still a medical student I had decided that general practice was not for me, and I did not see myself specialising in hospital medicine. Indeed, before I went up to the university I could not make up my mind whether to take up medicine or forestry. For the life of me, I do not know what made me think of forestry, when I did not know one tree from another. Perhaps it was the poet in me! That was the time when my friend Morris Smith, who had elected himself my agent, submitted, without my knowledge, one of my poems in a competition organized by the *Scottish Daily Express*. So it came as a surprise when he presented me with a five pound note, an incredible amount of money in our eyes. The poem was published at the top of an inside page under the title,

A Jesting God
To be a poet was my wish
To meditate and sing
Of birds, and trees, and windy leas
And every lovely thing.

To be a poet was my wish -
A jesting god sent down

87

My soul to earth, and gave it birth,
In the slums of a sunless town.

My mother, on the other hand, had no doubt whatsoever that my future lay in medicine. She reminded me repeatedly that my cousin Natie, who had a practice among the shipyard workers of Clydebank, was making a steady ten pounds a week!

In the end I opted for medicine. I have never regretted it. But such are the quirks of fate that, thirty years after I had made the decision, I found my lost wood with its profusion of wild garlic, bluebells, and blackthorn laden with sloes, a wood that became part of my existence for the next twenty-five years. But that is another story, which must wait its turn in the telling.

I saw an advertisement in the *British Medical Journal* for a senior medical officer at the Liverpool Children's Hospital in Myrtle Street. This was the kind of post I was looking for, since child welfare is an intrinsic part of public health. I applied, was interviewed and appointed. I was shown round the doctors' residence where I found I would be the only male among four newly qualified women.

When I entered the common-room, I was greeted politely except for one large girl who was obviously taking my measure. Her feet were planted firmly on a threadbare rug which lay in front of an empty fireplace. My own quarters consisted of an institutional bedroom and a small sitting-room brightened by a new red rug.

When I returned a few days later to take up residence, I noticed, when I entered the common-room, that the large doctor was sitting in front of the empty fireplace reading a newspaper with her feet planted firmly on the new red rug. This was a challenge I could not ignore. When my colleagues returned to the residence for lunch and found the worn rug back where it belonged, I was beset on all sides. However, their fury soon abated, and the pecking order having been established (after all I was two years their senior), it was not long before I became a father confessor, to whom they brought their personal and professional problems. I can recall the occasion when one girl sat on my bed and told me that her parents, who ran a modest restaurant in Lytham St. Anne's near Blackpool, were having difficulty with staff because of illness. The coming Monday was a national holiday and they did not know how they were going to cope. Another girl and I were off duty that day and all three of us went up to Lytham and were waiters and waitresses for a day. After that, in the eyes of my colleagues I could do no wrong.

Five mornings a week I held a clinic for those children whose parents were too poor to afford a visit to a general practitioner. When I thought a second and more experienced opinion was called for, I sent the child to the appropriate specialist. In effect, I was acting as a sorting-clerk for the more serious cases and the experience was invaluable because I was able to follow the progress of many of these children through the wards.

At the clinic's reception desk a card was completed for each child. For some reason I was never able to fathom, the father's trade or profession was also recorded. More often than not it read "Unemployed" for this was the time of world depression. Of the many children who passed through my hands, one little girl comes readily to mind because of two unusual features, neither of them clinical. The first was her father's trade. Instead of the usual "unemployed" on the card, I read "painter". The second feature followed upon the first. He must have had a good business because, even to my unpractised eye, his wife's clothes were of a superior cut and quality. Mrs. X explained that she had come to see me on the recommendation of a mutual friend. Despite the attention of doctors in her native Yorkshire, her daughter failed to thrive. It seemed to me that I was playing the part of any port in a storm. I examined the child and could find little wrong with her. Not to send Mrs. X away empty-handed, I recommended a few sessions at the ultra-violet clinic, a favourite therapy at that time in sun-starved Liverpool. The little girl, an only child, thrived in the company of the children attending the UV clinic. At each session, a grateful Mrs. X always arrived with an armful of toys. In the meantime I learned from our "mutual friend" that Mrs. X's husband was indeed a prosperous painter, not of houses, as I had thought, but of people. He was a portrait painter and had more commissions than he could deal with.

The next time I saw Mrs. X her concern was not for her daughter but for me.

"Are you married?" she asked. When I replied in the negative, she told me she would like to introduce me to a lovely Jewish girl whose father owned a big textile factory in Leeds. A really lovely girl who would make the perfect wife for a doctor. I thanked her for her kindness, but I had other plans. Her next proposal was that I should sit for her husband. Now, that I am old and in need of a little immortality, I am sorry I did not accept her invitation.

My plans included a shot at the examination for the Diploma in Child Health held by both the Royal College of Physicians of London and the Royal College of Surgeons of England. Afterwards, I might take a course leading to the Diploma in Public Health.

I settled down to a long haul. For my friends outside the hospital, I adopted the theatrical agent's rule: "Don't phone me, I'll phone you." I began to keep my own records of children with congenital anomalies. Some had initially passed through my hands, others had been sent directly to the hospital by general practitioners. Like a monk painstakingly transcribing a manuscript, I copied their case histories, the details of their anomalies, the pathology and X-ray findings, the treatment and the outcome. Today, all this information can be copied in a matter of minutes by exotic Japanese machines, but I wonder how much of it stays with the user. Many years later I handed over the collection to my wife's niece, a consultant paediatrician at the Hopital Brugmann in Brussels.

If I worked like a monk, it was not in my nature to live like one, and it was not long before Rita hung her clothes in my wardrobe. She was seventeen and lived with her grandmother in Liverpool. She was well aware of her Welsh good looks. She could not walk down a street without taking sidelong glances at her reflection in the shop windows. She had left school at fourteen and, as far as I could ascertain, she was not gainfully employed. I had met her at a *thé dansant* at the Adelphi Hotel. She settled in like a stray kitten that takes over a household. At first, my colleagues resented her presence but she soon won them over. Perhaps she reminded them of the carefree girls they once were, before they committed themselves to the responsibilities of a demanding profession. She even charmed our housekeeper, who set up another place in the dining room. But she could be infuriating at times, like reading the *Daily Mirror* when I was making love to her. When I could stand her no longer I would tell her to get out and she would leave with her scanty wardrobe, only to return a few days later as though nothing had happened.

I cannot recall when I applied for a visa to visit the Soviet Union. When it did not arrive, I decided to take a busman's holiday and attend a fortnight's course at the Children's Hospital, Great Ormond Street, for those intending to take the examinations of the Royal Colleges.

On returning to Liverpool, I was greeted with the sad news that Rita had left us, and was last seen in the clutches of the Cuban consul. It was my duty, they said, to free her and bring her back to the residence. At first, I demurred. If she was continuing to live in sin, she might as well do so in comfort, instead of having to make do in our shabby quarters. Then, responding to pressure, I agreed to have a word with her. I knew I would find her in the restaurant of the Adelphi Hotel. She came towards me in all her new finery. She looked marvellous. There was no need for me to ask if she was happy. There was no need for me to say anything. For old times sake we swam together in the hotel pool and then we said goodbye.

I did not see her again but I did hear of her, in most unusual circumstances, nearly twenty years later. In one of my rare visits to Scotland I was having dinner with Eileen and Joe Gerber in their lovely cottage at Newton Mearns. In the course of the evening I was talking about my early days in Liverpool, when Eileen recalled a conversation she had had with a next-door neighbour, a Welsh woman who was married to a Dutch sea-captain. The lady in question told Eileen, in confidence, about her friendship with a Glasgow doctor who had worked at the Children's Hospital in Myrtle Street many years ago. She often wondered what had become of him.

The picture of her neighbour that Eileen drew was indubitably Rita, hardly changed with the passage of years, except that the girl from the valleys had become a very proud *huisvrouw*. The couple, with their two children, had returned to Holland a few years ago. Eileen asked me if I would like to have their address in Amsterdam. I resisted the temptation to say yes. It was better to let sleeping housewives lie.

I sat the examination in child health and received the diploma in October 1938. By that time, I had enrolled for the course in public health at Glasgow University, and that diploma joined the others in the bottom drawer of my bureau in July 1939. I was working at Ruchill Fever Hospital and Sanatorium when War broke out. As far as I recollect none of the residents enlisted or were called-up. After six months of the "phony war" I made up my mind. On Tuesday, 12th March 1940, I enlisted at Edinburgh Castle.

Chapter 10

"Lt. Mair! LOOK AT YOUR COMPANY!"
and other misadventures in the White Man's Grave

The medical examination was perfunctory to say the least. A few incurious questions about my health, a stethoscope that barely stopped to listen, a glancing inspection fore and aft, and I was declared free of impediment and fit to become a soldier.

I cannot recall any questions about further qualifications and I know I did not make any mention of my diploma in public health. At the time it seemed irrelevant. I learned later, had I done so, I might have entered the Army as a specialist in hygiene with a crown on my shoulder, instead of the two pips of a lieutenant. In the event, I was told I would likely be posted to a field ambulance. When I mentioned this to a large, kilted, surprisingly affable sergeant-major, as we walked down from the Castle, his face lit up. In the clear, unaccented English of Inverness, he said, "Aye, that's a good unit to be in – plenty of casualties, quick promotion."

I was still chewing over the implications of that statement when I left the sergeant-major and hurried down the hill to Prince's Street and Waverley Station, and in the rackety old train carrying me to Glasgow I wondered how I should break the news of my enlistment to my unsuspecting family.

If my parents and sister were surprised and dismayed when I told them my news, my brother was not. Three years earlier, when civil war was raging in Spain, I had got in touch with Douglas Boddie about joining the International Brigade. I had first met Doug, a former Buckie

93

fisherman, when he was manager of Collett's bookshop in the High Street near the Glasgow Royal Infirmary. Later, he moved to London to take charge of the bookshop in Charing Cross Road. Doug took me along to see Harry Pollitt, general secretary of the British Communist Party. Pollitt, sitting behind a desk when Doug introduced me, looked at me coldly and asked if I was a member of the Party. When I replied I was not, he said, "How do I know you are not a spy?" I was so taken aback I could not answer him. After all, Doug, a not unimportant member of the Party, had vouched for me. Apparently, as far as the general secretary was concerned, only Communists were acceptable.

When I told Henny about my encounter with Pollitt. he said, with great prescience, "What's your hurry? If you want to fight fascism you will soon have a bigger war on your hands, maybe in two or three years' time."

In retrospect, I think Harry Pollitt, who did not find me suitable material for the International Brigade, would have approved my joining the British Army, because he openly supported Britain's entry into World War II. This did not accord with Soviet policy and led to his removal from the secretaryship of the party. He was restored to office in 1941 following the out-break of war between Germany and the U.S.S.R.

Towards the end of March I joined the newly-formed 195 Field Ambulance which occupied a large field on the outskirts of Wishaw, a small coal-mining town twelve miles from Glasgow. The unit consisted of two or three ambulances with freshly painted red crosses, several Nissen huts and a group of volunteers whose military experience was about the same as mine.

The commanding officer was a middle-aged regular of the Royal Army Medical Corps, whose career had been effectively stalled by long peace-time postings to Gibraltar and other quiescent overseas parts, where promotion depended on the demise by natural causes of the holder of a more senior rank. As I learned, he was obviously delighted to have been given command of a field unit and the rank of lieutenant-colonel. His second-in-command, a comrade of World War I, was a general practitioner called-up as a territorial army officer at the outbreak of war. I cannot recall their names or what they looked like. I can only refer to them as "the Colonel" and "the Major".

On the battlefield, the role of a field ambulance is to collect, treat and care for the wounded and sick until they can be removed to hospitals behind the lines. In the absence of a battlefield, the Colonel concentrated his energies on teaching us to march. Marching along the country lanes on a bright April morning, singing, "I had a good job and I left, I had a good job and I left", and stamping the left foot down at the end of each line, was exhilarating. It hardened us up, made us fit for the battles ahead. Had the Colonel been satisfied with this, all would have been well. But he was obsessed with ceremonial marches, perhaps a legacy of his earlier military experience. We marched in column, we marched in line abreast like Wellington's men at Waterloo, we marched in circles and formed squares. He even painstakingly taught us the grave, hesitant steps of the funeral march. Were it not for the Geneva convention of 1864, by the terms of which a field ambulance and its personnel were declared neutral and therefore were forbidden to bear arms, the Colonel would have had us marching with arms reversed, and had we looked back we would have found a farm horse following us with a pair of army boots placed reverse-wise in the stirrups.

One sunny afternoon I was promoted to leading "A" company in the field. At the command of the Colonel we were left-wheeling and right-wheeling line abreast. He was enjoying himself immensely. Suddenly there was an anguished roar, "Lieutenant Mair – LOOK AT YOUR COMPANY!" I looked over my shoulder. To the joy of the spectators and the fury of the colonel, "A" company was marching towards the sun and I was marching away from it. I knew then, all being well, I would wear my uniform to the bitter end, but at heart I would always remain a civilian.

After dinner, the junior officers would listen dutifully to the Colonel and the Major fighting World War I over and over again. As for the current war, the colonel assured us that the Germans would never breach the Maginot Line. They did not have generals of the right calibre; many of them were only privates or non-commissioned officers in World

War I. The fact that these erstwhile privates and N.C.O.s had seen off
the Polish Army in less than a fortnight did not seem to worry him. It
was only after the fall of France that he began to show some concern. By
then we were stationed in Essex on the east coast and ceremonial
marching had given way to digging trenches.

Meanwhile, the Field Ambulance had nearly doubled in strength. The
new "B" company was stationed at Billericay (site of Villa Erica, a
Roman settlement) some thirty miles from central London. The proximity
to London was a source of concern to the company commander, Major
Pennyfeather, because he was being constantly bombarded with requests
for weekend passes to "The Smoke". Pennyfeather was an Irish Protestant
whose family had provided many fine soldiers over the years to the
British Army. He was a good soldier and a religious zealot. He never
refused a request for a weekend pass, point blank. Not until he had
bowed his head and clasped his hands in prayer, did he finally look up,
and, as often as not, reject the request. One devious young man, who had
joined him in prayer, when told that this time he could not have a pass,
expressed surprise because he had got a message to the contrary.

One night when everyone in Billericay was abed, I was sitting talking
to Pennyfeather in his room when we heard a flapping of great wings.
The Angel of Death was near, but we did not know it. Then there was a
thud of something sinking into soft earth and the flapping stopped. It
was pitch dark outside and we could see nothing unusual in the hooded
light of our torches. Next morning at dawn I saw the monster lying in the
grounds of the house next door. It was a German "Big Fritz" five-ton
bomb dropped by the parachute we had heard flapping the previous
night. We notified the police, and soon everyone within a quarter of a
mile radius was evacuated to safety.

While we waited for the Royal Army Engineers bomb-disposal squad
to arrive, the phone rang. It was the lady from the house next door. In the
rush to leave she had forgotten to let the chickens out of the coop. Would
I be good enough to open the door and let them out? I went round to the
house and found the long black cylinder a few feet from the coop. I was
about to open the door when I had second thoughts. I did not think the

engineers would take kindly to a dozen Leghorns fluttering on and off the iron casing, while they struggled to disassemble the six separate anti-handling devices fitted to the bomb. The chickens would have to take their chances.

While all this was going on I was being posted to different units as a temporary medical officer. I served with the 46th Infantry Training Group in Cheshunt in Hertfordshire, the R.A.F. in Epping and the 11th Highland Light Infantry in Southend.

From my Regimental Aid Post (RAP) in Southend I could watch the RAF and the Luftwaffe fighting it out over the estuary of the Thames, and at night hear the drone of the German bombers following the river to London. I slept in the RAP which was some distance from the hotel commandeered for battalion headquarters. Hitler had not yet abandoned his plans to invade Britain so every morning the battalion 'stood to' just before dawn. I made an arrangement with the sergeant in the RAP to bring me a cup of tea at that time, and if there was no sign of an invasion, I would go to sleep again. On the morning of 15th September I got up, shaved and dressed and went along to the hotel for breakfast. On either side of the long table sat a group of unshaven, bleary-eyed Scots and none looked more hung-over than did the C.O. at the head of the table. Bright and cheerful, I said, "That must have been some party you chaps had last night!"

I sensed from the long silence which followed, and the baleful look of the Commanding Officer, that I must have said the wrong thing. The whole battalion, with the exception of the Medical Officer, had been standing-to since the previous evening for the great invasion that did not arrive, though the moon was full and the tide was right.

My next posting was to West Africa. I cannot recall if I volunteered or was pushed.

I. The Gold Coast

When Italy joined the Germans on the 10th June, the Allies could no longer be sure of the Suez route. At the same time, the establishment of the Vichy regime in France denied the Allies bases in North Africa. The destruction of the French fleet by the British at Oran on 3rd July, the attack on the *Richelieu* at the port of Dakar five days later, and finally the abortive attempt to land a British and Free French force on 24th-25th September at Dakar, with its attendant civilian casualties, hardened anti-British attitudes in French West Africa, which was to remain neutral, if not hostile, territory well into 1943.

In December 1940, Winston Churchill expressed his concern in a letter to President Roosevelt:

> "There is a second field of danger. The Vichy Government may, either by joining Hitler's New Order or through some manoeuvre, such as forcing us to attack an expedition dispatched by sea against Free French colonies, find an excuse with the Axis powers of ranging very considerable undamaged naval forces still under its control. If the French Navy were to join the Axis the control of West Africa would pass immediately into their hands, with the gravest consequences to our communications between the Northern and Southern Atlantic, and also affecting Dakar and of course thereafter South America."

British West Africa had acquired a new strategic significance. It was time to move the pawns to a different part of the board.

I joined the 5th West African Field Ambulance at Crookham, near Newbury, on 23rd October. My new Commanding Officer was known as Two-Gun Matthews from the pistols he was said to have worn cowboy fashion when he was in the Gold Coast colonial medical service. He was a plump, jovial, likeable character, full of tales about the delights and horrors of life in darkest Africa. In tropical gear, with his extra-long shorts and wrinkled stockings, he did not look particularly martial, but then none of us did. He was not the sort of man to insist on ceremonial marches, but he did inflict on us some hair-raising bush exercises, one of which I shall recount later. He was well-liked by everyone. We would have followed him anywhere – at a distance.

We embarked on the S.S. *Almanzora* at Glasgow. Walking along the quay on the way to the ship, I dropped out of the group to look at a heavily camouflaged cargo vessel whose lines seemed familiar to me. Any doubts I might have had vanished when a man, leaning over the rail high above me, waved furiously and signalled me to come aboard. It was my *bête noir*, the Chief Steward! But I was not taking any chances. I waved back, and hurriedly joined my comrades.

The *Almanzora* took up position off the Tail O' the Bank in a convoy which would sail due west out into the Atlantic, and then, somewhere beyond the sight of searching German reconnaissance planes, the *Almanzora* would break off and steam due south until, level with the bulge of Africa, she would turn again due east and make for the port of Freetown in Sierra Leone.

Our ship carried a large contingent of officers and N.C.Os. whose purpose, apart from defending the British colonies, was to train native troops for war in the Middle East, and later when Japan entered the war, in the Far East. According to Michael Crowder, in his book *West Africa Under Colonial Rule*, the strength of the West African Frontier Force was raised from a pre-war level of 8,000 to 146,000. For the first time West African troops were used outside the continent and acquitted themselves well: "In Burma, the African troops became indispensable not only as soldiers better suited to the conditions of jungle warfare than their white comrades, but as carriers who could transport supplies through territory where no vehicles could pass. The ability of the African carrier to move heavy loads over great distances in tropical conditions gave the Allies the initiative they needed over the Japanese."

As far as I can recollect, in those eighteen days at sea, we saw no aeroplanes or periscopes. From time to time, the *Almanzora* heeled over sharply and swerved to starboard or port, but perhaps this was to keep us on our toes. We were well aware of the lurking danger. We slept fitfully, fully clothed, and in our waking hours we did not talk much about the possible. The *Almanzora* was a 'wet' ship. There was plenty of liquor available, and I sometimes wondered how many would make the lifeboats or rafts if the ship was torpedoed at night.

During the day, we were entertained by amateur comedians and replicas of George Formby and his ukulele. Old "Coasters", military and civilian, talked to us informally or gave lectures about life in their respective colonies. The man who brought the house down was Colonel Matthews. His subject was, "How to finish your tour, in reasonably good health". He was talking about the fly as a vector of dysentery.

"If you go into the bush to relieve yourself, no sooner have you started than you're surrounded by hundreds of flies."

At this, a young officer piped up, "If you smoked a cigarette, Sir, wouldn't that keep the flies away?"

"Yes," said Two-Gun like a shot, "if you could manage to exhale through the right orifice!"

After listening to all these talks and lectures I came to the conclusion that in West Africa one would have to be perfectly fit to feel moderately unwell.

On the 17th November, eighteen days after leaving the Clyde, we arrived in Freetown. Hardly two months earlier, the 1/4 Essex battalion and a detachment of the Royal Marines had also arrived in Freetown for the Dakar show. By some oversight there were no mosquito nets for them. The Marines went ashore without nets and within a week eighty men were admitted to hospital with malaria. The Essex, more prudently, waited in the harbour till the nets arrived, then went ashore to take part in beach defence and bush exercises. Despite the nets, they too suffered heavily from malaria.

I do not know what happened to the Marines. Presumably they returned to England with the chastened General de Gaulle. The Essex battalion, joined by the 2/5 Essex, stayed on to garrison Freetown. At any one time more than fifty per cent of their personnel were off sick. Sierra Leone was living up to its reputation of being "the white man's grave".

On 17th February 1941, Churchill wrote to the Director Military Operations: ". . . if the West African Brigade were transferred from

Kenya to Freetown two British battalions now degenerating there could come forward to the Nile Army."

Five months later, the two battalions were shipped off to Libya where they were taken out of the line for three months to recover from residual malaria. Ultimately, they were decimated in the retreat to El Alemain.

On 27th November Lt.Colonel Matthews and his band of officers and N.C.O.s left Accra for Kumasi, the capital of Ashanti, with the purpose of raising the 5th West African Field Ambulance. The Ashanti had long had a reputation for military prowess and we had no lack of willing recruits; the only thing we and they lacked was experience, and this the Colonel was determined to provide.

We had hardly learned how to erect our camp beds and mosquito nets before he had us out in the jungle, in the heat of the day, teaching the natives bush-craft. Some unkind people have described Glasgow as a jungle but it was nothing like the jungle we practised in. On one occasion I was given the task of leading half a dozen stretcher-bearers through enemy lines to safety. The enemy were armed with grenades (compacted mud-pies), for throwing at us if we were intercepted. This tactic was designed to keep us on our toes. I was within fifty yards of the enemy lines. I could see a few bush hats bobbing above the high grass, when suddenly my bearers, who were crawling a few yards behind me, leapt up and pointing in front of me, shouted, "Master! Master!" and some incomprehensible Ashanti. I, in turn, shouted, "Get down, you silly buggers. I can see them." Meaning the enemy. But they kept shouting and pointing, until I realized that they were not pointing in front of me, but above me, where a swift and deadly mamba, swaying gently on a branch over my head, was about to strike. I leapt away, shouting, "We surrender! We surrender!" but the enemy still threw their grenades. Then, in a combined operation we attacked the snake with branches, but it escaped into the undergrowth.

After a month of training in the bush I was posted to the 7th Battalion, Gold Coast Regiment, at Kintampo. Depending on one's temperament there were differing views of Kintampo. The disgruntled British soldier, stationed there, might write to his mother, "Dear Mum, The Gold Coast

Captain Mair in the Gold Coast, January 1941

is the arse-hole of the Empire, and I'm 200 miles up it . . .", but I saw it in a different light.

Kintampo, situated on a plateau 1,500 feet above sea level, was a busy little market town, standing as it did on cattle routes from the Northern Territory and the French Ivory Coast. The battalion cantonment was about a mile from the town. To the south of the plateau a great forest reserve stretched as far as the eye could see, and to the north the flat savannah country seemed never-ending.

To sit on the verandah of my bungalow, sipping a pink gin after an arduous day, before that day plunged into night – no long twilights near the equator – was for me a constant delight. I can recall sharing such an occasion with Doctor Saunders, the local Medical Officer and international authority on sleeping sickness. I asked him how often he returned to Europe on leave. Looking pensively over the forest below, he said, "I haven't gone back for years. Europe is too much of a jungle for me."

I enjoyed Kintampo because, medically speaking, I was monarch of all I surveyed. I was solely responsible for all army personnel. With the assistance of an R.A.M.C. sergeant and a few African orderlies, I ran a twelve-bed hospital and a small operating theatre. The nearest hospital of any size was in Kumasi, 100 miles away.

It was not long before I was severely tested. A company had gone off on an exercise to the Black Volta river, about twenty miles to the west, when word came through that a black sergeant had been bayonetted in the abdomen by a young private who had apparently gone cafard. I jumped into an open truck with two orderlies and drove over the barely motorable roads until I found the sergeant sitting under a tree holding his bowels in his cupped hands. I tried to push the loops of intestine back into his abdomen but the wound was narrow and the abdominal muscles had gone into spasm. He was going rapidly into shock. The private was lying on the ground next to him, securely bound hand and foot. We lifted both of them into the truck and drove back to the cantonment. It seemed to my unpractised eye that the sergeant would never survive the journey to Kumasi. (There were no helicopters in these days.) I would have to operate. To complicate matters, my R.A.M.C. sergeant was down with malaria. I had to ask a fellow officer to act as anaesthetist. By this time the patient's pulse was barely palpable. I showed the officer how to pour the chloroform over the mask and, when I thought the patient was sufficiently under, I went round and made an incision to lengthen the wound made by the bayonet. As soon as I did this, the anaesthetist fainted. The orderlies had to drag him out into the fresh air. I gave the patient more anaesthetic and tried without success to push the bowel back and close the wound but each time I repeated the process the abdominal muscles refused to relax. Finally, running to and fro from head to abdomen, I managed to push the bowel back and close the wound. But, as the comics say, the operation was a success but the patient died.

The Sick Report

A play written initially for three voices but a fourth is heard briefly and the Deputy Director Medical Services and the Royal West African Service Corps are mentioned more than once.

Scene I

The Regimental Medical Officer (R.M.O.) of 7 Gold Coast Regiment (7G.C.R.) is in bed with sandfly fever, also known as break-bone fever, a painful tropical ailment. Enter the Regimental Adjutant (R.A.) waving a piece of paper.

R.A.: Hullo, Doc! I've got a message from D.D.M.S., G.H.Q., Accra. He wants to know why you didn't send the Sick Report for last week. The C.O. wants to know too.
R.M.O.: Tell them I've been in bed with Greta Garbo. I'm going to get up and phone the Report from your office.

Scene II

The R.M.O. is speaking on the phone in the R.A.'s office.

R.M.O.: This is R.M.O., 7G.C.R., Kintampo. Is that D.D.M.S., G.H.Q., Accra?

[He hears a polite African Voice (A.V.).]

A.V.: Yes, Sir, can I help you?

R.M.O.: Yes. Can you take down last week's Return of Infectious Diseases if I read it out to you?

A.V.: Yes, Sir. Will you please wait while I get a pencil and paper? [Pause] I have the paper and pencil now, Sir. Will you please proceed?

R.M.O.: Malaria, 4; Dysentery, 3 . . .

[There is a clicking sound from the telephone and the R.M.O. hears a New African Voice (N.A.V.)]

N.A.V.: This is R.W.A.S.C., Kumasi. Is that R.W.A.S.C., Takoradi?

R.M.O.: No! This R.M.O., 7G.C.R., Kintampo. Get off the bloody line, I'm trying to get through to D.D.M.S., G.H.Q., Accra!

N.A.V.: I'm sorry, Sir, I'm trying to find a missing truck. I think it's at R.W.A.S.C., Takoradi.

[The connection is broken and after several attempts the R.M.O. gets through to Accra. He wipes his sweat off the Adjutant's telephone and continues his litany of infectious diseases. As he goes on, his voice drops to a hoarse whisper and as he gets towards the end his voice rises again.]

R.M.O.: Gonorrhoea, 2; Syphilis, 1. Have you got that?

A.V.: Yes, Sir.

R.M.O.: Then read the lot back to me.

[The A.V. reads the Sick Report back to "Gonorrhoea, 2", then he hesitates.]

A.V.: S-S-S-. Can you spell the last one for me, Sir?

R.M.O.: S-Y-P-H-I-L-I-S, Syphilis, 1; read the last two back.

A.V.: Gonorrhoea, 2; S-S-S- Can you spell the last one phonetically, please?

R.M.O.: S for Sunday – have you got that? S for SUNDAY; Y for Young; P for Percy; H for Harry; I for Isaac; L for Love; I for Isaac; S for Sunday. Have you got that now?

A.V.: Yes, Sir.

R.M.O.: Then for God's sake, read the last two back, and we'll call it a

day.
A.V.: Gonorrhoea, 2. One on SUNDAY!
[Exeunt]

Just another hiccup in the war against Hitler.

When the sandfly fever was over, I returned to duty.

First, was the morning sick-parade of black other ranks. Most of them were healthy recruits complaining of the aches and pains inseparable from army training. It was they who gave me the nickname by which I was known among the rank and file. I do not know if it was Ashanti, Brong, Gonja or Dagomba but, translated into English, I was "Doctor-about-turn-quick-march". In the early days, when a patient returned for a check-up, I would ask him how he was keeping, whereupon I would receive a long list of new symptoms. When I got wise to this, I would look at the man, who a moment before had been jumping, laughing and joking with his comrades in the queue, and say, before he could open his mouth, "You're looking fine, about turn – quick march!" On most occasions he would leave the room with a big grin on his face and a shrug of his shoulders as if to say, "Well, I've had a go."

There was no quick dismissal for those who presented with yaws, subclinical malaria or the various worms they had brought from their native villages. They were admitted to the hospital which I visited next.

Confining a sick African soldier to his own bed was a Herculean task. My patients were constantly moving from one bed to another, playing cards, or checkers, or just talking. Suspected cerebrospinal meningitis, scarlet fever or sleeping sickness was no bar to social intercourse.

One day, I was told to expect a visit from General Giffard, Officer Commanding West Africa. Came the day when the General, followed by all his brass, stepped on to the sanded floor of my only ward. On the twelve beds lay twelve immobile black soldiers each at attention under a stiff white sheet drawn up to just below his nose. (I had warned them that the first one to move would be put on a charge.) General Giffard, the longest serving general in the British Army, who had spent most of his professional life in West Africa, looked at this sight for what seemed a long time, and then he said, pointing at the patients, "Doctor," (I remember he called me "doctor", not lieutenant), "is this usual?" I replied, "No, Sir, it's all for your benefit." He laughed heartily, and left the ward. I was to meet him again in entirely different circumstances.

Once a week I attended a parade where British other ranks were supplied with mepacrine tablets for the suppression of malaria. The tablets were issued but there was no guarantee that they were taken, because some of the men did not like the yellowish discolouration of the skin caused by the drug. There was one corporal, however, who always asked for more than the usual ration. I heard, on the grape-vine, he was convinced that mepacrine was an effective prophylactic against venereal disease.

It was in Kintampo that I began to fill two 100-page Army Field Message Books with notes on tropical diseases, minutely written in blue and red ink, with diagrams, illustrations, figures and charts. Did I contemplate writing a book on tropical diseases? On the first page is a table of contents beginning with Section I – Febrile Diseases caused by Protozoa, and then follows 1. Malaria, including Blackwater Fever, 2. Trypanosomiasis, Sleeping Sickness and Chaga's Disease, and so on.

Much of my information I obtained from the books on Dr. Saunders' shelves, much from my own experience of three years in West Africa.

When I look at the notes now, I ask myself, when did I find time to write them? But they also remind me that I did not spend all my evenings drinking in the various messes I passed through.

Of the numerous exercises and river crossings that took place in the three months I served in Kintampo, I can recall only two deaths by violence or accident, a statistic which was not excessive in view of the rawness of the recruits and the terrain in which the exercises took place. The first I have already described. The second was a recruit who drowned, or was pulled down by a crocodile in the Black Volta. He was a grandson of the old chief and his loss was deeply felt. We had given up all hope of recovering the body, when word came through that what appeared to be a corpse was lying on a shallow bank in the river, down-stream from where he had last been seen. I volunteered to collect the remains.

I drove in a truck to the village nearest to the sighting. The villagers were already waiting for me. I boarded a canoe which appeared to lie perilously low in the water. The members of the crew stuffed their nostrils with grass and we set off. We paddled slowly down the river until I saw, lying on a bank, an inflated, metallic-blue, Michelin man, shimmering and throbbing in the hot sun, an illusion created by millions of bloated flies fighting for what was left of him. We wrapped the corpse in an army blanket and placed it in the canoe. When we got back to Kintampo it was already dark. The whole village was out to meet us. I did not see any of my fellow officers, but there were many soldiers there. I had gone so far, I felt it was only right that I should be present at his interment. The corpse was taken into a house where it was washed and wrapped in a white sheet. It was then placed in the back of my truck and we drove slowly to the cemetery, followed by a large crowd of mourners.

At the cemetery, a wide grave had been dug to a depth of about six feet. At the bottom of the grave, a trench the length and width of a man had been excavated. It was, in effect, a grave within a grave. The bottom and sides of this narrower grave were lined with branches and leaves. The corpse, still wrapped in its shroud, was passed down to two mourners who laid it in the trench. Then, they placed branches crosswise over the corpse so that they rested on the ledge of earth on either side of the trench. In the manner of his burial, the earth did not touch the soldier in his narrow grave, nor did it lie heavily upon him when the larger grave was filled in.

After the incident of the drowned soldier there was no shortage of crocodile stories in the mess; suspicious-looking logs floating near the ford that suddenly submerged and disappeared; fearsome creatures that emerged from the river and attacked children playing on the bank. The truth is that, although fish form its staple diet, the West African crocodile will eat anything it can overpower. The unwary animal approaching within range of its powerful jaws is seized, dragged under the water and eaten. The crocodile recognizes man as its chief enemy and is wary of him but, given the chance, occasionally becomes a man-eater.

This was on my mind when I learned that a company had been ordered, as part of a larger exercise, to cross the Black Volta and forestall a hypothetical attack by the Vichy French from the neighbouring Ivory Coast. I was not told of this until they had been gone for several hours. I set out after them on foot, with four bearers carrying a stretcher and surgical supplies.

I was following the track the company had made through the bush, when suddenly I came face to face with General Giffard and a number of senior officers who were evidently observing the exercise. I think they were surprised to see me, as I was to see them. It was the General who asked, "What brought you here, Doctor?"

When I told him of my fears, he said, "Good thinking! As it happens, we have brought you a casualty," and he pointed up the track where four soldiers were carrying a white N.C.O. on an improvised stretcher.

"It seems," said the General, "he was pulled down by a crocodile." And with that, he went on his way.

The corporal, who was conscious and in much pain, told me he had demurred when he had been ordered to wade across the ford with his squad. When told he would be well-covered, he started off, and had gone only a few yards when a crocodile suddenly surfaced, grabbed him by the knee and pulled him under.

I learned later his squad had very bravely stood their ground, attacking the crocodile with their rifle butts until it released him and swam away.

We brought him back to the battalion, where I commandeered a car and driver to take him to the hospital in Kumasi. He was asleep when we reached the hospital. The surgeons were able to save his leg and he returned to the battalion. When I met him some months later in Accra, he told me he would never forget the terrible moment when the crocodile pulled him under the water.

"It just turned me over and over, and I could do nothing." He confessed that every time he went to bed, he looked under it, to make sure there was no crocodile waiting for him.

General Giffard must have put in a good word for me when he returned to G.H.Q. because my next posting was Temporary Deputy Assistant Director of Hygiene, Gold Coast.

Before I left Kintampo for Accra, I had one more task to complete. Jacob, my civilian batman, wanted to marry one of the old Chief's many granddaughters. Unfortunately he had only enough money to buy one cow, not the three the Chief would want in compensation. Could I (asked Jacob) persuade the old man to accept one cow as a deposit?

With Jacob's assistance I dressed for the occasion. In my well-pressed uniform with the three pips of a newly-promoted captain, the leather of my Sam Browne belt shining like my shoes, my cap at the right angle and swagger stick under my arm, I presented Jacob's petition to the Chief as he sat under a great baobab tree with the elders of the village. Perhaps he remembered how I had helped give his grandson a decent burial, because he agreed that Jacob could have his granddaughter. When I left Kintampo for the last time, Jacob and his bride-to-be came with me.

For five months, from the beginning of May until the end of September, I pursued, like a peripatetic circuit judge, a triangular course from H.Q., Accra, to 6 Battalion, G.C.R., Takoradi, to 43 Field Hygiene Section, Kumasi, and back to Accra. In that time, two incidents occurred which I have never forgotten.

I am in the club at Kumasi. There is an air of excitement among the army officers and the civilian gold miners. I recall the contemptuous, penetrating voice of a senior officer, "The Germans will go through them like a dose of salts", and my response, "Now we have a chance of winning the war."

It is Sunday, 22nd June, 1941. The BBC has just announced that the German Army has invaded Russia.

The second incident, which occurred in Takoradi in July, involved me in a near mutiny and a murderous riot. It began peacefully enough on a Sunday morning, when officers and N.C.O.s were swimming and sunbathing on the beach below the cantonment. The O.C. and his company commanders were attending a conference in Accra, leaving the battalion in the hands of junior officers. There was a holiday atmosphere in the air as they cavorted about like a bunch of schoolboys, which many of them were. Suddenly, a black corporal came running along the beach. Breathlessly, incoherently, he told us that fighting had broken out between soldiers and Krumen. (The Kru, a tribe inhabiting the Liberian coast, have furnished crews for English vessels since the eighteenth century. They are short, stocky and very hard-working, having established themselves in the ports along the Guinea Coast as stevedores as well as seamen.)

As far as I recollect, my fellow officers did not appear to be affected by the news. It was the old story: the local men resenting the attention paid to their women by "foreign" troops stationed in the town. It would blow over. But I did not see it that way. It was left to me, as the most senior officer present, albeit a medical one, to follow the Corporal up the cliff face to the barracks. There I saw a battalion in disarray. On the parade ground several hundred men were running about, gesticulating and shouting in a language I could not understand. I saw the African Sergeant-Major trying to pacify them. I asked him what this was all about. He told me the Krumen in the African township had fallen upon his comrades. In retaliation some of the men had broken into the armoury and helped themselves to weapons and were preparing to attack the Krumen. Most of the soldiers I saw were unarmed, but there were a number, large enough to be frightening, who were waving bayonets and rifles, and apparently screaming vengeance.

With help of the Sergeant-Major and other N.C.O.s the men were persuaded to stand to, while I harangued them about the gravity of breaking into the armoury. I told them if they were going to kill Krumen they would do it like soldiers, not like a bloody mob. It would be better for everyone if the arms were turned in immediately. When this was done, I would go down with a detachment to pick up the casualties. All this translated by the black Sergeant-Major.

Then followed a spectacle that to a disinterested spectator would have seemed very comical. Walking along the serried ranks, like inspecting royalty, I stopped from time to time to have a few words with some gigantic soldier, who would then hand over his weapon to me and I in turn would pass it to the Sergeant-Major walking behind me, with the bayonets and rifles cradled in his arms. All this time, I did not see a fellow officer.

I then took a large van with several men, and drove down to the African township. At the outskirts we were stopped by a European, nursing a broken arm, who warned us not to go any further. The Krumen were out in force, and very, very angry. We drove on and soon we came across dead, dying and wounded soldiers. With the tail-gate down, we picked them up and dropped them unceremoniously on to the floor of the van. Then, we could go no further. The street was blocked by a crowd of Krumen. I got out of the van, telling the driver to turn it quietly and keep the engine running. I walked towards the Krumen, repeating loudly, "I be doctor, I be doctor." Fortunately I was not in uniform. I was wearing the white shirt, shorts and sandals I had worn on the beach and could well have been a civilian medical officer whom they respected greatly. They moved apart to let me through, crying all the while, "They kill our brother! They kill our brother!" He lay, looking up at the sky, a dagger plunged in his heart up to the hilt. I shook my head and backed away until I was free of the crowd; then, my courage deserting me, I ran as fast as I could to the van, which drove out of the township in a hail of rocks and iron bars towards the African hospital.

The following night I was awakened by an officer who told me that an N.C.O. had been attacked at midnight as he was leaving the tent that served as the sergeants' mess. He was shaking when I saw him. He smelled strongly of beer and vomit. In the darkness he did not see his assailant who, he said, struck him a severe blow in the back, knocking him on all fours to the ground. There was no sign of injury. He was not hurt, only frightened. It was certainly getting serious if the Krumen were taking the fight to the Europeans in the cantonment. For the rest of that night I slept with a revolver under my pillow.

The next morning we could see where the sergeant, leaving the tent as drunk as a lord, had tripped over a guy rope and pulled its peg out of the ground.

I do not know if a court of enquiry was ever held about the riot in Takoradi, because a few days later I went on local leave to Prampram and immediately after that I left the Gold Coast and did not return for nearly a year.

Notes written on a trip to Paradise

29th September 1941

Going on local leave to Prampram, twenty-five miles up the coast from Accra, is like moving house. The Army provides a three-ton truck and the driver, Jacob and I load my camp bed, deck-chair, tin trunk, a chop-box filled with tinned salmon, soup, sardines, butter and tea, and a smaller box containing D. H. Lawrence, William Faulkner, Peter Cheney, Somerset Maugham, Richard Hughes, Voltaire and L. Rodger's *Textbook of Tropical Medicine.*

After leaving a barely motorable road, we turn off on to a muddy trail that seems to wander off across ploughed fields. Behind me, in the back of the truck, is Jacob and his affianced. They are not married yet, though she is getting near her time. Jacob, ever the sceptic, wants to be sure she is fertile before the knot is tied.

Prampram! Imagine a house built like a Beau Geste fort in the sand thirty yards from the sea. On either side of it, the flawless beaches stretch for miles, fringed by drooping palm trees. Behind the house the palms lean over its white walls and through their fronds one can see the mud huts of the village. The Rest House is clean and windswept. We three are the only ones there because the truck has gone back to Accra. On the upper floor is a room for my camp-bed, another for my kit and a balcony overlooking the sea, where I shall dine in solitary grandeur. Jacob and his lady occupy the ground floor where he prepares our meals. Darkness comes swiftly and soon I am having my usual struggle with the kerosene lamp, which lights after a series of explosions. (In West Africa kerosene is a precious commodity. It is a universal source of heat and light; refrigerators run on it; its containers are used for a multitude of purposes. The expression "fine past kerosene" is synonymous with excellence.) I am tired after the long day. The surf thunders beneath my open window. Time to seek the shelter of my net.

30th September 1941

From my balcony I watch the fishermen prepare to sail. There is a great surf breaking on the steep beach. One after another the combers come roaring in until there are as many as five or six chasing one another into the land. The first canoe is pushed into the sea. The five men who are her crew paddle furiously, though making little headway. The first breaker rears up in front of them but the canoe climbs it like the side of a hill and slips down into the valley following after. The next green monster comes rolling in and, like a swing boat at the fair, the canoe leaps up until it seems to be standing on its end, then down it comes with a splash that makes the men in her bob in their seats like marionettes. After surviving the next three breakers, the fishermen paddle away, then break sail and drift off towards the horizon. One after another the canoes go off but disaster overtakes the last. A great wave stands it on its stern and then topples it over broadside into the trough and she fills with water. The canoe is soon baled out and she goes off to join the others.

When the fishermen have gone the children come out to play. The boys swim out through the breakers and return like bullets on their home-made surf boards. The girls and women swim and dance a hundred yards up the beach. I never got any explanation for this separation of the sexes. The girls are lovely here. They seem happy, laughing and dancing all the time, so different from those one sees in Accra. With some cajoling and a few pennies I take some photographs. In one of his books Cedric Belfrage writes of the director who told his cameraman to "go to Bali and bring back a screenful of tits". He might as well have made the trip to Prampram where he would have found as fine a beachful of breasts as anywhere in Bali.

5th October 1941

A quiet Sunday morning, even the fishermen have beached their boats. I breakfast off newly laid eggs and freshly baked bread. I lie on my deck-chair and finish *Sons and Lovers*. The afternoon is equally quiet and the evening calm as a cathedral close. But it is all a hoax, a calm before the storm. At seven o'clock Jacob rushes into my room crying, "My wife go catch belly palaver!"

"Maybe it was the duck eggs we had this morning," I reply.

"No!" says Jacob emphatically, "This be proper belly palaver. This be pickin palaver!"

"Good God!" I cry. "Surely she's not coming off already!"

I am aghast. I haven't delivered a baby since my student days. When I go downstairs and enter the little room she and Jacob inhabit, I find her looking very pregnant indeed. She has the pains, she has the look, and so has the father. As she finds it more comfortable sitting up, Jacob brings down my deck-chair and we help her into it. With a few reassuring and meaningless phrases, I escape to my room where I gather my scattered wits and plan the coming campaign. Rodger's *Treatise on Tropical Diseases* is not much of a help. I am trying to recall all the right steps when Jacob interrupts with a message. A small boy has brought a note from the post-office some miles away. I flatten the creased paper and read:

Official Telephone Message from Colonel Donnelly
To Capt. N. S. Mair at Prampram
Transport arriving tomorrow 0915 hours to collect you Monday
6 October 1941. Posting Orders received
                    Signed
                        indecipherable
                        Cpl. of Police

You can guess how I felt when I read that message. Mrs J. ready to pop off and posting orders for me. I try to get back to my immediate problem but the message from the corporal of police keeps intruding. I begin to wonder. Where am I off to next? What have Fate and the British Army in store for me now?

When I go downstairs the lady's pains have subsided and she is sleeping quietly. I go to bed but I sleep badly, midwifery and secret movements keep colliding in my dreams. Finally I get up and the moon is full. I dress and go downstairs only to find that Jacob is also up and anxious like all new fathers the world over. His wife is still sleeping so we go for a walk along the sand. We find that others have also been awake but for a different purpose. Here a turtle is lying on its back, its stumpy legs waving futilely in the air. A villager has found it deep in a hole in the sand where it has been laying its eggs, has dragged it out and turned it turtle. No need to keep an eye on it, because no one would dream of stealing another's catch. Further along the beach we come across kerosene tins, their tops removed, sunk into the sand till the upper edge is flush with the surface. Inside are numerous small crabs. As they scramble across the sand the crabs fall into the tins. The sides are too smooth and steep for them to climb out. In the morning the women come and collect their haul. Finally Jacob and I turn in and snatch a few hours' sleep.

I am up early to catch the baby who may be coming, but the pains are now few and weak. With a bit of luck I might get Mrs. J. back to the village behind the cantonment in Accra, and safely into the hands of the local midwife. Indeed my luck is holding, because the three-tonner arrives an hour earlier than I expected. The driver warns me that after the overnight rain the road is bad. But I do not care what the road is like provided it leads to the village where deliverance is at hand. All my kit is put on board, followed by Mrs J., who is seated comfortably on my deck-chair. Jacob sits on my tin trunk and holds her hand. The gears crash and we are off! The journey back to the main road is a nightmare. What were furrows are now defiles and what were defiles are now small lakes. We slip and slide and skid. Only the skill of the black driver keeps us upright and going forward. Suddenly, over the roar of the engine, I can hear a frantic knocking on the rear window of the cabin. It is Jacob and he is shouting something I can't make out. With a sinking feeling I know the heavens have fallen.

"Stop! for Christ's sake, stop the bloody truck," I yell at the driver.

"There's a woman at the back having a baby!"

We stop. I am about to climb into the back of the truck when Jacob says, "Not go so fast. My wife break your chair."

"You mean she isn't coming off?"

"Pickin no come yet, but chair plenty broke."

"Damn the chair," I say happily and get in beside the driver.

"Softly, softly, driver," I tell him, pointing to the back. "I want only two passengers on this truck when we get to Accra."

And softly, softly we went. And in due course, Jacob's wife had her baby in the village behind the cantonment. And I got my posting orders. And here I am, at the end of one odyssey and the beginning of another.

II. The Gambia

Back at G.H.Q. in Accra I met Lt. Col. Donnelly who was responsible for maintaining the health of the troops in the four West African colonies. A lean, leathery South African, this was the man who was to change the whole tenor of my life. He greeted me warmly and told me that Brigadier Hepple, overall director of medical services, had just learned that I held a diploma in public health and was posting me to the Gambia as Donnelly's deputy in the rank of major. Meanwhile, he said, it would be a good idea if I took advantage of the excellent library at Achimota College, to learn something about the Gambia, and when I had done that I might join him for dinner and a game of poker afterwards. I was delighted with my promotion. I would not have gone away feeling so pleased with myself had I know of the appalling conditions in the Gambia, where the life-expectancy of the natives was only twenty-six years, less than the cattle they tended.

The first thing that struck me about the Gambia was its improbability. On the map it looked like a splinter in the vast bulge of French Senegal. The founding of the colony was a typical English gambit. The Portuguese discovered the Gambia River in 1455, and the English first traded there in 1587. After 300 years of struggle with the French, Portuguese and

Dutch, the English emerged victorious, claiming a strip of territory some 300 miles long and seven miles wide on either bank, thus depriving Senegal of what would have been its most valuable waterway. But it was a short-lived victory. When the French developed Dakar, all the trade of Senegal went through the new port. Although the Gambia River was navigable by ocean-going vessels for nearly 200 miles from its mouth, Bathurst, the chief settlement and capital of Gambia, was a port without a hinterland. It was a poor country. Its only cash crop was peanuts and there was barely enough rice, maize and millet for local needs. The weather was lousy. Torrential rain fell from early in July to the end of October and for the rest of the year life was hot and uncomfortable. In the wet season malaria was rife, especially in the mangrove-fringed marshes surrounding Bathurst.

One piece of interesting information I did not find in the books was told me by a naval officer who had served in the Gambia. He said that in the dry season the nights were sometimes so cold that the thin-blooded old hands could be found huddled over a flat-iron filled with burning charcoal, trying to get warm. I do not know if this was a sailor's tall tale, but I record it for what it is worth.

I disembarked at Bathurst from H.M.S. *Royal Scotsman* on 24th October in a tropical downpour that obliterated any chance of first impressions. Even now, I find it difficult to recall the cardinal features of this anonymous town. My first concern was to recover my tin trunk from the jumble of cargo lying on the quay. A harassed transport officer herded me and a group of newly-arrived pink-faced officers to a truck that brought us to a compound on a low promontory overlooking the sea. Through my streaming glasses I saw what appeared to be a native village of circular mud huts with conical grass roofs. Surely there must be some mistake? But there was none. The authorities had taken the wise decision to use local material and traditional design, proved through generations of use, and by doing so provided each of us with a cool, spacious and private hut. To reinforce our privacy, it was not long before we built low fences round our huts, thus turning our compound into a tropical suburbia. When the Americans came to Gambia, to take over the airfield at Jeswang, they brought with them prefabricated living quarters, small cabins off a central corridor. Each cabin was air-conditioned and accommodated two men with just enough room to move around. How the Americans envied us our primitive huts! The American padré often came to mine, not to save my soul but to get away from his claustrophobic quarters.

When I had set up my camp-bed and mosquito net, I reported to the A.D.M.S., who seemed a friendly sort of fellow. He gave me a brief rundown of the situation in the Gambia which was not very good, to put it mildly. Malaria, dysentery and beri-beri flourished. There was hardly a vacant bed in 55 General Hospital at Cape St. Mary. The War Office was complaining that troops and merchant seamen on vessels calling at the Gambia were subsequently going down with malaria. Everyone was grousing about the rations, or lack of them. The Vichy French, only seven miles away, maintained a strict neutrality but were decidedly unfriendly. They kept a firm watch on the border and it was impossible to get fresh meat from the Senegal. If I cared to go along to the Victoria Hospital, the African hospital in Bathurst, I would see what the military occupation of the Gambia had done for its inhabitants. So began my stint in the Gambia which lasted over a year.

It has been said, that of all the people born in the world since it began, more than half have died of malaria. After three years in West Africa, I am inclined to believe it. This recurring, prostrating infection was the most important medical problem the military had to face, particularly in the Gambia. Within two months of their arrival in the colony, seven out of every ten Europeans from military forward units were taken ill with malaria, and most had two or three attacks in that time. Much of what I had to say and do about antimalarial precautions was not so much educating, as re-educating. It had all been said before I came, and it would all be said again after I had gone. The battle against malaria, like painting the Forth Bridge, is never-ending.

The malaria-control officer was not particularly popular. He had to impress on all personnel the need to observe rules that many found irksome. It was not uncommon to find officers and other ranks – officers were the worst offenders – sitting about in shorts after dark, when the mosquitoes came out, literally, looking for blood. It was difficult to ensure that mepacrine was taken regularly. A tablet a day kept malaria at bay, but only if it was kept up. Mosquito nets were effective only if they had no holes in them. I made an inspection in one battalion and found that ninety per cent of the nets had holes in them, some large enough for a mouse to get through. And even when the net was intact it did not deter the blood-thirsty mosquitoes from waiting until the sleeper's limbs touched the netting, when they would begin feeding. In my investigations I collected satiated mosquitoes, sweeping them from the nets into wide-necked bottles in much the same way as my boyhood friends had collected bluebottles.

One can go on describing the various problems that had to be dealt with to achieve a reasonable standard of control. How, after months of agitation, mosquito wire gauze arrived in the Gambia and quarters were mosquito-proofed after a fashion. How, after a few months, time and climate took their toll. The wooden doors warped, the gauze rusted away, and worst of all, doors of mosquito-locks if closed sharply brought down the plaster from the bamboo lathes beneath, leaving holes large enough for a cat to jump through. But overall, with the considerable help of the Field Hygiene Section and the civil adminstration, we were able to reduce the incidence of malaria to manageable proportions.

There was another problem which, as far as I am aware, did not arise to the same extent in the other colonies. Put simply, we just did not have enough food for everybody. After the Dakar fiasco, the equivalent of two army brigades and nearly 1,000 airmen were rushed to the Gambia, with the result that the European population increased nearly 4 times; in addition to African troops there was a considerable influx of labourers from the rest of the country. On top of the French embargo, an outbreak of rinderpest in the local cattle curtailed meat supplies to vanishing point. Fruit, eggs and vegetables were practically non-existent. Owing to the shortage of shipping, imports had to be greatly restricted and the greater part of the food had to be obtained from our other African colonies. Unfortunately, the ships available for coastal shipping were neither fast nor fitted with extensive refrigeration. I can remember condemning a large consignment of canned meat which had arrived in the colony from Sierra Leone. If handled roughly the swollen cans were liable to explode, leaving a little piece of gristle at the bottom.

Nearly one third of the RAF personnel at Jeswang suffered from beri-beri because they refused to eat unpolished rice and other foodstuffs containing vitamin B, like peanuts, Marmite, egg-fruit and pumpkins when they were available. One foodstuff that we all looked forward to was our monthly bar of chocolate. Before we received it, we swore we would take only one small segment each day, so that it would last for at least a week or even a fortnight, but invariably our resolution wavered and the chocolate disappeared in one night.

If food was in short supply, whisky and gin were readily available. They were easily transported and did not need refrigerated ships. Liquor was so cheap on the Gold Coast when I was there, we did not take a bottle to a party, we took a case! If not so plentiful in the Gambia, supplies were still adequate. The officers' mess on a Saturday night was like a wild-west saloon. I suppose to some extent they were under stress and their behaviour was understandable, but sometimes it could take a nasty turn, as I was to discover.

The only other Jew in the mess was Monty Brill (only his forename is real). He was a major in the Royal Army Service Corps. He had worked his way up from the ranks and if he was not a likeable person he was efficient. The junior officers and other ranks were not allowed to forget he was Major Brill, a designation he kept even when he had become a prosperous developer in Manchester.

One particularly rowdy Saturday evening, about half a dozen officers were playing the game of going round the walls of the mess without putting a foot on the floor. Flimsy chairs were breaking under the weight of leaping lieutenants scarcely able to keep upright on the floor itself. Suddenly, a beery captain cried out, "Let's debag Major Brill," (with an emphasis on the Major), "and christen him with this," waving a beer bottle in his hand. For the uninitiated, to debag someone is Oxbridge for removing his trousers. Although he appeared drunk, I thought the Captain had chosen his words carefully. They left the mess to look for Brill and I went back to my hut and barred the door.

I could hear them looking for Brill, but apparently they could not find him, because the next thing I knew they were baying at my door. The Captain shouted, "Come out, you little prick, and take your medicine!" He was still choosing his words carefully. They pounded on the door. I could hear some of them scrambling over the grass roof. At that moment, out of nowhere, I remembered one of my father's favourite sayings: "If you forget you are a Jew, don't worry. Someone will remind you."

Then it struck me. This was my own personal pogrom. My father used to tell me, how, in Lithuania, neighbours who had been friendly all week would, after a night at the inn, turn on you like a band of drunken Cossacks. The only thing you could do, he said, was to close the shutters, lock the door, put out the lamps, and pretend you weren't there. Better a broken window or an overturned handcart than a broken head. Next morning it was as though the night had never been.

As I thought about this I became filled with a terrible rage. I opened my tin trunk and took out my revolver, which I kept to defend myself against an enemy. I called out so they could all hear me.

"I know it's Brill you want. If you think I will do instead you're mistaken. I've got a revolver here. If you don't get off that roof I'll fire into it."

There was a sudden hush. I could hear them scuttling off the roof, and the mutter of their voices as they went back to the mess. The next morning it was, "Sorry about last night, Doc. You know we didn't mean anything. It was just a bit of fun."

It was a long time before I spoke to any of them again.

By March 1942, I had been on the Coast for sixteen months, the last six of them in the Gambia. I had still two months to go before my tour of duty finished when I received a letter from Colonel Donnelly asking if I would be prepared to come back, after leave in the U.K., for another eighteen months.

Since Pearl Harbor and America's entry into the war, the ports and airfields of West Africa had become of prime importance as staging bases for American troops and supplies, and as air halts on the route to the Middle East and Far East. Between 1942 and 1943, something like 200 American aeroplanes a day used Accra airport and Jeswang was finally taken over by them. One story that went the rounds in Gambia and, I am sure, must have been told in a similar form elsewhere, was about the encounter between the pilot of the first American aeroplane to land at Jeswang on its way to the Middle East, and a British corporal painstakingly spraying the interior of the plane with insecticide. Impatient at the corporal's progress, the pilot said, "Come on, buddy. Dontcha know there's a war on?"

Back came the grumpy reply, "Yes, I've known it for two years now!"

When I got Donnelly's letter I was fit and well. Up till then, I had escaped malaria and dysentery and could see no reason to refuse. I told him so. A fortnight later, I had my first attack of malaria. It happened at a battalion jamboree on Cape St. Mary. It was a beautiful afternoon. I was standing next to a bonfire as big as a house. Nearby were two Queen Alexandra nursing sisters. Suddenly I felt a chill envelop me. I shivered as though someone were walking over my grave. I gritted my teeth to keep them from chattering. I could not understand why the nurses in their flimsy dresses were so oblivious of the cold. My head began to throb and my bones ached. I felt nauseated and tried not to vomit. The nurses were looking at me strangely, as though I had had one too many. I managed to get back to my hut and fell on my camp bed. A copy of the *Bedside Esquire* was on the tin trunk that doubled as a bedside table. The book was open at a very amusing article I had been reading when I left for the party. I picked up the book and began to read. Then I got up, went outside and was sick. Where I had been cold, I felt hot and my bones were breaking one by one. Though my head was throbbing worse than ever, I went back to the amusing article. They told me afterwards I was laughing hysterically when they carted me off to hospital.

When I came to I was still hot and very thirsty. I was given a small glass of bitter-tasting quinine which I promptly brought up, and which was as promptly administered again. Then I began to sweat profusely till the bedclothes were soaked through. When they were changed I fell asleep and when I awoke my headache was gone, my bones no longer ached, but I still felt drained and weak. The relief, however, was only temporary. Within ten hours the whole cycle began again. I was in hospital for about ten days before I felt well enough to resume duty.

On the evening of the day I was taken ill, I had been billed to give a lecture to a new intake on the avoidance of malaria. When a friend of mine – at least I thought he was a friend – announced to the assembled troops that there would be no lecture because Major Mair was in hospital with malaria, the hall exploded in laughter.

On the 14th June 1942, after nineteen months on the Coast, I went home on leave. I had been put in charge of a detachment of N.C.O.s from various units returning for good from their tour of duty. They were the pale yellow survivors and they wore their bush hats and tropical uniforms with jaundiced pride. As we sailed between the familiar banks of the Clyde towards our berth, I told them that in their outfits they should have no difficulty with the customs.

"Just declare what you've got except, of course, your great-coats."

At the mention of their great-coats, they all laughed. I was not supposed to know that the brass buttons of their coats had been removed and replaced with similar buttons of pure gold crafted by skilful Ashanti goldsmiths, which they were smuggling into the country. As for much of the rest, it was liquor bought in regimental messes. As I predicted, they had no trouble with the customs. I had left my great-coat with its original brass buttons in the Gambia, so that when it came my turn I told the customs officer I had only two bottles of Drambuie to declare.

"TWO bottles of Drambuie!" he said. "A don't believe you," waving me on.

The poor man had grounds for his disbelief. Drambuie, the liqueur of perfection, said to go back to Bonnie Prince Charlie, disappeared from the shelves in Scotland after the outbreak of war, exported for precious dollars.

My mother, who was already depressed because of my absence abroad, got more depressed when she saw how yellow I looked. It was hard to convince her that the Army had not sent me back because I was dying. It was the mepacrine, I told her, the "medicine" I had been taking, and continued to take while I was in the U.K. Father and Henny still got up at dawn and went to the workshop. Most of their workers were either called up or laid off. There was no demand for three-piece suites. They made ammunition boxes instead. Ray was her old dependable self, working in an office and helping at home.

When I was not lazing about the house or garden, I made the rounds of the family, wearing my bush hat which went down well, particularly with the younger members. I tried looking up old acquaintances but many of them were already in the army, and those that were not had their own problems. After two weeks I felt I had exhausted the domestic scene and went to London.

I saw my old friend, Doug Boddie. At my request, he had booked a room for me at the Regent Palace Hotel in Piccadilly; no mean feat, because at that time London was swarming with Americans and other Allies. In making the reservation, he had signed his letter, "Douglas Boddie, Secretary to Major Mair, Royal West African Frontier Force". I think this must have impressed the management of the hotel, because I got a very comfortable twin-bedded room.

Doug was no longer a member of the Communist Party. I do not know whether he was expelled on ideological grounds or for moral turpitude, because he had left his family and was living with the Countess of C, a divorcee and compulsive gambler, who would not walk 100 yards if there was a taxi at the kerb. I had got in touch with the passenger who had helped me with *Emphysema* on the Devon hills, and the four of us had a riotous time in London, until my leave and money ran out.

I returned to Bathurst at the end of August. In November we learned the Allies had landed in French North Africa and later in the same month that Boisson, Governor-General of French West Africa and a faithful ally of Vichy, was now reconsidering his position. Throughout the War the French in Senegal had remained strictly neutral, but now it appeared we would have even less to fear and the lights of Dakar, only forty miles to the north, seemed brighter and closer.

I was now a desk-warrior. I was quite happy to pass on the anti-malarial work in the field to the O.C. field hygiene section. My job was to prepare reports for G.H.Q., Accra, on the health, or lack of health of the men serving in the Gambia.

One item that did not appear on the list of maladies was prickly heat. As though malaria and dysentery were not enough for those condemned to serve in the tropics, the good Lord devised prickly heat, an ailment worthy of Job. Humans have about three to four million sweat glands and in the humid heat of West Africa they work overtime. The victim sweats and sweats until he becomes a miserable mass of red, itching, sodden skin. And for him there is no relief, except to pray for the cool days of the rainy season or until he becomes acclimatized, as I did.

I prepared reports on personnel declared unfit for further service in the tropics or anywhere else for that matter. They made melancholy reading, boys still in their teens returning like old men.

One report that caught my attention concerned a labourer employed at Jeswang airfield, who died in the African hospital four days after the onset of a fulminating fever. After an autopsy, the hospital pathologist was of the opinion that the cause of death was acute liver necrosis brought about by a toxic drug he had been taking for the treatment of tapeworms. But I believed the fulminating fever, the sudden death and the damage to the liver were also consistent with a diagnosis of yellow fever. If yellow fever had been shorn of its terrors by universal vaccination, particularly among Europeans, it was still present among Africans. Twenty years after the period about which I am writing, a devastating epidemic of yellow fever occurred in neighbouring Senegal with thousands of cases and hundreds of deaths.

When I mentioned yellow fever to the A.D.M.S. he became quite agitated. Our first priority, he said, was to intensify spraying of all buildings on the airfield and to continue doing so until further notice. I was to send specimens of the man's liver to the pathologist in Accra for a second opinion.

A few days later, I was in the mess, playing an after-dinner game of dominoes with the Intelligence Officer, when a puce, plethoric major came stumping up to us. He was trembling with rage. He wanted to know what was going on. He then described how he had been stopped on a road near Jeswang by an American G.I. armed with an automatic weapon. He was told he could go no further. The road was closed to all traffic and all ranks. The indignity of it – a Yank, and a private to boot, telling a British Major what he could not do in a British colony.

The Intelligence Officer said he would look into it. Then, for me, the labourer, the A.D.M.S., the major and the Yank, all fell into place. When the Major left, still muttering to himself, I said to my friend on the other side of the dominoes, "You would think Roosevelt was coming."

He looked at me over his half-moon wire spectacles, "You bugger!" he said.

It was a well-kept secret. The tight security that kept our irate Major away from the air-field also kept most of us from seeing the President. Much later, I learned, over another game of dominoes, that he had arrived in a Pan American flying boat after a nineteen-hour flight from Belém on the northern coast of Brazil. The presidential party then transferred to a Douglas C-54 standing-by at Jeswang, which we had so assiduously drenched with insecticide a few days before.

Brief though the visit was, it was enough to confirm the President in his anti-colonial views. He was appalled by what he saw and learned about the wretched life of the natives after 300 years of British rule. According to Elliott Roosevelt (*As He Saw It*), his father swore he would not "aid or abet the British Empire in its imperialist ambitions". However, it did not prevent him from flying on to Casablanca where he and Churchill decided on the landing in Sicily and on the systematic bombing of Germany.

The report from the pathologist in Accra had arrived in The Gambia a few days before Roosevelt's arrival. It read: "While the changes in the liver resemble those found in yellow fever I am of the opinion they are more consistent with carbon tetrachloride poisoning."

I still wonder if this was a medical diagnosis or a political decision, to ensure that there would be no hitch in the meeting of the Titans.

III. Sierra Leone

In the spring of 1943, after fifteen months in the Gambia, I returned to Accra. I had begun to count the days. By the beginning of 1944 I should be finished with West Africa and on my way home. But as I was to learn, the Coast had not finished with me.

The first warning came when I went out late one night to take off a seaman suffering from cerebral malaria on a ship lying off the shore. By the time the surf-boat with ten paddlers and a steersman had thrashed its way through the surf, I was chilled and soaked to the skin and on the following day I was in hospital with my second severe attack of malaria. This time it took me longer to recover and I wasn't the same man I had been two weeks earlier. From time to time, I ran a low fever which I began to accept as normal.

One day Colonel Donnelly called me into his office. He began with a compliment, which should have warned me, because he was a man not given to compliments. He called me his "trouble-shooter". He then asked me if I would be prepared to go to Sierra Leone. It would be my last move before I went home. We had reached a stage between us when he did not order me, he asked me, which in itself was also a compliment. I agreed to go.

He told me things were getting a bit awkward in Freetown. The A.D.M.S., it seemed, had crossed the border between eccentricity and dottiness. He was issuing orders that a concoction of sulphur and molasses was to be taken every day by all ranks to prevent constipation. There was also the usual business about malaria in merchant seamen after calling at Freetown. With a touch of sardonic humour, Donnelly agreed it was unlikely I would be able to clear that up by the time I went home. The deputy assistant director of hygiene had gone home sick a month ago and Major Bermingham, commanding the field hygiene section, was in need of support. A coaster was sailing for Freetown in the next forty-eight hours. He would reserve a cabin for me.

As soon as I left Donnelly, I began to pack my old tin trunk. Into it went my books, bundles of letters from home, the revolver I had never used except to knock empty cans off the rocks at Cape St. Mary and scare the "cossacks" off the grass roof of my house in the Gambia, my tattered tropical uniforms, and my immaculate dress uniform smelling of moth-balls, and last but most reverently my collection of Ashanti goldweights. I came across these little brass weights for weighing gold dust and gold nuggets when I first arrived in Kumasi and from that time on I began collecting them. Some I found in Kumasi but for the most part, I took the opportunity of my visits to outlying units to look for the weights in neighbouring villages. With Jacob, who spoke Twi, acting as my interpreter, I bought them sometimes singly, often in groups of five or ten, and once an incredible haul – a *futuo*, the equipment of a goldsmith wrapped in a white cloth. It contained his scales, spoons for lifting gold dust on to the pans of the scales hanging on threads, scoops for larger quantities, boxes for holding gold dust and nuggets, and about sixty brass weights. I cannot recollect what I paid for them but it was in pennies rather than in shillings and rarely in pounds. Later I learned that some of the weights were more than 300 years old. By the time I left the Gold Coast I counted 260 weights.

The weights were made by the lost wax process. A beeswax model of the weight was simply encased in a cocoon of plaster and charcoal. This was baked in a charcoal fire until the mould hardened and the beeswax ran out. The lost wax was then replaced with molten brass. When the mould was cool it was broken open and the weight removed. Only one weight at a time could be made by this method, and in this respect each weight was unique, for in the casting both wax model and mould were destroyed.

Models were either figurative or geometric. The figurative weights depicted a whole range of Ashanti life in peace and war and the artefacts that went with it. A language rich in proverbs provided a never-ending supply of subjects. Here is a man with a keg of gunpowder on his head and a flaming torch in his right hand, telling us that only a fool goes looking for trouble. A bigger fool has not only gunpowder and torch, but also a dagger in his left hand pointing at his eye. The miniatures are so fine, you can count fingers and toes. In addition, the goldsmith made castings of a wide variety of birds, animals and vegetables.

The geometric weights, by far the most numerous in the collection, range from a simple bar, through the swastika which the Ashanti likened to the hand of the colobus monkey, a stupid and malicious animal, to the most ornate and intricate designs which defy classification.

Finally, I wrapped in a towel the most prized piece of the collection, a three-legged brass pot about 8½ inches high and 4½ inches wide, of which William Fagg, Deputy Keeper of the British Museum wrote:

> "... It is certainly a *kuduo* or ritual vessel used for various purposes in Ashanti; sometimes they were used to hold gold dust for anointing of Kings and other important persons living or just dead, and sometimes buried with such persons and containing either fat or other things intended to be of use to the person's soul in the other world. I do not think we have any example of this exact type which is said to have been placed before the coffins of the Ashanti Kings in the destroyed mausoleum at Bantama ... It is an interesting piece and we should be glad to know if it is ever available for disposal. By the way, our technician points out to me that, as you are probably aware already, it seems to be in need of treatment for bronze disease."

As I write this, the kuduo, cured of its bronze disease, takes pride of place in the centre of the living-room mantelshelf.

When I look back on my five months in Freetown, I wonder how much I really accomplished. The problem of antimalarial precautions in troopships was formidable, and my contribution was minuscule. Freetown harbour is the largest harbour in the world after Rio de Janeiro and Sydney. When I was there, it was not unusual to see more than 200 ships anchored at the one time. Troopships like the *Queen Mary* and the *Queen Elizabeth* were anchored as far as possible from the malarious shore. Even then, lighters visiting a ship could still bring mosquitoes to it.

On the 21st of September 1943, I wrote to Donnelly:

"I understand that the D.D.M.S. will be visiting this Area about the end of October. I hope you will be feeling fit enough to accompany him, as I would like the opportunity to see you again before your tour finishes.

"This place is all you and Brigadier Hepple said it was. Since my arrival I have concentrated on shipping and malaria. There are other problems which require attention but I feel these two are the most important. At my suggestion the A.D.M.S. forwarded to G.H.Q. a few recommendations which should facilitate the work of the Embarkation Medical Officer, Freetown. Instructions to S.M.O.s' troopships, with special reference to coasting vessels, have also been compiled. I think we have got to grips with the problem of shipping." [On re-reading this, I am amazed at my optimism.]

"With the troops ashore, as far as malaria is concerned, I think we are making some progress. As you know, I made a census of antimalarial precautions in units and found nearly sixty per cent did not carry out mepacrine parades or weekly net inspections. Area was informed and immediate action was taken.

"My relations with Area staff and O.C.s medical units are amicable and I have found them most helpful. Major Bermingham is the best O.C. hygiene section I have yet worked with and we pull well together. He has put in a lot of work in this Area.

"I have been keeping fairly well but the continuous rains and the damp are rather tiring. Nevertheless, I hope when this tour finishes to be in there punching."

In reply, Donnelly wrote:

"I was glad to receive your letter of 21.9.43, and for the

useful information it contained of both your troubles and your progress.

"Unfortunately, I will not be able to visit your Area with the D.D.M.S. as I am suddenly 'off' elsewhere. Let us hope that some day we'll be working together as a team again but in some more operational sphere . . ."

I thought he was probably returning to the U.K. to take part in the "Second Front" we had heard so much about. The prospects of seeing him again in that vast undertaking seemed remote.

Meanwhile. the days that passed more and more slowly were lightened by the presence of Major Patrick Xavier Bermingham, the amiable Irishman with whom I shared a colonial mansion on the Hill. I liked him, for among other things, he liked to hear me sing Stephen Foster's "Beautiful Dreamer", which seemed to strike a romantic chord in him.

The house next to us was occupied by a Syrian merchant and his wife and children. We became friendly when Paddy diagnosed malaria in the youngest child and sent her at once to hospital. The merchant began to invite us across for drinks in the evening, and while Paddy and I looked longingly at his beautiful wife, the massive Syrian would pick up metal beer bottle caps and nonchalantly bend them double between finger and thumb.

Three months after my arrival in Freetown I suffered a severe attack of diarrhoea. So prolonged was the bloody flux, the physicians suspected amoebic dysentery. Then followed nights of nauseating emetine, mornings of bitter Epsom salts and afternoons of driving to the hospital to provide a specimen for the pathologist. The latter had chosen the magic number of seven stool examinations before he would commit himself to a diagnosis. After number six I revolted. I refused to continue with the regimen. The pathologist washed his hands of me, and I returned to my office. But I had no illusions. I was a sick man. I sweated at the least exertion and tired readily. I could sleep only by sitting up supported by three cushions. And even with that, I slept fitfully. Sometimes in moments of depression I felt I had had my fill of the Guinea Coast, its sun, its enervating humidity, its fevers and drenching rains. How often had there come to my lips the words of that unknown poet, crying down the centuries from some tropic shore:

> Western wind, when wilt thou blow,
> The small rain down can rain?
> Christ, if my love were in my arms
> And I in my bed again!

My African Odyssey was coming to an end, not with a bang but a whimper.

I asked the A.D.M.S. to apply for an immediate replacement. By the time he came, I had completed my second tour, and a week later I boarded a Norwegian ship bound for England.

I have warm memories of that voyage which went a long way to restore my flagging spirits. At Dakar we took on 400 Americans and at once the ship went "dry". Unlike the British, the Americans did not allow alcohol on troopships. It was amusing to see the "Old Coaster" standing at the bar, with foot on rail, sipping his soft drink. I spent mornings walking the deck with an American captain from Alabama. He told me about his encounter with a doctor serving in St. Helena where the troopship had stopped for a few days on its way to Dakar. The doctor admired the Captain's watch and wanted to buy it. The Captain agreed to sell it, for he could get another in the army PX. A price was struck. The Captain gave the doctor the watch. The doctor scribbled something on a piece of paper and gave it to the Captain, saying, "I say, old boy, do you mind taking my chit, for the time being?"

Said the indignant Captain to me, "Ah give him ma watch, and he offers me his shit! Sounds like Lend-Lease to me!"

It was Christmas when the ship put into Gibraltar. As a concession all personnel were given four cloakroom tickets with which they could obtain four alcoholic drinks. In no time the tickets became currency. I was initiated into the mysteries of crap by my Alabama friend.

"When the two dice add up to 7 or 11 that's a natural and you win the cloakroom tickets. When they come up 2, 3 or 12 that's a crap and you lose them. If the dice show any of the other numbers, that's a point, and you keep throwing till the same number comes up again, unless you're unlucky and throw a 7, in which case you go thirsty."

It seemed straightforward enough to me, but there was more to it than that.

Crap-shooters are animists who believe there are spirits in the dice which must be coaxed and persuaded to appear in their natural form. Pleas, like "Ma little baby needs shoes", precede the throwing of the dice. I do not recall where, in the ship, I played my first game of crap, but I remember the floor and the walls were tiled, so it might have been a large toilet which guaranteed a continuous flow of players. When I joined the circle of officers and N.C.O.s, squatting on their haunches, I was the only limey present. They welcomed me warmly, as they would a chicken ready for the plucking. In front of each, the cloakroom tickets. Play began with much pleading and cajoling and the occasional cry of triumph. Whenever my turn came I rolled the dice on the tiled floor without a word. More often than not I threw a natural or a winning point. Players came and went, the exhortations continuing without cease, while I sat quietly adding to my heap of tickets. While all this was going on two colonels stood watching the game. When I finally rose with my winnings, one colonel turned to the other, and in a slow Texas drawl said, "Just shows you, Joe. You don't have to talk to them!"

Chapter 11

Second Front

On the 4th of January 1944, I disembarked at Liverpool and on the same day was admitted to the Ormskirk Military Hospital. On the following day I was examined by a Medical Board and declared Category C, permanently unfit for general service.

After three months' sick leave I reported to A.D.M.S., 3rd Anti-Aircraft Group in Bristol. He was most sympathetic and asked what he could do for me. I wondered if he could find me a nice quiet spot near the sea. He suggested a reception centre at the holiday resort of Weston-Super-Mare in Somerset. The post of commanding officer was usually held by a captain, so I would have to go down one rung. I told him that was the least of my worries. A few days later I was comfortably installed in the centre, the personnel of which, I soon discovered, were with few exceptions, females! When I had left England in 1940, members of the A.T.S. (Auxiliary Territorial Service) were comparatively few in number. In 1943 the A.T.S. reached a peak strength of more than 200,000, and at least twenty of them were in the centre as cleaners, cooks, drivers and nursing auxiliaries!

But I was not destined to enjoy the delights of Weston-Super-Mare. I was feeling my way about, so to speak, when Fate in the form of Lt. Col. Donnelly decided otherwise. In less than a month I was posted to Bournemouth to take command of a field hygiene section mobilizing for D-day. So much for Category C.

The fighting had moved from the Normandy beaches when I got

135

orders to ready the unit for embarkation. All ranks had already received leave and I was about to make a flying visit to Glasgow when I learned I was to hand over command to an officer who would be arriving shortly. Evidently category C was still in effect.

I can truthfully say I was disappointed. A field hygiene section is a small unit, maybe fifteen to twenty men drawn from the medical and service corps. The Commanding Officer is a specialist in military hygiene and usually holds the rank of Major, and he may have a non-medical junior officer to oversee transport of which the unit has disproportionately a large number. The C.O. gets to know each individual, his strengths and weaknesses. None suffers the anonymity of service in a large unit like a battalion.

When my replacement arrived I said goodbye to each man and left for Darlington to mobilize the 55th Field Hygiene Section. Most of the men of this new unit were recruited from the farmers and miners of the northeast. Once again I went through the paper work, indenting for pots and pans, three-ton trucks and bicycles. Meanwhile, Staff-Sergeant Brewin trained the men and kept discipline.

In September we received orders to move south within a week. The men were sent on embarkation leave and I waited once more for an officer to replace me. But none arrived. I had a couple of hours with my parents in Glasgow and crossed the Channel with the 55th Field Hygiene Section the following day.

We went ashore at the artificial Mulberry Harbour constructed at Arromanches in Normandy, and were immediately directed into an area that was once a field and was now a sea of mud. Jerricans were used as stepping-stones between one vehicle and another. Our cook was rounded up to work in the large central kitchen serving the many units parked there. When we finally got orders to move, I sent out a call over the tannoy for Private Dickie at the cookhouse to report to 55 Field Hygiene Section at once. When there was no sign of Dickie I sent out the message again. Next to us was a Canadian unit. When the call came out a third time, I heard a Canadian, who was sitting on the running board of his vehicle with his feet on a jerrican, say to his comrade, "I guess they're dredging for him."

On the evening of the second day we set off. It was raining heavily as we made our way along roads littered with burnt-out vehicles and the debris of war. We had been travelling for about three hours when my truck broke down. Staff-Sergeant Brewin went on ahead with the rest of the unit while my driver tried to effect a repair. It was pitch dark and he found it difficult working by the light of a dimmed torch. Eventually he got the engine running again and, sooner than we expected, we caught up with the rest of the unit. Soaked to the skin, they had been struggling to keep a three-ton truck with much of our equipment from slipping into a bomb crater. With half of its load removed, the truck was carefully towed back on to the road. the only casualty was a green-painted, stripped-down bicycle which, in the darkness, was left inadvertently on the roadside. I recall this, because a major and a captain held a court of enquiry about its loss when we were in Belgium. I took over the lead again and led the convoy into a ploughed field. At this point I decided to call a halt. Everyone was cold, wet and miserable. We were on the outskirts of a village and I tried to find shelter in a barn but I banged on doors in vain. In the end, the men piled into the trucks, trying to find a place to rest. I ordered the drivers of the trucks to run up the engines and give up their cabins to the motor-cyclists who were dropping with exhaustion. One of the drivers, a feckless, foolish youth, resented giving up his place. In front of the others, he said to me, "I suppose you'll be sitting up in the front too."

When he said this, we were standing inside his truck at the rear. After the night's frustrations, I could not contain myself. I hit him so hard, he fell over the tail-gate of the truck and when he picked himself up I put him on a charge; my first and last violent act in more than five years of war.

When everyone was safely, if not comfortably, under cover I went over to a burnt-out truck I had earmarked for myself. The cabin had no windows to keep out the cold wind that blew off the field, but its roof was still intact. I waited for the dawn. I was back "in the field" but it was hardly an auspicious return.

In due course we arrived, without further mishap, at our destination, the ancient town of Ath, some fifty miles south-west of Brussels, our quarters a disused furniture factory.

The problem of the rebellious driver was resolved the following day when he walked out of the factory gate in defiance of an order confining him to the billet. To my surprise he returned an hour later, looking very pleased with himself. When I asked him to account for his absence, he said he had been for a haircut, adding, "San fairy Ann, one day is as good as another for getting your hair cut!"

I wanted to throw the book at him, but when I had calmed down, the doctor in me took over from the soldier. He seemed quite oblivious of the trouble he was storing up for himself. I re-read his record of service compiled by several units, in none of which he had stayed very long. He had a string of charges, convictions and punishments, which any soldier with a modicum of intelligence could have easily avoided. I referred him to an Army psychiatrist. Back came the latter's report which amounted to the fact that the Army had given an eight-year-old child the licence to drive a three-ton truck. He went back to the Army pool, probably to surface again with another truck.

(In the absence of footnotes, I would point out that "San fairy Ann", approximated into English from the French "Ça ne fait rien" meaning "It doesn't matter" or "Why worry?", was a popular catch phrase among Tommies in World War I. It was practically unknown in World War II.)

From Ath I made forays every day into the surrounding country-side to inspect service units, prisoner of war camps, and installations commandeered by the Civil Affairs Unit in Ath for refugees fleeing from the battle areas and liberated slave labourers making their uncertain way homewards. The workshop of the field hygiene section was stretched to the limit trying to cope with the demands made upon it following these visits.

About the middle of December I was called away to attend a top-secret meeting where R.A.M.C. officers were informed that, until ordered otherwise, they must carry side-arms, contrary to the Geneva Convention. The weapons were to be worn unobtrusively in order not to disturb the

Major Mair in front of the chateau where his unit was billeted, Renaix,
Belgium, December 1944

civilian population. The reason for this surprising volte-face was that the Germans had just launched what proved to be their last great offensive of the War in the Ardennes, later known as "The Battle of the Bulge". We were told that the so-called Panzer Brigade 150, led by Otto Skorzeny, the daredevil S.S. commando, had slipped into Belgium with the German armoured divisions. Skorzeny's men, wearing American uniforms and driving captured American jeeps, trucks and tanks, were said to be sowing confusion by posing as military police and misdirecting American military traffic. The occupants of any American vehicle entering our units were to be asked to show their dog-tags. Apparently, these had not been included in the disguise. For several days American soldiers as far back as Paris were challenged to answer questions about the World Series, an unlikely interrogation in the British sector. As far as I recollect, all our American visitors at that time proved to be authentic. The offensive finally petered out about the middle of January, leaving a large number of prisoners to swell the camps that were going up in Belgium.

A prisoner of war camp is not the best place to look for humanity. There, the struggle to survive is intense and invariably the weak go to the wall. The prisoner has always looked to the doctor, an internee himself, to provide the care and comfort so often lacking. In most accounts, the doctor has rarely failed him. In the P.O.W. camp at Enghien, on the road between Ath and Brussels, the doctor failed dismally.

On one of my routine visits to this camp, the R.A.M.C. Staff-Sergeant who usually greeted me in an affable manner was visibly angry. He urged me to go with him to the sick-bay, a large marquee containing about forty beds occupied by sick and exhausted prisoners of war. Between the beds, nearly as many lay on stretchers placed on duck-boards to protect them from the wet and muddy ground. It was all pretty primitive, but the camp was being overwhelmed by the enemy, who were surrendering by the thousand. At one place, however, the duck-boards had been removed. Six men, on their unprotected stretchers, lay soaking on the wet ground.

"Look, Sir!" said the Staff-Sergeant, "look at what these bastards have done"

The bastards, I learned, were four newly-arrived S.S. doctors whose duty was to look after their compatriots. They had the privilege of having their own tent and other comforts that go with being an officer. They had come to the sick-bay on the previous evening when the Staff-Sergeant had gone off duty, and told the German orderlies to remove the duck-boards from under the stretchers and to take them to their tent, so that their boots would not get muddy.

The four doctors were paraded before Colonel Helm, the A.D.M.S., not in his office, but on the open ground of the camp, so that the prisoners could hear what he thought of them. Speaking in German, the colonel recounted what they had done and ended by telling them they were a disgrace to the medical profession. I could see it was making an impression on the prisoners, some of whom turned away in disgust. The four S.S. men listened in stony silence, model soldiers in their uptilted caps, tight black tunics, wide stiff breeches and shining jackboots. When Colonel Helm was finished with them, they saluted, and marched off to their tent which had lost its duck-boards.

When I hear people say they cannot understand how physicians, of all people, could conduct sadistic medical experiments on concentration camp inmates and prisoners of war, I recall the four S.S. doctors who did not hesitate to abuse their own comrades.

Chapter 12

Hélène

Shortly after the incident at Enghien, I paid a routine visit to Civil Affairs, a visit with undreamt-of consequences. It was lunchtime, as good a time as any to begin a visit. I sat down beside the C.O. I was familiar with most of those present. There was the small, dark Indonesian from some Dutch colony in a Dutch uniform, the florid Cockney-speaking Australian, the Hungarian girl who spoke excellent English, and the young Russian officer who spoke no English at all. He had been at the military college in Kharkov when the Germans captured the city. He was taken to Belgium, but escaped and had been in hiding until the Liberation. He wore British battle dress relieved by the gold and red epaulettes of a Russian officer. Next to him, sat my current companion, Diana O., a Dutch officer who had come all the way from Hollywood to serve her country. She used to regale me with scandalous stories, in which she played the central role, involving British politicians and senior military types, who came to Hollywood, ostensibly to plead their country's cause. A number of British officers, men and women completed the group, except for one person, an attractive young woman I had never seen before. She was sitting quietly between two young men who were competing for her attention. She was in the uniform of the Belgian Red Cross and a dark blue beret worn at a saucy angle gave her oval face a piquant look. Nodding in her direction, I said to the colonel, "That's not a bad-looking ambulance driver, you have there."

He replied, "She is not an ambulance driver. She is our new medical officer, and I think she's beautiful."

At that moment, I knew what Sandburg meant when he wrote, "The past is a bucket of ashes."

This may seem paradoxical coming from one writing an autobiography, but at the time I was thinking of my amours, past and present.

A few days later, on the 5th February, I, who had always kept that aspect of my life to myself, wrote to my parents:

> "I cannot tell you where I am or the work I am doing. That would be a breach of security. But I can tell you that in the last place I was at, we were working in a camp for Dutch refugees. The interesting thing about this camp was that many of the paid helpers, all young people, were Jews. I went there a few days ago. Stayed for three days to make sure everything was running O.K. for a new batch of refugees who were coming in. While I was there, I met a doctor, a girl, very lovely but as still as a mouse. I became friendly with her and learnt she too was Jewish. She is one of the doctors in the camp. We went to an estaminet where she talked and talked. She told me she had not talked like this for years. She could trust no-one. She was like an empty shell. No confidence or faith in herself. She told me her father was in Buchenwald concentration camp and her mother was in hospital with a nervous breakdown. She herself had nowhere to go except to her old home in Brussels, a large house empty of furniture except for a few sticks in the kitchen. She hated to go there. The Gestapo had occupied her home when her father was taken. I took her to my place for tea. There she told me that she had just entered her fourth year at the University when the Germans invaded Belgium. For three years she dodged the Gestapo and at the same time attended different hospitals in the country, passing her finals in 1943. Don't you think that took some pluck?"
>
> "I noticed that the book she was using to learn English was

Hélène at her sister's wedding, August 1939: with her is her grandfather, who threw the postcard out of the window of the train taking him to Westerbork, the Dutch concentration camp, on 12th January 1943. Twelve days later he died in Auschwitz.

an old edition of a popular instructor used in that country, and that it was well annotated. It had been used by her father when he was learning English. I took it away from her and bought her a new edition."

"When I saw her at breakfast in the mess, I asked her what she was doing that morning. She said she was going back to her billet to mend her uniform, and to get some powder and lipstick. So you can see my treatment was showing some signs of success. I left her that day with the promise to look in, now and then."

The hints in my letter, which I thought were tentative, were evidently obvious to my family. They were delighted at the thought that at last I was going to settle down and, although they did not say so, in marrying Hélène I would not be marrying "out". I had not even asked Hélène what she thought about it, and here was the family jumping to conclusions!

We tried to meet as often as possible, but it was not easy. The Field Hygiene Section had moved out of Ath and taken over a chateau near Renaix some fifteen miles away. Hélène's duties sometimes took her thirty or forty miles from Ath, as I mentioned in one letter to Glasgow:

"Just now, she is stationed about forty miles from here, but we manage to see one another whenever we can. The other day we met at an estaminet about half-way. I came in my truck and she hopped two trucks and a jeep with a two-mile walk in between to get there. We had a drink and then we went back to my place where we spent a lazy day in front of the fire . . . We have much in common, professionally and otherwise, and I haven't come across anyone I would like to settle down with so much."

In our talks together, Hélène drew a picture of what it was like to be a crypto-Jew during the Occupation. One who, in her own fashion, refused to submit and resisted to the end. What follows is her own story, in her own words, which I persuaded her to write:

Hélène's Tale

This is a story of what happened to me and my family and my friends, not because it was so different from what happened to millions of other people in occupied countries, but rather, because it was so similar.

But first, let me tell you who we were, or rather who we were not. We were not Belgians. My parents, my elder sister and I were born in Holland. At the end of the First World War, my father had established his business in Brussels. There, I spent the first twenty-five years of my life, in the family house, going to French-speaking schools, then to the medical faculty of the Free University of Brussels.

We were not religious. Both my parents came from Jewish homes. My father, one of four children, came from The Hague. My mother, one of nine children, came from a tiny village in North Holland. Both shed their orthodox beliefs when they left home at the age of fifteen to make a living. We had a very liberal up-bringing.

The middle thirties were marred by the Spanish Civil War and many young men fell fighting fascism in Spain. I remember how we, as students, organized meetings and found families who would temporarily adopt Spanish children.

During these years, the shrieking voice of an obscure Austrian had made itself heard more and more. Often on Sundays he was shouting speeches in German, which I did not understand, and the wireless was turned off with the comment, "This madman won't last."

And so we come to the spring of 1940. One morning I was suddenly wakened by a continuous roaring noise. I jumped out of bed and raced to the open window to see the sky obscured by formations of low-flying planes. The people at their windows shouted, "*C'est la guerre*, it is War." The wireless, usually silent in the early hours, continually repeated, "Attention! Enemy parachutists are landing." And this is how it started on the 10th May 1940.

The Belgians, remembering the German Occupation twenty-five years earlier had only one thought – NOT AGAIN! Soon people started packing their belongings, and those with cars were loading them with prams and bicycles, in readiness to move.

It was my first year as an intern medical student and on that Friday I cycled, as usual, to the hospital to work on the ward. Later in the morning I was called to the phone; my father asked that I should return home immediately to go with the family to France. He thought and hoped that the army and the Maginot Line, the French fortifications, would hold the Boches. It was just a precaution and we would soon be back.

I was reluctant to go away. At the hospital I had already seen doctors leaving "just to bring their families to safety", promising to return without delay. But I had to give way under pressure to words like, "If you don't come, we won't be able to go." Soon the roads were packed with cars. We were diverted from one secondary road to another, having to leave the main arteries to military convoys. We drove the whole day getting nowhere and finally, still in Belgium, we stopped in West Flanders near Ypres, at a place named Poperinghe, and looked for a bed for the night. Every place was full and we were grateful to obtain any beds available offered by local inhabitants. Thanks to my Girl Guide training, I had packed a rucksack and a pair of boots. The next morning with my rucksack on my back, hitching lifts I returned to the hospital in Brussels.

Despite the most optimistic news about our military successes, it took only seven days for the first Germans to enter the capital. On Friday, the 17th May, I was waiting at Avenue Brugman, and there came down the street one heavy motorcycle with a sidecar with two Germans in their green uniforms.

That was all!

The same day, placards were fixed on street corners and official buildings, signed by the Burgomaster of Brussels urging the population to refrain from any action that might endanger them and to remain indoors as much as possible. As in a Hitchcock film, the normal business of life was suddenly interrupted by the abnormal, the unexpected.

Boche uniforms were around the town, in the streets, in the cafés, having a beer, fraternizing with the locals – "They aren't as bad as last time," many said. Why should they be? With little opposition they found themselves in the most desirable capitals of Europe – Brussels, Amsterdam, Paris. Nothing could hold them back. And London was next. They plundered our shops. For the first time in years they drank real coffee, not ersatz.

During the summer of 1940, I lived in the nurses' home. The Germans took over the hospital. One day a medical team arrived and in twenty-four hours, all the patients were sent out, surgical wards, medical wards, psychiatric wards were emptied and replaced by their own people. Our handful of doctors and medical students were restricted to one ward. We were to look after their wounded prisoners, mainly French North Africans, with one German soldier to keep an eye on us. He was a medical student, six months studying, six months fighting. This medical student boasted about the excitement of burning Polish houses down, while the occupants were forced to look on. One day he came along and said, "I have an order to arrest anybody of British nationality."

He was already walking out of the ward, when to my astonishment one of our doctors, a native of Ceylon, admitted he had a British passport. He was taken to a prisoner-of-war camp in Germany and died some time later, riddled with T.B.

My family had now returned from France. Money lasted only so long and the war was longer than expected. And so we were all back at our house, at 96 Avenue Louis Lepoutre.

While some people collaborated with the Germans, most remained neutral. Others found ways of expressing their opposition to the occupiers. While walking around the town, German soldiers would often ask the way to the "Grande Place" or the station, for example. When it happened to me, I would either say, "*Je ne comprends pas*", or send them away in the wrong direction. Packed like sardines in trams, they found cigarette-burned holes in their tunics. Soon there were trams for Germans only, and separate trams for civilians. Thus on a cold winter night, one had to let trams for Germans go by empty, and try to hang on somehow to the full civilian trams.

One day a doctor asked me if I could provide potassium nitrate and acid (essential ingredients apparently to make explosives). "How do you expect me to find such things?" "Well, one can never tell." By then the German civilian forces, and the party secret police or Gestapo, had pretty well taken over control of the country; it was forbidden to handle, sell or carry anything useful to the German forces, like these chemicals. Nevertheless, a few days later I proudly handed over one pound of nitrates and one pound of acid. How did I get them? Very simply, I asked my father. I still see him, carrying them with a lot of precaution, expecting them to explode there and then. He even had a try himself in the bathroom, preparing little black boxes that you could put in the palm of your hand and deposit in tram cars or sentry boxes. After a few near misses, the making of explosives was left to the experts.

In October 1940 the Nazis issued their first order in Belgium against the Jews, compelling them to register and excluding them from many offices and public services. A short argument in my home was rapidly settled; my father thought that in respect for his father living in The Hague, he should register. I exclaimed that never would I volunteer any information – let THEM find out. And so we did not register, and later did not have our identity cards stamped with the letter J.

The newspapers were censored. Many underground newspapers were produced at great danger to all involved. Like the B.B.C. they kept up the morale of the population. I helped with their distribution. At night I would meet at a pre-arranged street corner, and I would be handed a parcel containing about fifty news-sheets. I would put them in the side-pocket of my bike. No sooner did I get them than I wanted to get rid of them. They had to be folded and parcelled up five or six at a time for redistribution within the University to doctors, nurses and medical students. Sometimes news-sheets were left over. I just could not burn them – many people risked their life in producing them. I would fold the sheets like letters and push them at night through letter boxes. I also managed to stick slogans on lamp-posts, phone boxes and so on. At home whenever possible we listened to the strictly *verboten* B.B.C. news broadcasts, remembering to return the station indicator to the permitted wavelength.

On the 31st July 1941 the Nazis passed the decree to carry out "The Final Solution", which meant the total extermination of the Jews. In December 1941 they issued the *"Nacht und Nebel"* ("Night and Fog") order, which meant that arrests were to be made in such a way that next of kin remained uncertain of the fate of the arrested relatives.

For the Germans there were no labour problems. Anyone not working was forced to work for them. They took students, factory workers, young and old and everyone had to be registered. Many people lived away from home to avoid being picked up and forced to work for the Germans against their own country. Anyone could be arrested any time with or without reason.

And we were afraid too when, late on Christmas Eve 1941, the bell rang at our front door. Who could it be? When we opened the door there were two youngsters. Remember, everything was blacked out and dark. To our surprise we recognized one of them, John, our cousin from Amsterdam. They only carried one brief-case between them. We got them in quickly. They explained how they had passed the frontier from Holland to Belgium at night on bicycles. They wanted to join the British Army in England. My father contacted friends and gathered addresses through Belgium and France to Switzerland. After a few days hiding in our house, they went on their way. They wore two sets of underwear. We had sewn money in the seams of their jackets, and filled their pockets with food. Later we learned John was arrested in France and that was the last we heard of him.

These boys were only the beginning of a long procession of people. The word had gone round. Young people, whole families with children, older folk ill and afraid, unknown to us, came to the door. Some evenings we cleared the floor and accommodated them as best we could for the night. Then we had to find friends willing to shelter these illegal refugees. I accompanied them at night, through the dark streets, avoiding crowds and lights and was lucky not to have met German patrols.

One time, the bell rang at midnight. We didn't open, having a full house, wondering, what next? We were expecting the worst, but nothing happened that night. Next morning a young man arrived. He said with a Dutch accent, "I was here last night, but you didn't open. I got very upset, knowing no other address in Brussels. I walked up and down the street till a man passed by. I told him I was Dutch, I wanted to go to England. I had the address of a Monsieur Bolle, but he did not open his door. The man took me to his home and sent me away this morning."

Can you imagine if the passer-by had been a collaborator, what the consequences could have been?

We had to train people to keep silent. Careless talk has undone more resistance groups than anything else. This became a full-time job. With the help of others we were able to obtain for the refugees, identity and ration cards, food and medical help. But it all became too much and too dangerous; our address was too well known and we had to make the decision to leave the house in Avenue Louis Lepoutre. We each went to live separately in rooms, so that if one was caught, it would not affect the rest of the family immediately. We assumed different names. My father became "Monsieur Albert", my sister "Evelyn Bodart" and I, "Marcelle". (After the war, I named my first-born daughter, "Evelyn Marcelle".) My sister "Evelyn Bodart", and her baby daughter Denise, went to live in Bruges, first in a furnished apartment, then at M. Renard's bank, opposite to the Gestapo headquarters. M. Renard, a suave bachelor, gourmet, excellent cook and connoisseur of wine, handled the accounts of the German officers in the town. Once, after an excellent dinner, he took us down to the vaults where he opened one of the heavy doors. We went inside, sat round a small wireless set and heard the news in French from London.

In May 1942, a further order came for all Jews in Belgium to display a yellow Star of David on the left side of their coats. Just as we did not register, we did not wear a yellow star. In Holland, Jews were dragged from their homes, places of work and the streets often with the help of informers. A Gestapo car would tour the boulevards, and the local informer sitting next to the driver would point out Jews, who would be picked up there and then. My own grandfather, aged seventy-seven, was taken from his home in The Hague, together with three other members of his family. We know the date, the 12th of January 1943, because a postcard written by my grandfather, which he threw out of the train on the way to Westerbork, the Dutch concentration camp, reached us eventually at Avenue Louis Lepoutre. It read (translated from the Dutch):

> 10 a.m. Tuesday 12 Jan. '43
> Dear All
> The fate of so many has struck us too. Yesterday morning at 7.30 the four of us were taken and we sit now together in a compartment on the way to Westerbork. What is to follow we do not yet know, however we are in good spirits. Much love and kisses from your Father,
>> Grandfather and
>> Greatgrandfather

After that day, they were never heard of again. From Westerbork people were sent to the extermination camps. My grandfather was one of two brothers who married two sisters. Twenty-six members were taken to extermination camps; ten succumbed in Sobibor, fifteen in Auschwitz and elsewhere and only one, my father, came back from Buchenwald. He was the only one in the Resistance.

One morning, as I entered the porter's lodge at the hospital to clock-in, he presented me with a list of names, and asked me if my name was on it. I ran through the list and returned it to him. "No, my name is not on it. Why do you show me this?" He replied, "These are the names of Jewish students. We have received orders that from today they are not allowed in anymore." I went through.

One could feel the Gestapo closing in. The publication of the news-sheets had been badly shaken by the death of one of its printers, a doctor, who was killed while trying to repel a Gestapo attack on his premises in the Ardennes. A number of friends and helpers had been arrested. I was afraid to visit or even to phone in case I would fall into a trap. We heard of the fantastic escape of Youra, a final-year medical student, from the basement of the Gestapo headquarters in Avenue Louise. He had been arrested as he was leaving a garage, a secret arms store. He had been handcuffed but managed to free himself and by timing the Gestapo guard, who was walking up and down the corridor, managed to slip away unseen.

In the house where I lived, there was a woman called Claude. Like me, she had a single room off another landing. I learned she had strong reasons to want to leave the country, her husband having been arrested. Just before leaving she said she had been introduced to a sure escape line to London, with proof by radio links with England, of the safe return of allied airmen. Pre-arranged messages had been broadcast by the B.B.C., sums of money were received from London to cover costs. Claude had even been offered English cigarettes by the man in charge, a Captain Jackson, a Canadian who spoke English and French equally well. The drill was to stay in one of their boarding houses somewhere in Brussels until the group was ready to leave. From the boarding house Claude was allowed to write one letter. To be on the safe side we made an arrangement. If the letter started with *"Ma chère amie"* all was well. But if she wrote *"Chère amie"* I had to do everything to get her out. In due course I received a letter with *"Ma chère amie"*.

I understand that on the day Captain Jackson took the group of airmen and Claude to the station for the train to Paris, she thanked him for his help and kindness, saying she hoped maybe to see him sometime in London. He answered, "Never mind, we shall never meet again." In fact, we learned months later from a pencil-written message on toilet paper that the group was met in the Gare du Nord in Paris by somebody who led them across the city towards another station, where they were to continue their journey. In a narrow street they were met by a Gestapo patrol and arrested. Claude, who was a doctor, was the only one of the group to survive the war, after nearly two years in Ravensbrück, the special concentration camp for women.

After Claude, there was Lisette. Of strict Catholic upbringing, the niece of a Benedictine abbot, she was active in the underground. In

February 1944, a note in Lisette's handwriting was received from the prison of St. Gilles in Brussels. The note read: "I am expecting a baby. I have nothing."

A Red Cross representative went to the prison but was told, "Mademoiselle will be all right. No need to bother." Lisette had a baby boy in hospital one day, and next day was sent back to prison with the child. Later it was learnt that the boy's father was Captain Jackson.

Since September 1942 the Germans had been sending Jews in Belgium to the extermination camps. In April 1943, my father and other Jewish partisans planned an attack on a train taking 1,000 Jews from Malines to Auschwitz. This train was the twentieth transport of thirty-one which took 28,000 Jews to the extermination camps. From information obtained inside the camp in Malines, they got the date of the next departure and the route the train would follow. The night before, they went to inspect the track, to choose a favourable spot outside Lovenjoul. On the 19th April 1943, the train was stopped by the same Youra who had escaped from the Gestapo building. Youra stood on the line waving a red lantern and the train came to a halt. The guards took no action, since it was a slow train which often halted to allow troop trains to pass. This gave Youra and the other partisans the chance to open some of the cattle trucks. But it was not long before the guards jumped out and opened fire. Youra ran back and forth shooting all the time to give the impression that there were a large number of attackers. More than 200 prisoners escaped. Some were captured, some were wounded. Eight of those wounded were taken by the Germans to the nearby hospital in Tirlemont. A week later a second operation was launched to rescue the wounded. Three cars arrived at the hospital and with the pre-arranged consent of the medical director the patients were taken away. But the driver of one of the cars was a traitor, who had managed to infiltrate the group and obtained the password "Tunisie-Bizerte". The cars were ambushed in the town square. The partisans machined-gunned the Germans, a battle followed. Two patients, in one of the cars "borrowed" from the Red Cross, arrived back in Brussels. The car driven by the traitor took his prisoners back to Malines, and the occupants of the third car, all the tyres burst, ran for their lives.

The stopping of the twentieth convoy was the sole operation throughout Europe in which a train taking Jews to a death camp was attacked. By a coincidence it occurred at the same time as the Warsaw Ghetto uprising.

Youra was later arrested, incarcerated in Breendonck for a year, then shot at the Tir National, where another resister, Nurse Edith Cavell, was shot in World War I.

The Gestapo were getting close, but when they did pounce, they got my sister instead of me. My sister had already left her flat for two weeks and nothing had happened when we arranged to meet there one morning, because some refugees were in desperate need of kitchenware and she had plenty in her flat lying idle.

I went up to her third-floor apartment. She had left her two and a half year-old daughter with neighbours in another house. After half an hour I said I had enough to take away and we should be leaving, but she wanted to sort out some things.

I took a pail, brushes, pans, as much as I could carry. I walked down the stairs. At the front door I met two men wearing light-coloured gaberdines, carrying brief-cases. They came in as I walked out. I recognized instantly the "uniform" and looks of the Gestapo. A car was parked in front of the house. Had they come for me? Would they find my sister instead? Or by one of those coincidences were they after someone else in this block of flats? I continued walking, took a tram in the direction of town, got out at the next stop and hid behind the front hedge of a garden. In due course, the Gestapo car drove past. I could just get a glimpse of my sister, her hair undone. They had taken her. By what miracle had I escaped?

I fetched her daughter, Denise, and we spent the first night at the house of the Chief Girl Guide of Belgium, Mme. Morrel in Boitsfort. After a few days I obtained the address of a farm where Denise remained for the three months her mother was kept in the prison of St. Gilles. I managed to get my sister out of prison by bribing a Belgian collaborator whom I met three times in a cafe in the centre of the town. He was only interested in money, not in me. But not so the Gestapo.

I mentioned earlier that we had to enter the hospital through the porter's lodge. One day, just to change the routine, I decided to reach my ward through the School of Medicine, where in the basement a long corridor joins the building to the hospital. The morning's work done, I passed the porter's lodge on my way out. He called me back. "Mademoiselle Bolle, I didn't know you were in. Your sister called this morning asking for you but I said that you had not clocked in today." At that time my sister was still in prison. I thought it was not possible. It must have been someone else. I asked the porter if he was sure. "Oh yes," he said. "It was your sister."

"Was she alone?" I asked.

"No, there were two men with her."

The Gestapo never gives up. To be still around, one needed an awful lot of luck and that must have been my lot.

The year 1942-43 was my last as a medical student. The University of Brussels had chosen to close down in 1941 rather than have a German vice-chancellor and I took my finals at the University of Liège, playing hide-and-seek with the Gestapo. In July 1943 I finally became a doctor and returned to Brussels, only to learn that my father was in the hands of the Gestapo. After the first feelings of horror, there were two things I had to do – to find out where he was and to move house once more. Anyway, there I was, a doctor at last and nobody to celebrate with. My mother was in a psychiatric home because of her depression, as well as for her own protection from the Gestapo. My father had been taken away by them and I did not know where he was.

I thought it was important that my Uncle Nico should know of his brother's arrest as it presented a danger to him also. He was living with his wife in the village of Ave et Auf in the Belgian Ardennes. Their own home was in Scheveningen. I went to see them.

As I recall, it was a beautiful summer day. I wore a wide-brimmed hat and, since I never wore hats, this was my best disguise. In the compartment of the train sat a tall gentleman in a dark suit, writing letters. As we went along, stopping at small stations, the compartment emptied until both of us were left, sitting opposite to one another at the window. We were waiting for the train to restart. It gathered up steam, tried to pull away but came immediately to a standstill, with lots of rattling noises rippling along the train. When this was repeated two or three times, my irate companion stormed out of the compartment shouting, "The idiots! They don't realize that one of the wagons has its brakes on." I followed him, not without first having leaned over to read the address he had just written on one of the envelopes – Mme. X, rue François Stroobant, Brussels. Now, this was more than a coincidence. So, he was the lawyer notorious for having collaborated with the Germans in World War I! I surmised he was writing to his wife, and the address on the envelope was a side-street off Avenue Louis Lepoutre. The man was a neighbour.

While we waited for the train to restart he took out a box of chocolates and offered me one. Then he explained he was travelling to the Ardennes to join some members of his family and his grandchildren. They were staying at his country house. It was a marvellous place to relax, with a swimming pool. Then he stopped, looked at me as if to say, "I have told you about myself, what about you?" I said, "I too am going to visit my family. I have just finished my exams, and I need a holiday."

"Oh!" he said. "You are a student. What is your subject? Please have another chocolate, they are rather nice, don't you think?"

Munching the delicious chocolate, I said to him, "What do you think I am?"

After a few guesses, he said, "You are a nurse."

Laughing, I replied, "No! I am now a doctor!"

So, Maitre X, of all people, was the first to hear my good news.

It was soon time for him to gather his belongings. He said goodbye, told me his name, and invited me, if I had any time to spare, to come to his country house, maybe on my return journey. In any case, should I ever need him, I would always find him at the Palais de Justice in Brussels.

I returned from Ave et Auf still not knowing where my father was. If he was not in a Belgian prison, the most likely place was Breendonck, the only concentration camp in Belgium. In the 1914-1918 war Breendonk had been an underground fort for the defence of Antwerp. Now it was a vast expanse of green grass surrounded by barbed wire and watchtowers. I went to see it, to weigh up the possibilities. I was cycling back to Brussels when I got an idea. That man, Maitre X, had he not said, "If ever you need me, you will find me at the Palais de Justice." And that is where I went, walking up the stone steps, wondering what kind of welcome awaited me. I had little to lose.

I was admitted to his office without difficulty. He was writing, then looked up. I asked if he remembered the train journey into the Ardennes when the brakes locked. A few seconds of recollection – "Yes, indeed," he said. "Well, what brings you here?"

I told him that when we met on the train, I was really going to see my father's brother to tell him my father had been arrested by the Gestapo; that after all my enquiries, if my father was still in Belgium, he must be in Breendonck. Had Maitre X any contacts there? He said he was really busy that morning. Then consulting a diary he gave me a date and time to see him at home.

A few days later I entered a small room, full of papers from floor to ceiling with Maitre X behind his desk. Without further enquiries, he opened a drawer, took out note paper, wrote a letter and sealed it in an envelope which he addressed to the Burgemeester of Breendonck. By the way, I had been speaking to him in Flemish and that apparently went down well.

"You go there," he said. "He may be able to help you." I took the envelope, impressively embossed with words in gold letters, thanked him and left.

With the letter in my pocket, I cycled to the village of Breendonck and made my way to the Burgemeester's house. A young woman wearing a large apron was scrubbing the front steps. I said to her in Flemish I had come to deliver a letter to the mayor. "Oh!" she replied, "my father won't be home till this afternoon. Can you come back later?" "Sure," I replied, not really too pleased, as I did not relish staying around any longer than necessary. Having a few hours to spare, I cycled along and settled in a meadow close to a canal, looking at lines of tall poplars, eating a sandwich I had prepared and reading a thin volume of poems by

Emil Verhaeren.

I returned to the house, rang the bell, the daughter opened the door and took me directly to her father. He was short and fat, with an unpleasant appearance. He read the letter, got up and told me to wait for another person, who would come and show me the way. A man came and asked me to follow him. We walked a short distance to a large brewery owned by the mayor. There I was handed over to a third person, who led me to a house, saying it was the home of the village electrician who might not be in but his wife was. She was a large woman, with an open face and most talkative. "You must be hungry," she said, and without waiting for an answer she disappeared, to return with a plate loaded with white bread and thick layers of real lard between slices. What luxury! The room was ordinary, the mantelpiece bedecked with small objects. She talked non-stop. How her husband was the electrician for the fort of Breendonck, and of course this got him in contact with the prisoners. What was my job? "Oh! you are a doctor, then maybe you know Jean Casman?" I told her he was in my year. "Well, it is a shame. He and his father are here, both doctors. The father is not doing too well, but Jean, you see, has become my husband's mate and you won't believe this," (she chuckled), "he is the only prisoner in the whole of Breendonck to put on weight. You see, his mother comes and visits me, she brings food and flasks of whisky. Well, it is so damp in there, the Commandant is not surprised there are so many power failures!" She pauses for a second, turns to the mantelpiece and extracts a necklace from a little vase. "This is the last present Mme. Casman has given me, she is such a generous lady."

Anyway, after rattling off more names and stories, we came to the point of my visit. Could her husband find out if a certain Maurice Bolle was in the camp? He was my father, taken by the Gestapo within the last two months. She said she would tell her husband. "Come back in three weeks. It takes that long to find out. It is difficult, especially if they are in solitary confinement." Three weeks was a long time.

At my second visit, after what was to become a regular offering of bread and lard and more talk, she said, "I am sorry, but my husband hasn't come across that name. He will try again." It was disappointing. Was my father already out of Belgium, out of reach? Another three weeks, another negative answer.

"Try once more," she encouraged me, giving me examples of other people lost and found. When I came again, she told me her husband had found him.

"You did not tell me he was a Jew-man", she said, implying he would have been found earlier had I told her. Then she added, "In the camp he is known as 'The Millionaire'."

My father was rather big and his surplus weight must have helped him to get through the privations of the first few months. I was still doubtful that the man known as "the millionaire" was my father, until one day the electrician's wife handed me a scrap of paper on which was written – "hondepedodle", a nonsense word meaning "little dog", a name my father called me when I was a little girl.

I continued to visit the electrician's wife, until one day she told me that Maurice Bolle was not there anymore. He and others in his cell had been sent to Buchenwald.

With my father and some of my close contacts in the hands of the Gestapo, I felt it was time to "disappear". I was provided with a false identity card and given a job as a laboratory technician at the Polyclinic of La Louvière in the Borinage, the main coalmining centre of Belgium. I stayed in the small home of a coalminer and his wife. There were neither showers at the colliery nor a bathroom in the house. I can remember how she used to clean his leather boots under running water. At work I kept myself to myself, learning how to play my role, till one evening after several weeks, one of the nurses at the clinic came into the laboratory and told me people were talking. She had overheard a conversation in the local café, patronized by the Boche, about a laboratory assistant. That same night, without saying a word to the miner's wife, I packed my bags and left by train for Brussels. Again, I took refuge with my friends, wondering what to do next.

After my experience in the Borinage, I found myself with a different identity card employed as a domestic at an institution for girls on the outskirts of Brussels. It was run by two women. The head of the school, a strict disciplinarian, was feared by the girls and staff alike. Her friend was more of a mother figure. They appeared to devote more love and care to their large Alsatian dog and to one another than to the children.

Sunday, 3rd September 1944 was a day of brilliant sunshine. I was staying with my friend Suske in the rue de Venise, near the Maison Communale d'Ixelles. Suddenly she called me to the window. We could see flames rising from the golden cupola of the Palais de Justice.

"The Germans are burning the Palais de Justice," cried Suske. "Let's go and see. The Allies must be coming!"

We walked across the Porte Louise and down the Avenue de La Toison D'Or. Flags with red swastikas on a black background progressively gave way to the Belgian tricolor on the facades of all the buildings going down to the Porte de Hal. And then, amid a dancing, shouting, kissing population, the Allies in their open trucks came along the Boulevard du Midi towards us.

When we thought all Belgium was finally liberated, the Germans came back to the Ardennes in December. Many people in the "underground" had come out in the open (as I had done after 3rd September) and became easy targets for collaborators and the Gestapo. I felt betrayed. My friends did not worry, it was only a temporary setback. I heard that the Belgian Red Cross was sending specially equipped ambulances, each with a medical attendant, to the Ardennes. I volunteered to go but was told that I was too late, the last ambulance had left that morning. But doctors were needed in other parts of the country. Would I be prepared to go to the Civil Affairs Unit in Ath? Reluctantly, I said, "Yes."

Chapter 13

The Rhine Offensive and a Wedding

When I was a soldier bold
I seldom did what I was told.
When I was asked to fight the foe
I swore that I would never go
Until I'd wed my Hélène fair
And changed her name to Mrs Mair.
So others crossed the River Rhine
But she was mine, but she was mine.

I had heard only the early part of Hélène's story when I realized I had found the woman I had been vainly seeking all the past years. We were living in a rapidly changing world. Either of us could be sent away at a few hours' notice. Unless I acted at once she might be gone as quickly as she had come.

The day Hélène accepted my proposal I applied (in duplicate) to 21 Army Group in Brussels for permission to marry a foreign national. The same day I had an appointment with a notary about arrangements for a civil marriage. He seemed to be more concerned about the difficulties that might arise after marriage than before it. He said the first thing we should do, as we were both physicians and evidently people of substance, was to draw up a marriage contract. I told him we were not about to build a bridge, and if we did, it would be a metaphysical one. I did not get very far with him. I wrote to my family in Glasgow, enclosing a

163

photograph of Hélène. My father took it upon himself to reply on behalf of the family in the only letter he ever wrote in English:

"Just a line or two to express my feelings we are all glad and hapy that you have found the girl you deserve you have added another jewel to the family treasure you may be sure she will be dear to us as you are to us you should see mother looking at her photo and she looks at the photo every houer of the day and her eyes so much happiness in them only a mothers eyes can have that look we are all waiting for the time when you and your dear girl will come home for good let us hope it will be soon or there will be nothing left of the Pesachdeke wine can your girl speak Yiddish?"

If we had received the family's blessing, the 21 Army Group's blessing was slow in coming. However, it did send a Jewish chaplain but Hélène did not want a religious ceremony and I was lukewarm, so he left wishing us well. I waited impatiently for a reply from Brussels. It came three weeks after I had submitted the application. The delay was due to an amendment which called for submission of the application in triplicate. The third form was at the moment following the officer who had counter-signed the first two!

One day, early in March, a car drew up in front of the chateau. The driver leapt out and opened the rear door. If anyone was ever fitted to play the role of *deus ex machina* it was my old friend Donnelly as he stepped out of his motor-car. He was now a full colonel on the staff of headquarters on his way from Brussels to Tournai. There was a sly smile on his face as though to say, "You didn't expect me, did you?" It was good to see him again and for a few minutes we swapped reminiscences of West Africa. Then he said, "What was that nonsense, about a reception centre in Weston-super-Mare? I saw your posting at the War Office and told them to give you a job in the field." I did not tell him about Category C, that I was in Belgium on false pretences.

I took him round the unit. In the workshop, he asked me if we had enough tools. I made noises indicating that we had enough. He said, "What a question to ask you. Knowing you, I ought to go round to the unit next door and ask what tools they are short of." Considering that practically all our furniture and a good deal of our stores had been "won" since landing, he was not far out.

He then went on to tell me to prepare for an important move. By the heavy traffic moving north it was apparent that a big offensive was in the offing. I asked him if we were going to cross the Rhine. He did not answer. Then, I told him about Hélène. About the application I had submitted for permission to marry. I expected an answer at any time. If I went into Germany it might be months before I saw her again. I was afraid I would lose her. There was a long silence, then he said, "I will send another unit, but I cannot guarantee to do this a second time."

On 25th March I stood beneath a wonderful blue sky to watch our airborne divisions on their way north. Mussolini once boasted that his air force would darken the sun. I saw it that day. There were hundreds of great planes with gliders in tow all over the sky. All flying towards the Rhine. Although I did not take part in the Rhine offensive, I became one of its casualties. I was sitting at my desk in the chateau, looking out on the wide field of a neighbouring farm, when I heard the scream of an approaching plane. As the noise of the engines increased, I was sure we were about to be dive-bombed. I was diving under the heavy oak table when I caught a glimpse of one of my men running in front of the window, looking up as the plane came nearer. I remember thinking, "That's a damn silly thing to do!" A second later there was a loud crash as though a building had collapsed. I climbed out from under the table, and through the window of my office I could see an American B-17, its nose embedded in the barn of the farm, its tail pointing to the sky. A plume of smoke and licks of fire were rising from the fuselage. I grabbed a first-aid kit and together with several of my men began running across a ploughed field towards the plane. No one had emerged from it, when suddenly the world exploded. Those of us nearest the barn were lifted up and hurled to the ground. I do not remember much of what happened afterwards. I was badly shaken. I had no apparent injuries except that my ears ached. For a while I could not hear anything for the ringing in my ears. Sometimes the ringing stopped and was replaced by the sound of escaping steam. The doctors call it tinnitus. That evening, I visited Hélène in Termonde. She said to me, "You are shouting." On and off, I have been shouting ever since.

Shortly afterwards my unit crossed the border into Holland and set up house in St. Angela's School in a residential area of Eindhoven. The school had been run by an order of nuns who still lived in the adjacent cloister. One day, the Mother Superior, who spoke excellent English, asked me if we could let her have the left-overs from our meals, rather than dispose of them in the swill-bins. The children, she said, were very hungry. I recalled the anger we felt with a contingent of Americans who occupied the house next to my unit in Bournemouth. They would open up cartons of canned fruit, puncture the cans with a bayonet, drink the juice and throw the cans still full of fruit into the dustbins. Thereafter, every evening when the Mother Superior went over the left-overs she found unopened cans of bully-beef among them.

The children, whose school we occupied, would try to get into the premises to pilfer whatever they could find. In a half-hearted attempt to keep them out we ran up strands of barbed wire at the entrance and other vulnerable places. One afternoon I came across the Mother Superior deep in conversation with a little boy at the entrance to the school. He kept pointing at the wire we had erected and making circular movements with his hands. I asked her if he did not like the barbed wire all over his school. She replied, "No, he is not complaining about that. He says the straight wire is useless. Anyone can get through. What you need is concertina wire."

He was evidently speaking from experience!

By 28th April most of Holland had been liberated except for a pocket in the northwest where the cities of Utrecht and Amsterdam were still in German hands. On that day the fighting ceased in West Holland. A truce was arranged and several days later food supplies began to move through the lines in order to feed the starving population.

Meanwhile, we learned over the radio that Buchenwald had been liberated and later the names of those returning to Belgium were announced. To our joy, Hélène's father was among them. I can well remember with what excitement she and I, together with my cousin Michael Toshner whom we had just met in Brussels, leaped into my truck and rushed off to Le Cirque Royal where the prisoners were arriving. Many were still wearing the striped garb of the camp and all were wizened by starvation. Hélène could not find her father among them so we went off to the airport. The road to the airport was lined with thousands of people waiting for the cars with the prisoners to pass, and as we were on our way, another convoy of cars approached. Hélène got out and stood in the middle of the road, scanning each car as it passed, but again, no luck. We went on to the airport. It was now seven o'clock. There we met another lady who was waiting for her husband. She told us M. Bolle had not yet arrived. I went to Movement Control but they knew as much as I did. All the while, Dakotas were landing every few minutes, and French, Belgian and British prisoners-of-war were disembarking and being taken away in lorries. We waited till ten o'clock and then left. I had to get back to Holland. I was very sorry for Hélène, but she took it bravely. "I have waited for two years," she said, "another day makes no difference."

At the beginning of May I was notified of an impending move to Norway. It was a sore disappointment to me, since it would mean further, indefinite postponement of our marriage. At the eleventh hour the move was cancelled. It was then that I made up my mind that I must go to Brussels and obtain the necessary permission. Surprisingly there was little difficulty at that end. It seemed that now the war in Europe was over for all intents and purposes, it was safe for me to marry despite the missing form. I rushed back to Avenue Louis Lepoutre to tell Hélène the glad news, only to be told there was another obstacle to surmount – she did not have a birth certificate as required by law. All her family's papers had disappeared when the Gestapo took over her home. Only a tribunal could decide her identity and that meant another delay. One thing was clear, Hélène was born in Utrecht where the original record was made, and that was where I had to go.

On the morning of Thursday, 10th May, two days after V-E day, I left Eindhoven in a jeep with a driver and another of my men, armed with a Sten gun. Except for essential purposes, there was a restriction about driving into areas occupied by the Germans. I could not think of a more essential purpose than mine. We drove north to Arnhem, where in September 1944 the Germans won their last battle of the war, then we turned due west to Utrecht. The roads outside the town were full of Germans. The once mighty Wehrmacht was crawling slowly out on foot. Some pushed hand-carts and bicycles. I saw a few battered trucks. Their guns were drawn by farm horses. They were still armed but they looked a fairly dispirited lot. In the streets of the town, and in all the roads leading to the centre, the people wore their summer best and everyone we passed gave the V-sign and cheered. One young man who spoke English hung on to the jeep and guided us to the Stadhuis. The town council was in session. I asked someone if I could see the burgemeester. He came out and gripped my outstretched hand. The Germans officers who passed us saluted punctiliously. I am sure the mayor must have thought I had come to take over the town, for I could not see any Canadians whose sector this was. When I told him of my predicament, that I had come to Utrecht for a copy of a birth certificate in order to get married to a Dutch girl, he burst out laughing. I have never seen a man laugh so heartily. I could imagine him going back to the council chamber to tell the members about the mad Englishman. In retrospect, it really was a ridiculous situation but at the time it did not seem so to me. He sent for a clerk who took me to another building to a room filled with leather-bound tomes. And there, as his finger moved along a page dated 17th October 1918, I saw the name Hélène Julia Bolle, and the names of her parents, Maurits Bolle and Grietje Stoppelman. Armed with a copy of the birth certificate, I returned to the jeep to find it surrounded by a large crowd crying for tobacco. All three of us gave away our cigarettes. Afterwards a man offered me a silver spoon for a packet of cigarettes, so desperate was he.

As soon as we got back to Eindhoven I sent a motor cyclist to Brussels with the birth certificate. The next day, Friday, he returned with a message from Hélène – I must be in Brussels by Saturday morning, when we would be married. I left for Brussels on Friday night and the next morning, on the 12th of May, we were married at the Maison Communale d'Ixelles. The only people who were there were Hélène's father, who had come back from Buchenwald four days before, her brother-in-law, Adrien, newly released from a German prisoner-of-war camp, and her friend Suske. An official, dressed in a blue uniform with plenty of gold braid and wearing a gold-handled sword, stood on a dais with an assistant by his side. As the ceremony was in French we had arranged that, when he asked me the important question, Hélène would nudge me and I would answer "Oui!". But we found ourselves seated on low, cushioned stools about three feet apart. In his introductory speech – I was told later – the official said how pleased he was to participate in the marriage of one of our brave liberators and, when I began to wonder if he would ever come to the point, my smattering of French came to the rescue and I said "Oui!" at the right moment. Then he put the rings on our fingers and we were married.

When everyone was abed at 96 Avenue Louis Lepoutre, we dragged a mattress on to the balcony overlooking the garden and spent our first night as husband and wife under the stars.

Chapter 14

Last Act in the Arctic

The move that was suddenly cancelled was as suddenly on again. We managed to enjoy four blissful days at Han-sur-Lesse in the Ardennes before I returned to Eindhoven and Hélène to Brussels.

A few days later, I saw Donnelly for the last time. He was pleased to learn I had got married at last. Then he briefed me. My unit would be taking part in "Operation Apostle". In Norway there were an estimated 350,000 armed Germans, and more than 70,000 Russian ex-prisoners of war. It was the job of the British Army and its Norwegian allies to ensure that the Germans maintained discipline while they were disarmed, screened, searched and deloused before they were sent back to Germany. The Russians were to be sent home as soon as possible. There was not much time, because half of the Russian camps were in the North and winter comes early in the Arctic. I was to make sure all our vehicles were in good trim, and that went for the men too. We were going to show the flag. It struck me that the code name for the operation had been well-chosen. We were bringing the good news to the Norwegians and, incidentally, to the Russians.

Hélène came up to Eindhoven for a few days. We hired a couple of the high Dutch bicycles and pedalled gently – for I was a very uncertain rider – round the cobbled streets of the town and along the still canals. On Friday, 25th May, I said goodbye to her again. I can still see her standing in front of the school, waving as we left for Hamburg. I am sure she was still waving when the last vehicle turned the corner. She still waves to departing guests in exactly the same way. Two days later I wrote to Hélène:

> "You should see the German countryside. It is lovely. But the towns! At the entrance to a town the Military Police usually erect a large sign with the words painted in white on a black background – THIS IS . . . When we crossed the Rhine the first thing we saw was a large sign reading – THIS WAS REES. Not one building standing! It was a small town. Next we passed through Osnabrück – worse still, if possible. Then Bremen and today, to cap it all, we drove into Hamburg. It must be seen to be believed. For nearly seven miles I drove through utter destruction. The streets are covered with mountains of rubble. I think nine out of every ten buildings I saw had been blasted. People were living(?) in blocks of flats three-quarters of which had been blown away. The town is a desolation, made alive only by the streams of Allied troops passing through. At first, I was elated by what I saw, but after a while I began to feel depressed. It was unnatural. Truly had the German people sown the wind of Rotterdam and Warsaw and reaped the whirlwind of Bremen and Hamburg."

On 30th May we embarked on a U.S. tank-landing ship, a large merchant vessel converted to carry tanks and used for assault purposes in amphibious operations. The men slept in their trucks. I shared a cabin with a U.S. naval officer. When he saw Hélène's photograph, he said she was beautiful. Placating the gods, I said she was lovely rather than beautiful. The naval officer in the next cabin disagreed. He insisted she was beautiful and he was sorry he had not met her before I did.

Once out of Hamburg we ran into foul weather. I found my sea legs quickly enough but many of my men in the trucks were glad to see Oslo. Two weeks later we were at sea again, this time on a German merchant ship with a German crew, bound for Tromsø, 300 miles north of the Arctic Circle.

Before we left Oslo on 17th June I inspected the holds, in which several hundred other ranks were to eat and sleep. I was accompanied by the First Mate, a surly ruffian. When we came to the first hold he pointed to an iron ladder running down into the depths, indicating that I should precede him. I declined the invitation and told him to go first. There was definitely no fraternizing or trust on that voyage.

When a large detachment disembarked at Bergen, those of us bound for Narvik and Tromsø were not allowed to go ashore. This order did not seem to apply to a group of commandos, who swarmed down the hawsers and kept the citizens of Bergen awake until we sailed for Trondheim at 0300 hours. On the evening of that day, the 21st of June, we saw the bonfires burning on the beaches and the hills, celebrating the summer solstice, a custom forbidden during the German occupation.

The further north we sailed the longer the days became until, when we reached Tromsø on 24th June, there was no night at all. I spent most of the days on deck writing to Hélène. (Indeed, in the four months I was in Norway, I wrote her more than 100 letters and received as many in return.) When I was not telling Hélène how much I missed her I was advising her how to go about obtaining and completing the necessary forms so that she could enter Britain. I anticipated the same delays as had occurred with our marriage application. I should have known better. On the 6th of June, two weeks after I had left for Hamburg, Hélène returned to Eindhoven, charmed the brigadier commanding the area and, without filling up a single form, was granted approval, as the wife of a British Officer, to be repatriated to the U.K.; the Army would provide transport!

Many years later, in a letter to our daughter Evelyn who had just emigrated to Canada, Hélène describes her own arrival in Britain on the 4th July, 1945:

"I can remember it as though it all happened yesterday. On Wednesday morning, 4th of July, my father brought me to the Grand Hotel, Boulevard Adolphe Max, where about twenty soldiers and officers and two or three civilians were waiting to fly in a military aeroplane to England. We were told that when we got to Croydon a bus would take us to London. When I come to think of it, it must have been my first journey in an aeroplane and the novelty of it was exciting. It was a beautiful clear sunny day with no wind. No one was sick, except me I am ashamed to say. In Croydon I had to go through security and immigration, and by the time they were finished with me, the bus with all the passengers had gone to London. There I was on the tarmac with my two black heavy suitcases filled with clothes and medical textbooks, wondering what to do next when, out of the blue, a young woman in uniform approached me and said, "Are you a doctor?" I could not believe it, because nobody, absolutely nobody in England knew I was coming. How did she know? Hesitantly, I said, "Yes, but . . ." Before I could say any more, she grabbed my cases and said, "Follow me. I have a car waiting for you. You are going to London, aren't you?" Again I said, "Yes, but . . ." still not believing my luck when she continued, "I was sent to Croydon this morning to fetch a doctor coming from Brussels. I have been watching all the planes from Brussels – not a doctor among them. So I am pleased to have found you. Now I can go back."

"So off we went to London with me in the back. I even remember the name of the car. It was a Panhard, the same car my father drove. She asked me where I wanted to go. I had no idea, except that I wanted to go to Glasgow. She said she would take me to a reception centre in town and I could go on from there. At the reception centre a lady with grey hair helped me put my luggage in the cloak room and asked if I would like a cup of tea. I was attended to, hand and foot. A deep comfortable armchair covered with an incredible flower-patterned cloth, dainty triangular thin sandwiches without crusts, a two-tier cake stand with creamy small pink and pale mauve square petits-fours, and lots of silvered-haired ladies with big smiles. Having told them I wanted to go to Glasgow, they advised me to leave my cases and walk to the station to get my ticket and the time of departure. With the only money I had in my handbag, a £5 note, I bought my ticket and was left with £2 and 10 shillings. I went back to the reception centre, and in the evening when it was time for me to go the ladies saw me and my luggage into a taxi.

"The train left Euston station at nine o'clock and arrived in Glasgow at six o'clock next morning. I followed the instructions your father had given me before he left for Germany and Norway. I crossed the street in front of the station and asked for a tram to Rouken Glen. On the tram I told the conductor I wanted to get off at Woodlands Road. Well, the tram went and stopped, and went and stopped for nearly an hour through miles of built-up areas until we came to a tree-lined road and the conductor said, "Here you are!" He had specially stopped at Woodlands Road, between two regular stops. He helped me with my cases, and off I went. The road ran uphill and before I got to No. 20 I had to stop a couple of times, the cases were heavy. The curtain was slightly drawn. A man was standing behind the window looking down the road. That must be his Dad. The curtain fell. A second or two later the front door opened. I had arrived."

On Sunday, 24th June, 55 Field Hygiene Section disembarked at Tromsø, the whaling and sealing port of Northern Norway. In 1945 Tromsø was a small town of weather-beaten wooden buildings, perched on a rocky islet protected in the west by the island of Kvaloy and in the east by a mountainous mainland. Its inhabitants, nearly 11,000 of them, weather-beaten as its buildings, taciturn, unforthcoming, were regarded as the finest Arctic sailors in the world. I sometimes thought, in my few contacts with them, that they were as wary of us as they were of the Germans. I learned later that this mistrust was reserved for everyone, even their own countrymen, from anywhere below the Arctic Circle.

Our new billet was in a former Luftwaffe seaplane base, about three miles north of the town on the shores of Tromsøsound. German naval personnel, who were still present when we arrived, helped us unload our stores. A young lieutenant in charge of the detachment, speaking fluent English, was most co-operative. When I complimented him on his command of English, he told me his father had been a diplomat at the German Embassy in London for several years and had never been an enthusiastic Nazi, nor was he. (The number of lukewarm Nazis and German pacifists that I came across in Norway was formidable.) Before he was due to be repatriated the lieutenant came to my office and handed me his binoculars. He said he had no further use for them and besides they were stamped "Dienstglas" (service glasses), and as such, he would have had to give them up anyway. Repatriated Germans returned to their homeland with the bare minimum. All service issue in their possession was confiscated, as was anything they might have bought or "won" in Norway. If a man had two combs he came away with one. He might be able to keep a Leica but not a silverfox fur. When a man appeared with a pillow in his kit-bag you could be sure there was a fur among the feathers. As a result, exchanges between British and German soldiers were common-place. When my German driver was about to return home, he asked me if I would exchange my ordinary steel watch for his, a German Army issue for Alpine troops. It was, he assured me, rustproof, waterproof, shockproof, anti-magnetic and also kept good time. I do not have the watch now, nor do I know what happened to it. But I still have the naval binoculars. I use them for bird-watching.

I occupied a cabin which had belonged to a Luftwaffe officer. So close was the cabin to the water's edge, that from its casement window I could drop a stone into the sea when the tide was high. Its furniture consisted of two scruffy armchairs, a table, a hard bed-base, a chest of drawers and a wardrobe. The latter provided a pleasant surprise. Apart from a few clothes-hangers, it was crammed with bottles of Burgundy and Bordeaux. I could hardly believe my eyes. If my memory does not deceive me there were also whole and half-bottles of champagne. I am sure it was the latter I opened when, wakened by the sun streaming through the window at three o'clock in the morning, I needed something to assuage my thirst. It was apparent that my predecessor had planned for a long stay.

Once settled in, we devoted our initial efforts to the 49,000 Russians and other ex-prisoners of war spread out along the highway stretching from Narvik in the south to Hammerfest in the north, with German lagers and X-P.O.W. camps often facing one another.

On paper, delousing is a simple procedure. A three- or four-man squad from the Field Hygiene Section arrives at a camp where the inmates are lined up in a disciplined manner outside a hut or marquee where the action is to take place. A petrol-driven air compressor linked to three or four D.D.T. "guns" is set up outside the hut. Inside, the squad, wearing white operating gowns and gas-masks, starts firing the white powder into armpits and crotches until the recipients take on the aspect of ghosts. A well-trained squad can process several hundred persons in a matter of hours.

Sometimes it did not happen that way with the Russians. Our first assignment was to examine and delouse 1,400 Russians awaiting repatriation in a lager on the mainland about 100 miles north of Tromsø. We made the journey in two of our three-ton trucks through the most magnificent country, along the blue fjords and over mountains covered in snow, until we came to a small fishing village where the Russians were going to embark. Like a travelling circus, we set up our tent and all the paraphernalia for delivering the D.D.T. The Russians, happy at the thought of going home, formed a straggly column, but as soon as they saw the spectral figures of the D.D.T. squad in their protective overalls and masks, armed with what appeared to be guns, they broke for the woods. Who knows what horrors these men had suffered at the hands of their captors? Those that stayed proceeded to nullify our efforts by immediately beating their clothes against the nearest tree to get rid of the pesticide. When I complained to the Russian camp commandant that we were several hundred short of the expected number, he smiled indulgently, offered me a glass of vodka which I accepted, then enlightened me with the help of an interpreter.

"I can understand why you are annoyed," he began, "because England is a small country with maybe thirty, forty million people, so to an Englishman 200 is a lot of people. But Russia is a big country. There are maybe 200, 250 million Russians. So for a Russian 200 is nothing."

As though to contradict his last statement, he took me to the local cemetery, where he showed me a common grave surmounted by a cross, on top of which was a red Soviet star. There was a list of the Russian dead attached to the upright of the cross, and next to it an obelisk in construction to mark more permanently their last resting place.

In my reconnaissance of the Russian camps, I had occasion to travel to Bardufoss, the vast airfield the Germans built to bomb our Murmansk convoys. The camp I was seeking was somewhere in the woods on the periphery of the airfield. After an hour's fruitless search, I came across a compound surrounded by barbed wire. A wisp of smoke was coming from the chimney of a building in the centre of the compound. I went up the steps and opened the door. Several Luftwaffe officers and N.C.O.s were sitting at a table playing cards. One of the officers got up, approached me with outstretched hand, and said, "Can I help you?"

Ignoring the outstretched hand, I replied, "I'm looking for a Russian camp and I can't find it on your bloody airfield." He clicked his heels, bowed slightly and said with great emphasis, "YOUR airfield."

His reply brought to mind an incident in the submarine yards in Bremen, when we were on our way to Hamburg. I was in the office of a British quartermaster staff-sergeant when a German watchman came in greatly perturbed and said to him, "They are stealing your stores!" It transpired that "they" were some of the battered citizens of Bremen pilfering pots and pans and other items to help eke out their existence. "Your" stores were German stores hardly a month before. The Luftwaffe officer at Bardufoss and the watchman in Bremen truly believed, "To the victor, belong the spoils of the enemy."

The measures taken with the Germans in the lagers were much more stringent than with the Russians, because they were not only disinfected but interrogated and searched. However, but for one exception described below, everything went smoothly. They were as anxious to get home as we were to get rid of them. They came naked into the delousing hut, clutching their clothes and meagre belongings. We looked for signs of infection and for the blood group tattooed under the left arm of those belonging to the S.S., or for the scar where the tattoo had been removed. Anyone suspected of being a member of the S.S. was promptly detained for further investigation. Delousing was followed by interrogation by an intelligence officer or N.C.O. while clothes and kit bags were searched for prohibited articles.

Staff-sergeant Brewin, my right-hand man, who had been with me since we formed the Section, took an active part in these sessions, particularly in the search for contraband. Usually he returned from them with what he called "souvenirs", until one day he came back, empty-handed and depressed. I asked him what was the matter. He said, gloomily, "I'm in trouble. Champagne Charlie is going to put me on a charge."

Charlie, notorious for the amount of champagne he could drink at one sitting, and for the amount of loot he sent back to Scotland in the Sunderland flying boats, was supervising officer at these sessions.

As far as I could gather from Brewin, a German who had just been screened complained to the supervisor that the sergeant had confiscated his Rolleiflex, which was his personal property and was not Army issue. Apparently this man knew his rights. Ordered by an outraged Charlie to return the camera to its owner, Brewin went over to his hold-all and fished out a camera which he offered to the German. The latter looked at it, turned to Charlie, and said, "But this is not mine!" At which Charlie turned the hold-all upside down and out rolled several cameras, including the Rolleiflex. The German went away with his camera and Charlie went away with the rest.

After the sergeant had told his story, I advised him to curb his enthusiasm for photography. As for Charlie, who approached me in the mess that evening, I told him that when he turned in all his loot, I would put the sergeant on a charge. That was the last I heard from Charlie.

By the end of July, all the Russians and most of the Germans had gone. With them went the General Hospital, which had come over from

Scotland ostensibly to treat the numerous Russian sick as well as Allied personnel. I often wondered why such a big hospital had come to Tromsø in the first place, because there were never more than half-a-dozen patients in it at one time and none of these were Russians. The Russians evidently preferred to treat their people in their own camps.

With the departure of the colonel commanding the hospital, I was appointed senior medical officer of the Tromsø zone. One of my first duties was to inspect a concentration camp on the mainland just across the fjord from Tromsø. During the years of occupation it had been used to imprison Norwegian patriots. Now its inmates were sixty-three Gestapo officials and S.S. weeded out of the German lagers. And they had a complaint. It was voiced to me by a Gestapo official who addressed me in German. With his rimless glasses he could have doubled for Himmler. I asked the interpreter what he was complaining about.

"He says the Wanzen, the bedbugs, are biting him."

The chutzpah of the man!

"Tell him," I said to the interpreter, "tell him I am sorry for the Wanzen." Then I turned on my heel and walked away.

If nothing else, Tromsø became famous as the graveyard of the *Tirpitz*. To the west of the island, near its southern tip, the upturned hull of the great battleship lay like a stranded whale. Little launches buzzed round it, their bows making V-signs on the placid fjord. From time to time a brave soul would walk precariously along its red, rusted bottom rising above the surface of the water. The story of this leviathan is worth telling, because like most fables it has a moral for our times.

The 42,500-ton battleship, the pride of the German Navy, was completed in 1941. She served in Norwegian waters from January 1942 to November 1944, a permanent threat to the British convoys to North Russia. For the first and last time, the *Tirpitz* fired her heavy guns on 9th September 1943 during an inglorious raid on Spitzbergen. Thereafter this great fish lurked in the fjords harried by smaller fish – frogmen sitting astride torpedoes with detachable magnetic mines and midget submarines manned by Royal Navy volunteers. On 22nd September 1943 a great hole was torn in the side of the *Tirpitz* by two tons of explosive laid by the crew of a midget submarine. No sooner were temporary repairs completed than further damage was inflicted by three aircraft of the Fleet Air Arm. The forepeak had to be filled with cement before she could be towed to Tromsø, her final resting place. On 29th October, RAF Lancasters flying all night from their base in Scotland found a layer of low cloud over the *Tirpitz* and the attack was aborted. With winter closing in, another raid seemed unlikely – from the beginning of December there is little or no sun in Tromsø. However, the weather took a turn for the better and on 12th November the second attack took place. The first bomb struck the *Tirpitz* amidships. Her guns stopped. Two more bombs struck, while spouts of water rose all around. Fires blazed amidships. In a few moments it was all over. The ship turned turtle and half an hour later the reconnaissance plane flew through the rising smoke, to photograph her bottom. More than 1,100 men were still inside her when she rolled over. Rescuers heard faint tappings from the inside. Holes were cut in the hull with oxy-acetylene burners, and a few escaped that way. Then the gas ran out. The tapping went on for four more days, then stopped.

On July 1990, I wrote to the editor of *Nordlys*, the local Tromsø newspaper, asking, among other things, what had become of the *Tirpitz*. He replied: "To your question about the battleship *Tirpitz*. It was sold to Hovding Skipsopphugging after the war, and most of it was cut, and the steel plates exported, mostly to West Germany where they made plows and tools of it."

On the 10th of August I went on leave. The passengers for the Catalina which was to fly us to Oslo were assembled on the jetty when a car drew up and three British soldiers and a German emerged. The latter wore his greatcoat round his shoulders like a cloak. His S.S. uniform was immaculate. His breeches stuck out like elephants' ears. His riding boots shone. He might have been going to a Nuremberg rally, were it not that he had been stripped of his badges of rank. He gave me an impression of someone of importance or notoriety. I wondered what crimes warranted an escort of two military policemen and an officer. The passengers sat opposite one another along the length of the plane. I began to read *Les morts nous regardent*, the French translation of Gerald Kersh's *The dead look on*, published in 1943. The jacket of the book showed people engulfed in flames, and in large letters the word "*Lidice*", the Czechoslovak village wiped off the face of the earth and its inhabitants massacred by the S.S. in revenge for the assassination of Reinhard Heydrich, the ruthless governor of Bohemia. Directly opposite to me, his face a few inches from the book, sat the S.S. officer. He knew what I was reading, but his face maintained a stolid impassivity as I read the book all the way to Oslo. He and his escort left the plane first and I never learned who he was.

I was fortunate to find a berth on a destroyer of the Royal Navy and arrived next day in Leith and within a few hours I was home. Hélène was blooming. Pregnancy suited her. In the short time she had been at Woodlands Road she had become one of the family. So much so, my father said, he hoped the Army would not be in a hurry to get rid of me, so they could have her to themselves a bit longer. But for the fourteen days of my leave she was mine. We talked and talked as though a letter had never passed between us. We talked about "Rondolet George" (who became Evelyn Marcelle) and every day we walked along the winding stream in the Glen that had become Hélène's favourite haunt. We visited Edinburgh Castle and I showed her the place where I had been inducted into the Army. It was over all too soon and I was on my way back to Norway.

At the end of September, when spicules of ice were coming through the water-tap, we handed over our transport to the Norwegians. Tromsø was shrouded in mist when we embarked on N.Y. *Stella Polaris* for Oslo. In England, we gathered for the last time at Halston Hall Camp, near Oswestry, in Shropshire. Day by day my men left, most with jubilation, a few with apprehension about entering the new world, until, apart from my clerk, there was only one man to be accounted for. He was a driver who had spent seventy days in detention in Tromsø and had now overstayed his leave. I phoned the police in Fife to find out what had happened to him. They phoned back later to say that he was on his way to Oswestry and would be back in camp that evening. When he left

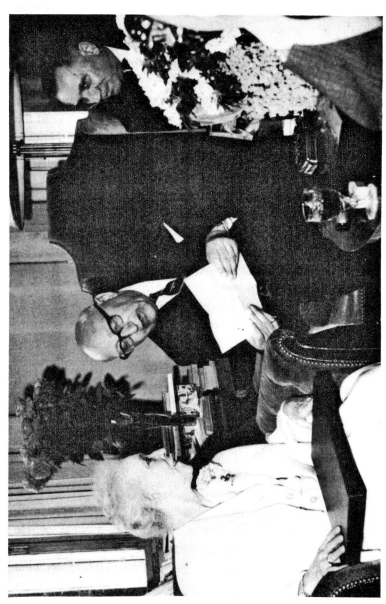

Maurice Bolle with Queen Elizabeth (grandmother of King Bauduin) at the Royal Palace of Laeken, Belgium 1960

with the clerk that would be the end of 55 Field Hygiene Section. On that day I wrote in the War Diary, "Disbandment of the Section was completed on 13th November 1945", and at the bottom of the page I added, "R.I.P."

"You can't do that, Sir," said my clerk. "This goes to the War Office."

"Never mind," I said, "if they don't like it they can get in touch with me in Civvy Street."

The Army released me on Sunday, the 2nd of December. I had to hand in my gas-mask, steel helmet, gas cape, webbing equipment and the revolver given to me in West Africa. In return I received a railway warrant to Glasgow and a ready-made three-piece suit which fitted where it touched. The "Thank you" letter from the War Office, which said I could call myself Major Mair if I wished, came two months later.

The end of the war in Japan brought rewards for some and retribution for others. Hélène's father, Maurice Bolle, returned from Buchenwald, physically a shadow of his former self, but in spirit indomitable. He built himself a splendid home on the outskirts of Brussels, and devoted the rest of his long life to helping the survivors of the concentration camps and the relatives of the dead. He travelled the length and breadth of Europe with his exhibition of the Nazi Concentration Camps, drawing the attention of a horrified public to the infamies of the Holocaust. For his service in the Resistance and to the Dutch people in Belgium during the Occupation, he was appointed an Officer of the House of Orange-Nassau. He died in 1976 full of years and honours. In recognition of her services, his daughter, Hélène Mair-Bolle, received from Queen Wilhelmina of the Netherlands a silver medal depicting Androcles removing the thorn from the lion's paw.

In March 1947, Prosper de Zitter, also known as "Captain Jackson" or "The Canadian" was tried for treason by a military tribunal. Beside him in the dock were his accomplices, Florence Giralt and Jean Nootens. De Zitter was born in Passchendaele, West Flanders. From all accounts he was most convincing and attractive to women. At his trial, a procession of widows, resistance fighters and concentration camp survivors recited a litany of betrayal – evidence of his success as an informer and agent-provocateur. It did not take long for the tribunal to find the accused guilty of treason. De Zitter was sentenced to death, his accomplices to fifteen years' forced labour. The night before his execution de Zitter was told what was in store for him. He would be shot in the police barracks. It seems that despite everything he had done, he still expected a reprieve. When he heard the news, he fell to the floor in a dead faint, deaf to the consoling words of the prison chaplain. He was lifted on to his cot where he spent the night crying without cease – "Fusillé, fusillé". In the morning, still prostrate, he was strapped to a stretcher and taken in a truck to the police barracks where a double row of gendarmes and several military and civil dignitaries awaited him. He was lifted from the stretcher and tied upright to the execution stake. At the word of command the gendarmes took aim and fired. De Zitter slumped in his bonds. He had paid his monstrous debt.

As for myself, I have no medals, service or otherwise, to show for my five years and 256 days in His Majesty's Army. If I was entitled to any, I never claimed them. My role was hardly valorous – taking up the rear of every advance. When I come to think of it, no one ever fired at me in anger except one lone German fighter pilot who strafed my truck when I was driving into the factory in Ath. I went into the war with my eyes open. There was a job to do, and I did it to the best of my ability.

Chapter 15

A Laboratory Service for the People

The day after I left the army, still in my uniform, I set out for Rochdale in Lancashire, a town I had never seen in my life. A month before, I had answered an advertisement in the *British Medical Journal* for an assistant medical officer of health and I was on my way to convince the health committee of that borough I was the right man for the post. Perhaps the uniform helped, because I got the job.

Rochdale, like Rome, is hilly. There the resemblance ends. In 1945, the mills dominated the skyline. They manufactured cotton, wool, rayon and especially flannel, for which Rochdale was famous, sending their products all over the world. Rochdale had two other claims to fame. It was the birthplace of the Cooperative Movement, founded in Toad Lane by the Rochdale Pioneers in 1844, and of Grace Stansfield, better known as Gracie Fields, the great music-hall artist who was born over a chip shop and died a Dame of the British Empire in her magnificent villa in Capri.

I took up my appointment on the first day of 1946 and on the second day I learnt that Evelyn had been born in the nursing home in Glasgow. I now had a family to care for.

Although Britain was no longer at war, everything was in short supply. It was the time of one egg per person per week. Accommodation was difficult to find with so many men coming back from the services, many to set up home for the first time. Buying a house was out of the question, because we had no intention of staying in Rochdale for any

187

length of time, and anyway, we did not have the money to buy one. I searched the "for rent" columns of the *Rochdale Observer* without success. Either the rooms were unsuitable or already taken. It seemed that one had to have inside information and as a stranger to the town I was at a disadvantage. I pestered everyone I met to let me know of rooms about to fall vacant – colleagues, nurses, newsagents (who would know when newspaper deliveries were cancelled) and the milkman, likewise. None was spared. Then, one wintry evening when the streets were like glass, a young man called at Marland Fever Hospital where I had taken up temporary residence. His mother, he said, had fallen, injuring her leg and since her general practitioner was not available he had called at the hospital to see if anyone could help her. Since I was the only doctor in the hospital at that moment, I agreed to go with him. We walked a short distance to his home, where I found his mother lying on a sofa. After applying a dressing to the bruised leg, and assuring him that no bones were broken, I was about to leave when he took out his wallet. I told him to put it away, and made my plea once more. Two days later he came to see me at the hospital. There were rooms for rent at 3 Oakenrod Villas. I should go there at once because the advertisement had just been submitted at the *Observer* office where he was employed. It would be in the paper tomorrow. And that is how we came to live with Mrs. Ormerod.

The name "Oakenrod Villas" was misleading. There were no villas. On a low rise at the end of a long drive off the Bury road stood a large, imposing, granite Victorian mansion which, in the past, had encompassed three contiguous yet separate Ormerod households. These three houses in one had been built by Mr. Ormerod, a prosperous leather factor. With the passage of time his fortunes had declined until death and departures left only old Mrs. Ormerod, who now lived alone in her part of the building while two other families occupied the rest. Mrs. Ormcrod was prepared to let us have two of her numerous bedrooms, a cavernous bathroom, a small living room and the use of her kitchen, which was separated from the rest of the house by a green baize swing-door. As I talked to her in the ill-lit hall, I saw, in my mind's eye, a succession of cooks and housemaids pushing the door open with laden trays, and I thought of Hélène (whose mother had hardly approved of her going "downstairs" when they lived in Avenue Louis Lepoutre) on the other side of that green baize door, sharing the kitchen with Mrs. Ormerod and half-a-dozen hungry mice.

I have warm memories of 3 Oakenrod Villas. Our landlady was eccentric, to put it kindly, but she was kindness itself. She took to Hélène and could not do enough for her. Determined to ensure that Hélène started on the right foot as far as housewifery was concerned, she insisted on lending her *Beeton's* Book of Household Management. The book, published in 1861, had belonged to Mrs. Ormerod's mother. Its 1,100 pages proved to be a mine of information as regards the duties and the qualities expected of the housekeeper, butler, valet, footman, upper- and under-housemaid, lady's maid, waiting maid and maid-of-all-work. We felt that in time we might be able to afford the last-named, whose mistress, Isabella Beeton declared, was usually the wife of a tradesman, like a butcher or baker, and as such was likely to be only one rung above her maid on the social ladder.

My favourite was the under-housemaid, who was expected to be at work by six o'clock in the summer, and half-past six or seven in the winter months. Earlier than this, wrote Mrs. Beeton, "would, probably, be an unnecessary waste of coals and candles, in winter." In the under-housemaid, with whom I felt an affinity, Mrs. Beeton had found a model for perpetual motion. Her duties are described in ten closely printed pages. She is expected to "do" all the lower rooms before breakfast. In the breakfast-parlour, library and drawing rooms she opens shutters, takes up hearth rugs, cleans out the fireplaces, saving the cinders for the kitchen and the copper, sets and lights fresh fires, sweeps the carpets sprinkled beforehand with well-squeezed tea leaves, then, having washed herself free from the dust arising from the morning's work, she collects the breakfast things on her tray and proceeds to lay the table; having given the signal for breakfast she is ready to serve.

Breakfast over, she then proceeds to the bedchambers, where she airs the rooms, empties the slops, turns the bedclothes down and then remakes the beds according to the preference of the occupants. (Any feathers which escape during bedmaking, a careful servant will put back through the seam of the tick.)

Here, we must leave our under-housemaid. She has still much work to do. And when it is done, we find Mrs. Beeton has something else up her sleeve:

> "On leisure days, the housemaid should be able to do some needlework for her mistress – such as turning and mending sheets and darning the house linen, or assist her in anything she may think fit to give her to do. For this reason it is almost essential that a housemaid, in a small family, should be an expert needlewoman; as if she be a good manager and an active girl, she will have time on her hands to get through plenty of work."

If Mrs. Ormerod was preparing us for the future, our present was in the safe hands of Ed and Dot Davies, who lived in a terrace of humble houses across the Bury road. As children they had done their spell in the mills, working at the looms in the early hours of the morning and falling asleep at school in the afternoon. Ed was now caretaker at the public health department. A bit of a dandy, he always wore a collar and tie. I rarely saw him in overalls. My wife often complained that Ed looked like the assistant medical officer of health and I looked like the caretaker. Forty years later, a similar sentiment was expressed by Professor Sir Robert Kilpatrick, the dean of the medical school, on the occasion of the farewell dinner held in our honour at Leicester University on 10th January, 1986: "Hélène is a charming person who always behaves and looks as though she has stepped out of the pages of *Vogue*. The same cannot be said of Nick . . ."

Mr. and Mrs. Davies went on to become wardens of old-age homes in Leicester and Torquay, where Ed died in 1966.

I had been in Rochdale for just over a year when I noticed that I was listening but not recording. The simple act of hearing what was said to me was becoming an effort. Since the incident of the downed bomber in Belgium, I had become accustomed to the constant tinnitus which, while a nuisance, did not seem to interfere with my hearing. But now, the tinnitus was increasing in intensity and variety – cymbals clashed with the hiss of steam escaping under pressure. When a person, speaking to me, turned away for a moment, the words turned away also – I might catch a word or two but for the most part what came to my ears was gibberish. The speaker only had to turn again towards me and I "heard" every word, or almost every word that was being said, enough to make sense of them. I was lip-reading.

As I was to learn later, lip-reading has its hazards also. David Wright, poet and literary figure, begins his book *Deafness – a personal account* thus: "'Where's the baby?' 'I put it in the dustbin.'"

In a footnote he explains that to a lip-reader the words baby and paper are indistinguishable.

I have had my own disasters. I met a female virologist in the corridor of the hospital. She was in a hurry but stopped to explain at great speed, which made lip-reading impossible, that she was off to catch a train to London. I gathered that she was going to join her father for the weekend, a matter which did not interest me in the least. I did not like the woman, but being polite, I said, "I think the weather is going to hold. Have a good time."

I know she did not like me either, but I did not expect the look of loathing with which she greeted my remark. Only later did I learn that she was on her way to attend the funeral of her beloved father.

While I was grappling with the problem of my impaired hearing, I had come to the conclusion that I did not intend to spend the rest of my life in a child-welfare clinic, dispensing cod-liver oil and orange juice to young mothers and giving the same answers to the same questions, day after day. The work made few demands on me and, although in a way it might have been the answer to my problem, it was not what I wanted.

My inclination was to work as a bacteriologist, preferably in a hospital or a university department. I saw myself at the laboratory bench painstakingly identifying the bacteria which cause infection in the individual and outbreaks in the community. Was I seeking to emulate Pasteur, the father of bacteriology, or Robert Koch, the German country doctor who discovered the bacillus of tuberculosis, or was I looking for the seclusion of an ivory tower? If it was the latter, I could not have been more mistaken about the role of the medical bacteriologist. In the course of time I worked as a bacteriologist for more than thirty years, and never once did I find that ivory tower.

When I told Hélène of my intention to change horses and go off in another direction she didn't turn a hair. After all, she had coped with more important things in her young life than having a husband who would earn no money while he attended the nine months' postgraduate course for the Diploma in Bacteriology at the London School of Hygiene and Tropical Medicine. I wrote to Dr. Graham (later Sir Graham) Wilson, Director of the Public Health Laboratory Service, who had initiated the course with Professor W. W. C. Topley before the War. I have not got a copy of my letter but the gist of it can be gathered from Dr. Wilson's reply:

Keppel Street
(Gower Street)
W.C.1
5th February 1947

Dear Dr. Mair,

Thank you for your letter of January 27th.

I am sorry to hear about your deafness which is bound to incapacitate you to some extent in medical work. I am doubtful about the wisdom of your desire to take up bacteriology, partly because you are already too old to start on a highly specialized subject, and partly because deafness is a serious handicap both to the hospital pathologist who has to discuss cases with clinicians inside and outside the hospital, and to the public health bacteriologist who has to undertake field investigations.

It is difficult for me to advise you what branch of medicine to take up, but I do feel fairly strongly that bacteriology is not one in which you would be likely to achieve great success.

I may add that even if you do decide to take up bacteriology there would be no possibility of your taking the course for the Diploma in Bacteriology this year as it is already booked up.

Yours sincerely,

G.S. Wilson.

I was disappointed with Dr. Wilson's reply, to say the least. I had just turned thirty-five and he was writing me off. Was family history about to repeat itself? While I pondered the implications of his letter, Hélène's response was more immediate.

"*Merde!* Don't take 'No' for an answer. We'll find another place that will take you."

And miraculously we did. Only ten miles down the road from Rochdale, the department of bacteriology at Manchester University was about to resume its own postgraduate course, which had been discontinued during the War. I applied for a place and was accepted. Professor Hugh B. Maitland was head of the department but the driving force behind the course was David Gwynne Evans, a fiery, extrovert Welshman. David, as he became known to us, lectured at break-neck speed. How most of the members of the class, who came from what we now call "The Commonwealth", understood his Welsh accent, I do not know. I had not yet resorted to a hearing-aid, but by sitting in the front row I was able to follow most of his lectures. There were times, however, when only a sustained effort of concentration on my part enabled me to follow what he was saying, and when I had a head cold there was nothing I could do except to sit back and spend the hour up-dating nursery rhymes for my little daughter, like "Simple Simon and the Black Market":

> Simple Simon met a pieman
>   going to the fair,
> Said Simple Simon to the pieman
>   "How much are the pies you've there?"

> Said the pieman to Simple Simon
> "One Coupon, and two a penny"
> Said Simple Simon to the pieman
> "Coupons I have not any."
> Then said the pieman to Simple Simon,
> "No Coupon – and one for tuppence!"

Thanks to the generosity of a fellow student, Dr. John O'Hara Tobin, whose notes I borrowed, I was able to make up for the "missed" lectures. John, a medical officer in the Parachute Regiment, had been dropped at Arnhem and taken prisoner by the Germans. We had a lot to reminisce about.

The last two weeks of the course were taken up with revision in preparation for the final examination. David never told us what questions he was going to set but hinted what questions were unlikely. He would come into the laboratory, sit on a bench with his foot on a stool, put his hand out blindly for someone to put a box of matches in it, light up his inevitable cigarette, and then say to us, who sat at his feet like disciples, "What shall we talk about this morning?" If someone suggested, for example, *Mycobacterium tuberculosis*, (the T.B. bacillus) he would shrug his shoulders and say, "We'll talk about that if you wish, but . . ." Conversely, if he adopted the suggestion of the diphtheria bacillus as a topic for discussion, one concluded that in the examination stakes the latter was a more likely starter than the former, although that was no guarantee it would be one of the runners, there were so many to choose from.

At the end of the course we all went our respective ways. The only dentist among us became, in time, dean of dentistry and professor at University College Hospital, London. The refugee from Iraq who, at the beginning of the course, took the cotton-wool plugs out of the sugar tubes with his teeth, became a respected microbiologist at an east-coast hospital. John, turning to the developing discipline of virology, later also made his reputation as an authority on Legionnaire's disease. As for David, he left Manchester to make his academic fortune in London. The activities that earned him international praise and recognition, and his smoking that never stopped, made him a predictable candidate for knighthood and cancer, both of which came his way in due course.

After the examination I departed with yet one more diploma for my bottom drawer and the bonus of John's friendship that has lasted more than forty years.

Hélène had set her heart on practising medicine in her new country. On the 29th January 1946, four weeks after Evelyn's birth, she wrote to the registrar of the General Medical Council enquiring about the equivalence of her Belgian degree in Britain, only to learn that it was not registrable in Britain. She was prepared to take the five-year medical course all over again but the medical schools to which she applied could not find room for her because of the great demand from service men returning to civilian life. When she had just about given up all hope, fortune smiled in the form of the Medical Practitioners and Pharmacists Act, passed in October 1947, which made registrable the degrees of those foreign practitioners, mostly refugees, who had temporarily replaced British doctors called up for service with the armed forces. The same concession was offered to foreign doctors who had cared for British internees in the Far East or had served in the British Army, as Hélène had done. She was now able to practise in the U.K. In September 1948 she took up an appointment as part-time medical officer in the Blood Transfusion Service.

I had not seen Hélène at work when I learned of her skill as a phlebotomist from a grateful patient, who could not praise her highly enough. It was a Saturday night, and the inn was packed with a shouting, cheerful crowd. We found a vacant corner of a table and I left Hélène to stake our claim to it while I fought my way towards the bar. Standing behind it was the landlord, a vast, florid man with arms like hams. As I approached, he pointed in my direction and shouted above the hubbub, "The best ever! The best ever!"

There was a sudden silence, and everyone looked in my direction. Still shouting the publican went on, "I'm a blood donor. I go to the clinic every month or two. They can never get into a vein. Three or four go's they have – no use. Then along comes this girl–" (he snaps his fingers), "she's in the vein first time!" Then, I realized he was not pointing at me but Hélène, who had deserted her post and come up behind me. Many doctors do not like taking a blood sample because of the difficulty it sometimes presents. Hélène had the gift and she never lost it.

I was working as a lecturer in the department of microbiology in the University when Dr. M. T. Parker offered me a job in the public health laboratory he was setting up in Monsall Hospital in Manchester. But first, I had to get the approval of the director of the service, who only twenty months before had told me that I was too old and too deaf to cope with such a highly specialised subject, one in which I was unlikely to achieve great success. (I knew it all by heart.) Of course, I did not tell this to Tom Parker, who must have written to the Director because I received a letter signed by his secretary to the effect that "Dr. Wilson would like to have a talk with you himself to discuss the possibility of offering you a post as assistant bacteriologist in the new public health laboratory at Monsall Hospital. Could you come up to London to see him at 2.30 p.m. on Tuesday, the 28th September?"

G. S. Wilson was a name to conjure with. If British bacteriology needed a guru, it had found one in Dr. Wilson. He was co-author with W. W. C. Topley of the world-famous bacteriologists' Bible: *Principles of Bacteriology and Immunology*, first published in 1929 and which has since run into 8 editions under different editors. He was among those who laid the foundations of the Emergency Public Health Laboratory Service. In the late thirties, before the outbreak of World War II, it was recognized that the laboratory facilities for the investigation of infections and epidemics were inadequate to cope with the threat of bacteriological warfare and the possibility of epidemics arising from the mass evacuation of women and children from the threatened cities to the country, from overcrowded air-raid shelters, and from the dislocation by air bombardment of water supplies and sewage disposal. The E.P.H.L.S. was established in September 1939.

In the event, the fears proved groundless. There was little if any increase in infections or epidemics, but the studies applied to the normally prevalent diseases by the experts in the various laboratories were so revealing and successful that they led to a permanent service in November 1946.

G.S., as he became known, ran both services almost single-handedly from 1941, when there were fifteen area and regional laboratories, until he retired in 1963 when the P.H.L.S. consisted of nearly seventy laboratories providing a medical microbiological service for England and Wales. He also hand-picked his trainees, interviewing each one. After the interview, the applicant underwent a variety of aptitude tests conducted by a psychologist. G.S. always maintained that these tests confirmed his assessments. I had heard a lot about this ordeal by interview from other members of the P.H.L.S., and to add to my trepidation I was sure he had not forgotten the letter he had written to me, for he had a phenomenal memory. I wondered if he had asked me to come so that he could meet the fellow who had refused to take his advice.

When I was ushered into his office that Tuesday afternoon, I saw a tall cleanshaven man, spare and austere, with a high-pitched voice, who greeted me affably and set me at ease by talking about the weather and the inconvenience of travelling up to London in dirty and overcrowded trains. When it came to the purpose of my visit, the hour-long interrogation was thorough and exhaustive, covering my personal and professional life, including my experience in the army. I remember he was intrigued to learn how Hélène had obtained her registration, and when I told him that she was now with the blood transfusion service he remarked prophetically, "She won't be with them for very long." At the end of the interview he asked me if I had any questions to ask. I told him I had heard about the psychologist and her aptitude tests. The thought of them terrified me. Did I have to take them? He laughed for the first time in the long interview and waved me away, saying, "There will be no tests for you."

I became a member of the P.H.L.S. on the 1st November 1948 and Hélène followed suit five months later. Her move was instigated by Dr. Wilson himself. He was making his annual visit to Monsall, during which he asked me if my wife was still with the blood transfusion service. On being told that she was, he said to me, "Do you think she would like to work for us?"

I was sure she would jump at the chance, and I told him so. Tom Parker, who was present at the time, wondered if it was a good thing for a husband and wife to work in the same laboratory, forgetting that Dr. Wilson had done exactly that. G.S. saw Hélène in London a few days later. She had a good interview. When it came to the matter of how she would be employed, he assumed that having a young child she would prefer to work part-time, but she told him she wanted to work full-time and to take the course at Manchester University that her husband had just finished. He asked her if she intended to increase her family. When she said that she did, he took a sheet of paper and made some notes. At that moment Hélène thought, "Now I've had it." Then he made her understand the interview was over. Six days later she received the offer of an appointment as a trainee in the P.H.L.S.

Between May 1949 and October 1951, when she began the course leading to the Diploma in Bacteriology, she worked in the Royal Infirmary and in the P.H.L.S. in Monsall, with time off to have Ann Margot in October 1950. All this would not have been possible without the help of Riet Nonnekens, a buxom forty-nine-year-old woman from Bergen-op-Zoom, who answered the advertisement Hélène had inserted in *Elsevier*. Riet had a family of Argentinean half-brothers and sisters living in Buenos Aires, whom she had never seen but hoped to visit. She came to us to polish up her English, which she believed was the language spoken in South America. She stayed with us for three years, sailed on the *Andes*, saw the family her father had raised in Argentina, and returned to us for another two years.

Hélène was working steadily through the diploma course when she received an unusual request from Professor Maitland. He had been invited to give a lecture in Paris, which he proposed to deliver in French. Could she help him with the pronunciation? So, for one hour on three consecutive days, Hélène sat in the front row of an empty lecture theatre listening to her professor revive his almost forgotten Canadian-French.

Apparently his effort was much appreciated in Paris, and he in turn responded by inviting us to dinner at his home, where for the first time we met the other half of Maitland and Maitland, the husband and wife team which pioneered a method of culture that later formed the basis for the preparation of the Salk vaccine against poliomyelitis. Mrs. Maitland was a very charming person, who steered the conversation away from microbiology and appeared to be more interested in learning how Hélène was coping with married life in Lancashire. During dinner, Maitland told us how he went Sunday-painting with his friend, the famous painter Laurence Stephen Lowry who lived, a recluse, in a little stone house in the village of Mottram-in-Longdendale. Afterwards the professor took us round the house to show us the Lowrys he had collected over the years. Most of them he had bought, many were gifts of the artist. Landscapes, portraits and street scenes, large and small, hung in every room, some up to the ceiling. In the street scenes, he showed us the painter's "trademark", the little stick-like men in oversize bowlers held up by their ears, clumping their way in outsize black boots across grey-white streets, against a background of factories and mills. When it was time for us to go, the professor handed Hélène a small flat package that was evidently a painting wrapped in brown paper and tied with string. We could not get home quickly enough to see our Lowry. Once it was unwrapped, we saw a typical Lowry scene: a lock-gate and a cobbled path alongside it, in the background a derelict building. It was a Sunday-painting by H. B. Maitland.

In the four and a half years I was in Monsall, thanks to Tom Parker I squeezed in twice as many years of experience. He was a perfectionist, demanding high quality work in all areas, but he himself set the pace. He it was who gave me my first taste of research.

One morning when I had been working at Monsall for nearly two years, Tom came to see me with the news that there was an outbreak of smallpox in southeast Lancashire, probably imported in bales of cotton. A large number of patients had already been admitted to Ainsworth Smallpox Hospital about twenty miles west of Manchester. Later, I learned that 135 persons had been infected. Today, smallpox has been eradicated, but at that time it was worldwide. It was regarded as one of the most deadly of the infectious diseases, able to survive in the air and dust and to infect at a considerable distance. A case of smallpox has been recorded where the only known source of infection was when the victim passed by a smallpox hospital on a bus.

I was not unfamiliar with smallpox. I had seen several cases in West Africa, the last of them a young English officer who, somehow, had missed vaccination before being sent to Nigeria. He had suffered all the stages of the fearful smallpox rash: first the spots (macules) all over his body, then the macules swelled to the size of peas and became filled with clear fluid (vesicles) which soon turned to pus. At this stage his temperature rose and he became delirious. I can remember standing at the foot of his bed with Brigadier Findlay, consultant physician in tropical diseases. Through the open window we could hear the laughter of the officers and nurses on the tennis court. There was nothing we could do except watch him die and it was an ugly death. The virus which caused his death was known as *Variola major*.

The cause of the Lancashire outbreak was soon identified as *Variola minor*. This virus, as the name implied, caused a disease which was a weaker mirror-image of the smallpox that killed the young soldier. The rash was as profuse but more superficial and left few pock marks and very few died of the infection. It seemed to Tom that here was a golden opportunity to carry out a bacteriological investigation of the smallpox rash at each stage of its development. The medical textbooks claimed that invasion of the rash with *staphylococci* and *streptococci*, pus-forming bacteria from the patient's skin, caused his delirium and subsequent death. Antibiotics known to be capable of controlling bacterial infections were becoming available, and it was now a matter of importance to find out what part, if any, they could play in the treatment of smallpox.

We agreed that I should carry out the investigation. I began by revaccinating Hélène and Evelyn, and the laboratory staff. Tom and I had been vaccinated so often we hardly took. Every morning I drove to the smallpox hospital, a bleak collection of buildings, standing well away from the nearest built-up area. I passed through the guarded gate where everything from the world outside was left for collection by the hospital staff. Wearing sterile trousers, cap, mask and gown, I began taking specimens from the patients in various stages of the rash. In some, the pustular rash was so extensive, I was reminded of the soldier in Lagos, yet they were not seriously ill. In others, the rash was sparse and it was evident that as soon as the crusts, which were still infectious, had disappeared, they would be discharged.

The method of collecting the samples was simple. A sterile glass capillary tube with a small rubber teat at one end was inserted into the skin, and the fluid, either clear or pustular, was withdrawn and expelled on to the surface of a special growth medium. I had no doubt that, while I took every precaution, I was expelling large quantities of virus into the air at the same time. Within four hours I was back in the laboratory with the culture plates for incubation. During the next two weeks I collected specimens from forty patients from the date of admission until they were discharged. In only two of these did I find any pus-producing bacteria and these were scanty in number. We could only conclude that pustulation was due to the destructive action of the smallpox virus on the tissues rather than to secondary bacterial invasion; a conclusion that was generally accepted after the paper was published.

Having disposed of that problem, I was about to start on another, when I was struck down by a shattering headache that left me prostrate. I rarely suffered from headaches, but this time I felt as though my head was being squeezed in an ever-tightening vice. I told Hélène to stay away from me. The water she brought me was placed outside the bedroom door. From time to time, I crept out of bed to peer into a looking-glass for signs of the tell-tale macules on my forehead, where they first appear in smallpox. The physicians from Monsall Hospital put their heads together and decided that I was suffering from a rare condition, *Variola sine eruptione*, or in the Queen's English, smallpox without the rash, an allergic reaction occurring in highly-immunized persons exposed to the virus. I recall they mentioned the long convalescence necessary to ensure complete recovery. Tom was told about this and, when I returned to work after a week, he offered me sympathetic support, but this only lasted for a few days and soon we were back to frantic normality.

I was still under the weather when I travelled up to Glasgow to see my father who had just suffered a severe heart attack. It was evident that he was dying. I kept the night watch, reading stories by Shalom Aleichem. In the early hours of one morning he asked me to look into the inside pocket of his jacket hanging in a closet. I brought out a five-pound note.

"Take it", he said. "Take it."

My legacy. But I had already received my legacy over and over again. When I was a little boy, my father used to give me a three-penny piece, saying, "Don't spend it all in one shop."

I would like to write that I kept the five-pound note as a souvenir but I spent it, though not all in the one shop. My father was the last person for whom I sat shiva.

Thirteen years later, on the 14th April 1963, after years of frenetic searching, my mother found peace at last when she died suddenly in hospital after falling and breaking her leg. I was in California at the time. I learned about her accident and her death two days after she was buried beside my father.

Chapter 16

Working Together

On the 28th June 1952, I was promoted to consultant bacteriologist and appointed Director of the Leicester Public Health Laboratory. Two days later, Hélène received her diploma from Manchester University and was offered an appointment at the same laboratory, with the grade of assistant bacteriologist which she accepted. For better or for worse, we were to work together for the next twenty-six years in a laboratory improvised from a disused ward in Groby Road Isolation Hospital.

"Ward 5", as our laboratory was known in the hospital, differed little from other improvised laboratories in the Service, except that it contained an unique piece of equipment, or rather furniture. In its last incarnation Ward 5 must have been the hospital social club because, occupying a considerable amount of floor space in what had once been the female part of the ward near the staff tea-room, stood a full-size billiard table, massive, immovable like the Rock of Gibraltar. It reminded me of my younger days in the Glasgow University Union. For some unknown reason it had been left behind when the P.H.L.S. took over. We were very proud of our billiard table, on which we played after working hours. What public health laboratory, or for that matter any laboratory in the United Kingdom, could boast of such a table on the premises? My only concern was what G.S. might think of it when he made his annual visit. When he did see it for the first time his only response was a slight raising of his eyebrows and the faintest glimmer of a smile when he saw the picture my chief technician, Eric Fox, had affixed to the wall next to the score-board. It showed Alexander Fleming, discoverer of penicillin, playing his favourite game – billiards.

When I write we were to work together, I should make it clear that while we laboured under the same roof, providing a microbiological service to the Leicestershire hospitals, general practitioners and local health authorities, our jobs were different, but complementary. A high wooden partition that ran the length of the laboratory where the benches were located emphasized the separation. On one side of the partition I practised diagnostic bacteriology. On the other side Hélène, starting from scratch, set up a thriving unit devoted to the diagnosis of diseases caused by viruses.

My discipline was in the tradition of Pasteur, Lister and Koch, whose discoveries in the 'nineties had begun to revolutionize the entire science of healing. Much of the progress in the subsequent fifty years was in the fields of isolation, identification and classification. The tools of my craft were simple, consisting of two resistance wires and a loupe, the watchmaker's magnifying glass. One wire was about two and a half inches long and had a loop turned on it. "Taking a loopful" is a phrase constantly used. The other wire, about three or four inches long, was used for picking colonies off a plate or making stab cultures. We grew the bacteria in broths and jellies made firm with agar-agar derived from the stems of various seaweeds growing in the Chinese seas. The basis of our media was ox-heart broth made by Geoff, our oldest hand. Geoff never sat any examinations but where making media was concerned he was *"un cordon bleu"*. When I introduced him to visitors I pretended I could not remember whether he had worked for Alexander Fleming or Louis Pasteur, although in truth he had spent some months in Fleming's laboratory at St. Mary's. About twice a month Geoff went to the slaughterhouse and bought ten pounds of ox-hearts. In the media room he removed the fat, sliced and minced, added cold water to the minced meat in a stainless steel bucket with lid, heated the contents carefully to 80° C., stood the bucket in a sink with cold running water, added sodium carbonate and, when the contents had fallen to body temperature, added trypsin to digest the meat and chloroform to stop any growth, incubated the lot for six hours, tested a sample for digestion with copper sulphate which turned the sample a nice pink colour if digestion was complete, added concentrated sulphuric acid to the broth, put the bucket in a steamer for two hours, took the bucket out, stood it on a stool and went home. The next day he filtered the broth first through muslin, then through paper pulp, bottled it and sterilized it in an autoclave. I should mention in passing we never bought commercial trypsin. Geoff made it himself from pig's pancreas. I should also add that it was Geoff's know-how that helped me to make "Mair's Medium".

In the course of time we managed to drag Geoff into the twentieth century. Almost all our media were obtained from commercial sources in the form of dehydrated powders and granules. All he had to do was add distilled water. My assistant bacteriologist needed no persuasion. She came into virology after Enders, Weller and Robbins, three American scientists working in Boston, showed that poliomyelitis virus could grow on human and monkey tissues artificially cultivated as a single layer of cells on the sides of flat bottles or on the walls of test-tubes. With this revolutionary discovery, for which Enders and his colleagues received the Nobel Prize, tissue culture of viruses became a procedure well within the scope of a routine bacteriological laboratory.

I can remember how I went down to the pharmacy at the bottom of Groby Road and asked for six hexagonal Pyrex feeding bottles. The pharmacist looked surprised but with admirable reticence refrained from comment. A few days later I returned and asked for another six. He said he had exhausted his stock but would get them for me. This time he asked me what I was going to do with them. I told him we were about to carry out an experiment at the isolation hospital. For the experiment we had built an incubation room in which we installed a machine like the Ferris wheel one sees in amusement parks. It was made from a child's Meccano set and was fitted with a small electric motor, pulleys and reducing gears. Four baby bottles were fixed to the periphery of the wheel like passenger cars. Each bottle contained a suspension of the cells to be cultured with serum and lactalbumen for sustenance and antibiotics to maintain sterility. It was an odd contraption, but it worked.

The wheel turned slowly so that the bottles rolled about twelve revolutions per hour until after about five to seven days, complete cell sheets were formed on all six sides of each bottle. From these bottles secondary cell cultures were prepared in test tubes for virus isolation. Eventually, we used four different "lines" for tissue culture; monkey kidney cells, amnion cells from human placenta, human embryonic cells and HeLa cells, named from the fore- and surname of the cervical cancer patient who provided the cells which have been used continuously in laboratories all over the world for the last thirty-five years – a bizarre immortality.

The work on both sides of the partition was increasing to such an extent we were hard put to find room for extra staff and new equipment. Hélène had no office except a desk in her laboratory. It was evident that our billiard table would have to go.

One morning a truck pulled up outside Ward 5. Four men in overalls got out, entered the laboratory and surrounded the billiard table. They unbolted the cushions and removed the six pockets. Two of them detached and rolled up the green billiard cloth to reveal five slabs of Welsh slate fitting so snugly they looked like a single piece. The slabs were so heavy, the four men could barely carry each one to the truck. Then, having dismantled the frame and taken away the eight beautifully carved mahogany legs, they gathered up the cues, the billiard and snooker balls and, not forgetting the score-board, got into the truck and left.

"Abortus! Abortus! what is this Abortus?
In Holland we pay for it!"
(Riet Nonnekens, 1953)

Shortly after our arrival in Leicester, I was informed by Dr. Gibson, the county medical officer of health, that bovine brucellosis caused by the bacterium *Brucella abortus* was rife in Leicestershire herds, showing itself in abortions, failure to thrive and low milk yields. A later survey showed that 30,000 herds in the U.K., a third of the total, were infected. These herds presented a hazard to those in direct contact with them, farmers, slaughtermen, butchers and meat packers and indirectly to laboratory technicians. Individuals who drank raw milk exposed themselves to infection. Those affected suffered severe headaches, generalized aches and pains, and drenching sweats, which sometimes lasted several months.

The bacteriologist, attempting to isolate *Br. abortus* from herd samples of milk by culture, usually failed because of the presence of large numbers of contaminating organisms in the milk. Under the best conditions it took about four days for *Br. abortus* colonies to appear and by that time the culture plate was covered with contaminating colonies and moulds. The usual method was to use animal inoculation. A guinea-pig was inoculated with a mixture of cream and centrifuged deposit. Six weeks later the animal was killed and the organism cultured from its spleen.

The medical officer of health receiving the report from the laboratory had the power to stop the sale of milk from an infected farm until it had been pasteurized. This penalized the farmer producing the more expensive high grade, tuberculin-tested, unpasteurized milk which many people preferred. The medical officer himself was often hesitant about applying the stoppage notice because the laboratory report referred to a sample taken six weeks earlier, and since the excretion of brucellae is intermittent it was difficult to decide if the milk was still infected at the time the report was received.

It seemed to me that there was a need for a quick and reliable test for the detection of brucellae. More and more antibiotics were coming on the market. Perhaps they could be substituted for the aniline dyes that had been used up till now to suppress contaminants. I intended to go in at the deep end. I would try to devise a selective medium for the isolation of brucellae from herd samples of milk. The milk officer would merely dip his collecting cup in the milk churn and go away with the sample and within a week he would have an answer. G. S. Wilson expressed his doubts. He thought I was excessively optimistic.

A selective medium works on the principle that one man's meat is another man's poison. If the antibiotics I chose were not exactly the brucellae's meat, they were certainly the contaminants' poison. After much trial and error, and many discussions with Hélène, I finally arrived at the right recipe. Riet, our help, who had heard all about it, morning and night for weeks, and could not contain her curiosity any longer, cried from the bottom of her heart, "Abortus! Abortus! What is this Abortus? In Holland we pay for it!"

Our preliminary trials were proving highly successful when I got a telephone call late one Saturday evening. It was from Dr. Gibson;

"Is that you, Mair?"

"Yes."

"I've just been pulled out of my bath by Lady Rumbledum. Farms near the Lincolnshire border. She's flaming mad. Says she's going to sue us. The local M.O.H. put a stop on her milk after he got your report. She says it's Strain 19 you've isolated and you and the M.O.H should know better. What are you going to do about it?"

Strain 19 is a live, attenuated strain of *Br. abortus* used extensively by veterinary surgeons to immunize young calves against brucellosis. Sometimes the vaccine is given to older cows coming into the herd for the first time. On rare occasions, it has been known to enter the milk. It is not regarded as harmful.

In devising my medium I had not taken Strain 19 into account. I could imagine what counsel would make of that in a court of law. The only thing to do was to forget about it till Monday, when I could set about obtaining ampoules of the vaccine from various sources. I tested them against the complete medium and separately against each of its ingredients, penicillin, the broad-spectrum antibiotic polymyxin B sulphate, the antifungal agent actidione and a weak solution of gentian violet. The vaccine failed to grow on the complete medium and therefore the strain isolated from Lady R's herd was not a vaccine strain but a wild one. The ingredient responsible for the failure of the vaccine to grow on the medium was penicillin. Further investigation showed that the vaccine strain was extremely sensitive to very low concentrations of the antibiotic. This was an interesting observation because the existing method of differentiating wild strains of *Br. abortus* from the vaccine strain involved growing them on a complicated battery of media containing aniline dyes at different concentrations. I was about to rush into print when I learned that American workers had published a similar observation several months before.

Mair's medium was accepted by the P.H.L.S. and other laboratories as the medium of choice for the isolation of *Br. abortus* from milk. It remained so for several years until it was superseded by a better one building on mine, which is the nature of science. In 1981, except for a single source, brucellosis was eradicated from all herds in the United Kingdom.

If I had escaped one lawsuit, I found myself embroiled in another. This time it concerned water and Mr. O'Brien, who owned an off-licence in Leicester and an inn on the road to Oakham. Mr. O'Brien was in trouble with the County Council. The water supply for the inn came from a well on the premises. According to the local medical officer of health the water was polluted. He had grounds for this view because he had received reports from us to that effect. The Council wanted the inn to go on the mains water supply but O'Brien, stubborn Irishman, refused. Matters came to a head when the Council threatened to close the inn as a danger to the public health. Counsel on both sides were briefed and a date was fixed for the adversaries to meet in the courthouse at Oakham. I was asked by the Council to attend as an expert witness, my expertise extending to confirmation that my laboratory had done the tests and that the results were accurate. But before that happened I received a visit from my friend, Ted Kelly, general practitioner and police surgeon, about whom you will hear more later. Ted recited the woes of his fellow Irishman O'Brien, and asked if I would do him a favour. There was a second well that had never been tested. Were he to collect a sample from that well, would I test it? I told him it was probably as bad as the other, because there was a sealed cess-pit nearby; his friend was throwing good money after bad. I gave Ted a sampling outfit and in due course he learned that the second well was as polluted as the first. The report was for his eyes only as the sample was his.

If one has to spend a morning in court there is no better place to do so than the courthouse in Oakham. Long known as Oakham Castle, it has a fine banqueting hall, a remarkable survival of domestic Norman architecture, probably the best thing of its kind in the country. Should the attention wander there are the horseshoes of Oakham Castle, more than 200 of them nailed to the walls of the hall. Through many centuries it has been one of Oakham's customs to demand a horseshoe from every peer of the realm passing through the town. Some of the shoes are very small and others over a yard high. Most are ornamental.

Surrounded by this remarkable sight, Mr. Skinner Q.C., the Council's advocate, put up a strong case for closing the inn. Mr. O'Brien's counsel tried to bamboozle the county sanitary inspector, who was even more deaf than I was, by dropping his voice several decibels from time to time. Towards the end, when it was evident that O'Brien was going to lose, his counsel declared that his client had decided to go on the mains. If the Council agreed he would like to keep the inn open while the new pipes were being installed. There was another well he could use. There were no objections from the Council. No one asked me about the potability of the water in the second well, so I kept my mouth shut. A short time later I received my fee as an expert witness from the prosecution, and a bottle of Irish whisky from the defence.

Chapter 17

Giselle

Gilmour had three initials, C. C. B., preceding his surname. In the few years that I got to know him I never learned what they stood for. He was always "Gilmour" to me, as I was "Mair" to him. I met him for the first time in 1952 when I attended my first directors' staff-meeting at the Central Public Health Laboratory in Colindale, North London. He was already in his sixties, not far from retiring age, a lean, white-haired, grizzled Scotsman, a former colonial medical officer who had joined the P.H.L.S. when he came back from Malaya after the War. He was not given to much idle talk, but when he learned that I had been in Malaya before the War he became quite affable, having found a kindred soul. We were sitting together listening to a dull paper on bacteriological standards for ice-cream when, out of the blue, he told me about his boat. She was a five-ton, twenty-five-foot, gaff-rigged vessel designed for deep-sea sailing. I had no idea what a five-ton, gaff-rigged boat looked like since most of my sailing had been on ships of several thousand tons. His boat was moored on the River Nene not far from Peterborough where he had his laboratory. He wondered if I would care to join him in some sailing on the Wash. Leicester was only forty miles from Peterborough. If I left early, we could get in a day's sailing, and I could be home the same evening. I told him I was willing to give it a try.

When I saw *Giselle*, for that was her name, she looked very small. In the tiny cabin there was a framed, enlarged photograph of a scene from the ballet *Giselle*. Gilmour's daughter, Sally Gilmour, prima ballerina of

211

the Ballet Rambert, occupied the centre of the stage. She was very beautiful.

When the table in the centre of the cabin was cleared away, there was room for two to sleep and in the fo'c's'le room for two more if they did not mind the anchor chain and life-jackets. It took several turns of the handle to start the engine in the open cockpit, but once started it was fairly reliable.

By river, Peterborough is about thirty miles from the Wash, the shallow bay of the North Sea between Lincolnshire and Norfolk. Much of our sailing was really cruising down the Nene between the high banks that protected the low-lying fields on either side. For much of the journey, the mast lay on the deck so that we could pass under the bridges which spanned the Nene. Once we reached the open sea we raised the mast, unfurled the sail and enjoyed the last few hours of light before returning to the estuary, which was so shallow that more than once we had to anchor off for several hours until the tide was right. The return journey to Peterborough was often made in darkness.

In the summer Gilmour had another proposition to make. He planned to sail up the North Sea to the Firth of Forth, cross the Forth and Clyde Canal and spend his vacation in the west of Scotland. Would I be prepared to crew for part of the way? Besides us, there would be two others. I agreed. A few days before we were due to leave, I learned the others had called-off. I went round the students' halls of residence in Leicester looking for a volunteer. I found Wally, a London Cockney reading English. He had never been to sea before but he was ready and willing. I advised him to bring some wet-weather gear. He brought a bicycle cape.

We set off from Peterborough in bright sunshine which turned to clouds and rain before we reached the Wash. Once clear of the last bridge over the Nene we raised the mast, and fixed it in its seating with a large bolt. A strong easterly wind had whipped up the sea and we cruised under power, making no attempt to raise the sail. The weather grew worse and the skipper decided to return to the shelter of the Nene. We waited for two days. Then having convinced ourselves that the wind was abating, we set off again. But the calm of the Nene, sheltered between its banks, deceived us. If anything, the weather was worse than before, but this time Gilmour was determined to go on.

Before we set out the first time, I had persuaded Wally to take avomine, an anti-seasickness pill, which seemed to have been very effective. This time he refused, saying he saw no need for it; a display of bravado for which he paid dearly. I do not recall how long we had been running, our little engine chugging away bravely, when Wally was overtaken by a prolonged bout of sickness. At the sight of Wally, Gilmour followed suit, but in a more professional manner – a short, sharp expulsion on the lee side. Suddenly he clapped his hand over his mouth and between his fingers, said, quite calmly – "I've lost my teeth!"

When he took his hand away I could see his upper plate was missing. To me it seemed a devastating stroke of ill-luck but Gilmour took it in his stride. He shrugged it off as though it did not matter. There were more important things to do. The sea was rising and seemed to be coming at us from all sides. *Giselle* was dancing as she had never danced before. The mast was swaying and straining against the stays as though at any moment it was going to go over the side. Gilmour went forward to have a look and came back with grim news. The bolt which held the mast vertical had worked itself out of the seating and half-way through the width of the mast. Apparently, when we had raised the mast after passing under the last bridge over the Nene, the bolt had not been tightened sufficiently. We had to get the bolt back through the mast and screwed tightly into the seating or we were lost.

Wally was lying in the lee of the cabin, soaked, sick and miserable. Gilmour went over to him and told him what he had told me. The transformation was instantaneous. Wally stopped being sick. He leaped up and joined Gilmour at the foot of the mast, which was swinging like an inverted pendulum. I was trying to keep the boat head-on to the wind. I watched them battling on top of the cabin while the seas broke over them. At last they rose, thumbs up. At least one disaster was averted.

About an hour later, I was still at the wheel trying to keep the bow head-on to the waves when suddenly I saw a pink creature like a tiny crab sliding up and down the deck on the port side. As the bow rose, it scampered towards me and as the stern rose it scuttled away. I could not see it clearly through my streaming glasses and I was afraid to touch it. I wiped my glasses, and even then I could not believe my eyes. I grabbed it before it got away. In my hand I held Gilmour's upper plate! I can only surmise that when Gilmour had thrown up, his teeth had dropped on the deck and slipped towards the bow, probably becoming entangled in the anchor chain there, only to be released shortly before I saw it. The gunwale had prevented the plate going over the side when it started sliding up and down the deck.

We looked on the return of Gilmour's teeth as a good omen. Surely, things could only get better now. It was dark when we followed a ship into Grimsby. We tied up at a jetty, hung our soaking clothes over the boom and tumbled into our bunks. When we got up next morning, *Giselle* and our clothes were covered in an inch-thick layer of coal dust. A collier in the next berth had been discharging its cargo down a chute while we slept. An inspection of our boat showed that during the storm the anchor had slipped over the side and, suspended by a short length of chain, had been chipping away at the hull.

Later we met in an hotel lounge, bathed and fed, and over our drinks we discussed the habits of those who sailed or fished for pleasure. I told them about a Leicester colleague, a chest physician and avid angler, who on the second day of his honeymoon had gone off to fish in the morning, leaving his bride in the hotel. It was getting dark when a search party found him at the edge of a reservoir waiting for another bite. Gilmour's comment on this was, "Aye, these fishermen, they're mad."

Two days later in lovely sailing weather we reached Bridlington, about fifty miles up the coast. We went ashore and joined the holiday-makers on the promenade. We stopped at a fortune-teller's booth. I suggested to Wally that he should go in and find out what the future held for him. We joked about what he might find out. Gilmour was not amused. Then, hesitantly, he told us his story. In Singapore before the War, he and his wife were attending a government garden party. A native seer, much sought after by the ladies, was telling fortunes. Gilmour persuaded his wife to have her fortune told. She came out of the booth, pale and distraught. Though at that moment she was surrounded by the luxury of colonial power, the seer had told her she would die alone, in hunger and misery. When the Japanese entered Singapore, Gilmour and his wife were interned in Changi Gaol, she in block A and he in block B. He never saw her again. (When I was researching this episode, I came across a book, *British Civilians and the Japanese War in Malaya and Singapore, 1941-1945*, by Joseph Kennedy. In it he mentions C. C. B. Gilmour as one of fifty-seven civilians who were taken for interrogation and detained in police cells in Singapore, where they suffered appalling torture.)

Gilmour decided not to go any further and we returned home. He retired from the P.H.L.S. in 1956. Later the same year he tried again. The least I could do was accompany him. This time we took John Tobin along. The voyage was uneventful until we passed under the Forth Bridge. I remember it was a misty dawn. The river was full of the sound of foghorns. We were drinking coffee laced with rum, toasting our triumph when *Giselle* ran aground on the banks of the River Carron. It took two days of pushing and pulling before we got her afloat again. John and I returned to Leicester by train. Gilmour went on through the canal by himself, until he reached his destination in the Firth of Clyde where he married his childhood sweetheart, the purpose of all our efforts.

Chapter 18

The boy who did not have appendicitis

In the Spring of 1959 a chance encounter set me on a course of investigations and research that lasted nearly twenty years. On second thoughts, perhaps "chance" is not the right word. My office door was rarely closed, an open invitation to anyone who had an axe to grind. So, when Dr. Kelly dropped in to tell me about the boy whose acute appendicitis had turned out to be something else, I was prepared to listen. He was most emphatic about the accuracy of his diagnosis.

"Sure, I've been in the business long enough to recognize a case of acute appendicitis when I see one."

But to his surprise the hospital report had come back, "Acute mesenteric adenitis: Normal appendix".

This was something new to Dr Kelly. In fact, probably more than a third of children admitted to hospital with a diagnosis of acute appendicitis suffer from mesenteric adenitis, a gross inflammation of the lymph glands in the region of the appendix, which on the whole remains unaffected. The signs and symptoms of mesenteric adenitis and acute appendicitis are so similar that the surgeon has little choice except to operate.

Dr. Kelly wondered if it might be a reaction to pasteurized milk, a suggestion no less fanciful than others made over the years. It seemed to me that it would be worth investigating the possible viral origin of mesenteric adenitis.

With the co-operation of the resident surgical officer and the consultant bacteriologist at the Royal Infirmary, arrangements were made to collect specimens of glands, appendix, faeces, throat swab and serum from patients in whom the diagnosis of mesenteric adenitis had been made at operation. We had no sooner started our investigation than G. S. Wilson drew our attention to the work of a German bacteriologist who had isolated an organism called *Pasteurella pseudotuberculosis* from the glands of children with mesenteric adenitis. Moreover, the glands showed tissue changes, in the form of micro-abscesses which seemed to be characteristic of this infection. I obtained a copy of this paper and I recall how Hélène and I sat that summer on the beach at Lerici in the Gulf of Spetzia translating the German article with the aid of a dictionary, and reading up *P. pseudotuberculosis* in "Topley and Wilson" when we got home. The organism had a long pedigree going back to 1883, when it was isolated from a guinea-pig inoculated with experimental material. The lesions in the guinea-pig resembled those found in tuberculosis, hence the species name. By the middle of this century only fifteen cases of human pseudotuberculosis had been recorded in the medical literature, most of them of a typhoid-like nature. The only other observation I would make about this organism, in view of what the future held, was that it belonged to the same family and closely resembled *Pasteurella pestis*, the dreaded bacillus of plague.

Between May and October 1959 we investigated seventeen children for the presence of virus and for evidence of pseudotuberculosis infection. We failed to find any evidence of virus infection, but to our selfish joy three of the children showed that they were infected with *Pasteurella pseudotuberculosis*. The paper, "Three Cases of Acute Mesenteric Lymphadenitis due to *Pasteurella pseudotuberculosis*" by N.S. Mair, Hélène J. Mair, E. M. Stirk and J. G. Corson was published in the *Journal of Clinical Pathology* in 1960. It was the first publication of its kind in the English language. *The Lancet* followed with an annotation drawing the attention of the medical profession as a whole to a newly discovered cause of an old disease.

The response to the paper and the annotation was almost immediate. I received a telephone call from a pathologist in the north of England.

"I am sending you a serum and a section of a lymph node from a young man, diagnosed as abdominal Hodgkin's disease. He's down for deep X-ray therapy, but I've read your paper and I've asked for the treatment to be held up till I hear from you."

Hodgkin's disease is a cancerous disorder of lymphoid tissue characterized by progressive enlargement of lymph nodes throughout the body associated with weight loss and anaemia. In the early sixties deep X-ray therapy offered prolonged remissions, but the side effects of the treatment – nausea, vomiting and colitis – were most distressing.

The specimens arrived next morning. A simple slide test indicated that the patient's serum was strongly positive for *P. pseudotuberculosis*. When I examined the section of the gland under the microscope I could see the typical micro-abscesses. I immediately phoned my findings. Two weeks later the pathologist wrote to tell me that the patient was responding to antibiotics, adding, "You have given this young man a new lease of life."

These were the first of a host of specimens that were submitted to us from all over the U.K. Within a short time the Leicester laboratory was designated the U.K. reference centre for *Pasteurella* infections, one of the few reference facilities developed outside the Central Public Health Laboratory.

I was interested not only in the diagnosis of pseudotuberculous adenitis but in its epidemiology, because the link between the human disease and animals soon became apparent, pseudotuberculosis having been long recognized by veterinary pathologists. There was the little boy, the son of a doctor, who shared a kennel with a labrador. The little boy got mesenteric adenitis and the dog's blood was positive for pseudotuberculosis. There was the outbreak of acute appendicitis at a boys' boarding school in the south of England, or so it must have seemed to the school doctor who sent three boys to hospital on the same day and kept an eye on four others in the school sanatorium. At operation two of the boys were found to have acute mesenteric adenitis and a normal appendix. The third boy had palpable glands in the appendix region, and the penny having dropped, was kept under observation. We received serum samples from all the affected boys and all were strongly pseudotuberculosis positive, while the organism was isolated from a gland taken at operation. I was invited to visit the school to help find the source of the infection. On these occasions, particularly in private schools, there is a tendency to conceal rather than reveal. In this preparatory school, the headmaster was most co-operative. He told me that members of the Royal Family had been pupils and he was anxious for the matter to be cleared up as soon as possible. It turned out that the only time the seven boys were together, excluding the dining hall, was a biology class where they had been dissecting a rabbit. The biology master, who kept rabbits on a small-holding, had supplied one for the class. We took samples of blood from the rabbits and most were pseudotuberculosis positive. He assured me the boys were told to wash their hands after the class. I do not know whether they washed their hands, but I know on that particular day they had sticky buns for tea.

After the outbreak at the school I began an investigation into the prevalence of pseudotuberculosis in animals in co-operation with several veterinary centres. I also wrote to the pathologist at the London Zoo asking for any cultures he might isolate. He replied that pseudotuberculosis did not seem to be a problem but he would now look out for it. Three years later, in 1964, he wrote in his annual report:

> "Pseudotuberculosis, caused by *Pasteurella pseudo-tuberculosis*, began to appear in the Gardens in disturbing numbers of cases some three years ago. Since then a number of cases have been regularly encountered and it would appear as if this disease must now be regarded as endemic and likely to cause a number of losses each year."

Our records show that, in the twenty-one years between 1961 and 1982, the Leicester laboratory, in collaboration with veterinary centres, identified 570 strains of the organism. About a third came from mammals and birds in zoological gardens and just under a quarter from farm and domestic animals. Among those identified for the first time in the U.K.

Dr. Hélène Mair in the virus laboratory, Leicester 1956

were the bovine foetus, cats, a foal and a fox. In Leicestershire, a great hunting county, the fox has an almost sacred, sacrificial status. When a fox is found dead in an open field without signs of external violence, it is a matter of concern. On such an occasion a furious master of hounds brought a carcase of a fox to our local veterinary investigation centre convinced that the animal had been poisoned by anti-hunting activists. An autopsy revealed gross enlargement of the abdominal glands from which we isolated *Yersinia pseudotuberculosis.* (The genus name was changed to *Yersinia* in the 1980s.) During the same period 395 cases of human pseudotuberculosis were diagnosed by culture and serological tests.

There would never have been a Yersinia Reference Centre in Leicester were it not for the magnificent work of my chief technician, Eric Fox. He had just completed his national service with the R.A.M.C. in Egypt when he joined the Leicester laboratory in 1950. He was a tall, gangling young man who spoke little and smoked too much. I liked him from the start. Unlike the other ex-service men on the staff he did not address me constantly as "Sir!" It was always, "Doctor Mair." If he was a little weak on administration, that was of minor importance to me for he was a superb "bench" man. His name appears with mine on several papers and the monograph *Yersiniosis* finalized our work. He enjoyed the respect of his colleagues in the P.H.L.S. and the hospital service. When I retired in 1978 it was he who said, "You know, Doctor Mair, you never did anything by the book." Who could ask for a better epitaph?

Eric suffered from an inherited defect, an excess of cholesterol in the blood. He underwent open heart surgery in January 1988 and died of heart failure in May of the same year at the age of fifty-four. After his death, the Yersinia Reference Laboratory moved to Colindale.

Chapter 19

Escape to Keeper's Cottage

One wintry afternoon in February 1962, I stood on a snow-covered hill with Ted Kelly, who appears for the last time in this chronicle. He had stopped his car before a five-barred gate at the entrance to a wood. He pushed the gate open against the wet snow and we began to trudge downhill, crouched against the wind, to where the trees began.

That morning, Hélène and I had talked over plans for the summer holiday. For the last few years we had gone either to the south of France or to Italy, finishing with a visit to her family in Brussels. For the coming summer Hélène proposed a different vacation. Our daughters kept two ponies in a stable near the Leicester racecourse. If we could find a farmer, preferably in the Cotswolds, who would take the horses and provide us with accommodation at the same time, the girls could have a riding holiday. Ted came to the laboratory, for what purpose I do not recall, but I remember it was a Thursday, his half-day. I told him about Hélène's proposal because I knew he often explored the Cotswolds in his caravan. He made some suggestions, then he said, "If you are looking for a place in the country, there is a derelict cottage in a wood near Tilton-on-the-Hill hardly a dozen miles from where you live, right in the heart of the Fernie country." (The Fernie is one of the most famous hunts in England.) He went on to tell me that in 1948, at the time of the Berlin Air Lift, he had taken over the cottage for a refuge should war break out between the former Allies. He gave it up in 1949, and as far as he knew it had been empty ever since. I had never heard of Tilton-on-

223

the-Hill, but I had a sudden urge to go there. I said, "Look, Ted. It's your half-day. It's snowing. You can't play golf. Will you take me there this afternoon?"

Tilton and its wood are mentioned in William the Conqueror's Domesday Book. It looked as if it had never been disturbed since. The wood we walked in was ancient, wild and abandoned. Dead trees leaned at every angle against the living. It was not possible to leave the track and turn into the wood without meeting an impenetrable barrier of thorny undergrowth. We must have walked for about twenty minutes when suddenly the track opened out into a clearing in which a house stood, stark and brooding, at the edge of the wood.

From where I stood I could see the front door hanging askew from its upper hinge. Above the door on the upper floor was a tiny window about a foot square, the only intact window in the building. The rest of the house had mullioned iron window-frames in which most of the panes had been broken. To the right of the door, at the corner of the building, was a Victorian brick annex which contained an overflowing chemical closet.

We squeezed past the hanging door and found ourselves in a stone-flagged chamber hardly bigger than a scullery, its window draped in cobwebs, and its floor knee-deep in old newspapers, magazines, empty cartons, bottles, cans and discarded clothing. In one corner stood a copper-boiler with a little fire-grate under it and next to it a block of black slate hollowed out to serve as a shallow sink, with a hole in the centre to take a cork.

Underneath the sink there was space for a bucket to collect the waste water when the cork was removed. Ted did not remember using either. They had been there long before his time. The rest of the ground floor consisted of a kitchen with a cast-iron grate, rusted in places but still serviceable, a cavernous room with a floor of red brick and a sloping ceiling that went right up to the roof, and a snug little parlour in which Ted had built a brick fireplace. (In May 1979, when we were staying at the cottage, two brothers, Charles and James Burton, came knocking at our door. Charles told us that their father Alfred Burton brought his wife and children to Keeper's Cottage in 1930 when he came to work on the farm. They lived there for eight years. Mrs. Burton raised five children there and they were always clean and proper. They can remember their father hanging the pheasants in the room with the sloping ceiling because it was always cool in summer, and their mother using the sink and the copper in the "scullery". Twice a day she went down to a well in the wood for water.) In 1962, thirty years later, there was still no water in the cottage.

The windows of the kitchen and the parlour looked south over a wide field to Skeffington Wood and beyond it to the village of Skeffington a mile across the valley. Nichols, the Leicester historian, records that when the plague raged at Skeffington in 1665, the villagers took to the wood and built themselves huts in order to avoid the contagion from travellers on the high road which runs from Leicester to Uppingham. Some parts of Skeffington Wood are still called by the names of those who stayed there until the plague had burned itself out.

The upper floor of the cottage, reached by a narrow, winding staircase from the kitchen, contained three bedrooms. One, as small as a monk's cell, had a stone floor and the tiny window, and in another the floor boards were so wide they must have been laid when the house was built 200 years ago. It was from a beam in this room that a gamekeeper called McDougal hanged himself after a drunken quarrel with his wife. The last bedroom had a trap-door in the floor. I was told that this was to lower coffins into the parlour because it was not possible to take them down the winding staircase. If nothing else, the cottage had atmosphere and an unique solitude, miles from the nearest main road.

We returned to the car and drove down the hill to Grange Farm, where I met the farmer Jack Holm and his wife Nora. When Mr. Holm learned I was interested in the cottage he said the place was a mess. It had been occupied by squatters after Dr. Kelly had left and the windows had been broken by the lads of the village. It was five years since he had been down there. He had no intention of selling any of his land or buildings. If I wanted to do something with the cottage, I was welcome to it, rent free. I had no illusions. I would be paying rent, and more, with the improvements I intended to make. There was no formal contract. We made a gentleman's agreement which we both kept until Hélène and I left England twenty-four years later.

When Hélène saw Keeper's Cottage for the first time, the winter sun was setting behind Skeffington. In the valley the sheep and cattle were standing still, waiting for the night. Further west, the city of Leicester could have been a thousand miles away.

"You have found a lovely place," she said, but she had some doubts about the cottage. "If you think you can do something with it, you're welcome."

I was sure I could. The forester had found his forest.

As soon as the snow had gone I began the rehabilitation of the house. The roof appeared in good repair – no obvious leakage in the upper floor, but the tall brick chimneys would probably need replacing in the future. The soft ironstone had crumbled round the window frames and sills and at the corners. I would have to learn how to point. If the house looked melancholy on these February days, the ironstone would shine like old gold on summer evenings. On closer inspection I saw what looked like rifle cartridges here and there in the stone. They were marine fossils, belemnites or thunderbolts as they are sometimes called, a reminder that a hundred million years ago central England was under the sea.

I went to the village to find Ben Curtis. Ben was well-known in Tilton and in all the surrounding villages, for he was not only an excellent carpenter and handyman, he was also a master undertaker. He had a box-file full of letters from the grateful sons and daughters of the local aristocracy thanking him for the efficient and dignified manner in which he had interred their elders. Ben made his own coffins. The day he had to buy a coffin for a client, said Ben, was the day he would retire. Like all those who have intimate contact with Death, Ben was full of jokes about it, most of them irreverent. I was reminded of my days in the anatomy department. He agreed to secure the door, install new window-panes and do any other repairs between burials.

We went to the Rose and Crown to cement what became a long-lasting relationship. There, Ben introduced me to the landlord and the latter's mother-in-law who, armed with a cloth and a tin of Brasso, constantly polished the 485 pieces of brass in the pub. The Rose and Crown was very old. Upstairs I was shown a room, the walls and ceiling lined with oak beams, where Oliver Cromwell is said to have slept while his men stabled their horses in the twelfth-century church of St. Peter beside the pub. The inn catered mostly for a mix of the local gentry, farmers and labourers who shared the same settles. With the passage of time brass gave way to chromium, and settles to chairs set round little tables in a separate lounge for visitors from the city.

All through the spring I went to Tilton immediately after work. By the light of paraffin lamps and the headlights of my car, I scrubbed whitewash from the beams in all the rooms, revealing some magnificent oak. I ripped off layers of damp wall-paper and tried to fix the crumbling surfaces with plaster and emulsion paint. My constant companion was an ungroomed, standard poodle. I had bought him four years before, a pitch-black ball in a shoe-box, in an attempt to persuade my daughters that a poodle like those dandies we saw parading on the quays at St. Tropez was preferable to a pony. They could not agree more. But I was to learn that I was living in a conspiracy of women. A few months later they got their first pony and I got Pitchou.

Water to Grange Farm came from a spring in a nearby field. The water was pumped uphill to a tank next to the entrance to Tilton Wood. Mr. Holm agreed to let me tap this tank and his son Richard ploughed a deep furrow down the side of the track through the wood and across the paddock to the back of the house. I obtained a kitchen-sink unit. I can remember clearly the day I brought it down through the wood sticking up out of the back seat of my open convertible. As I was going down, the Fernie was coming up. I shall never forget the look of distaste on the faces of the riders as they picked their way between the kitchen sink and the thorny undergrowth. In the furrow we laid two 200-yard lengths of green garden hose joined together by a piece of copper tubing. We connected one end of this long pipe to the tank and the other end to the kitchen sink, turned on the tap and after a short interval a steady stream of water emerged. Then we buried the hose. We had our water supply which would remain unused until our housewarming three weeks away.

We were in no hurry to install electricity. The cottage was some distance from the power lines and a generator would spoil the calm of the wood. The refrigerator, cooker and space heater ran on Calor gas. Pressurized paraffin lamps provided light for reading at night and storm lamps and candles lighted us to bed. There was an unlimited supply of wood for the fireplace in the parlour, which worked perfectly once we had pushed the bird-nests out of the chimney. The "pheasant" room became a "bistro" with small round tables and assorted chairs and horsy paraphernalia round the walls. The house was furnished with donations from friends, one of whom provided us with an iron three-tier bunk bed, which had been used in an air-raid shelter during the War.

I bought a broken-down war-time American Army jeep, borrowed a flat-bed trailer from the farmer, and with the help of my daughters got the lads of the village to gather stones from a nearby quarry to fill the ruts on the road through the wood.

On the afternoon of Sunday, 29th July, we held a house-warming. Ben was there as "mayor" of Tilton. He wore his black top hat and funereal tails. From his chain of office hung a large copper seal struck by the makers of Elect Cocoa to commemorate the coronation of H.M. King George Vth and H.M. Queen Mary in 1911. The rest of the party, farmers and their wives, members of my staff, and those who had helped in the restoration were in conventional attire. All went well, until in response to Ben's toast, we drank our whisky topped with water from the tap. It took all my will power to swallow the first mouthful, it was so nauseating. Was there something wrong with the whisky? I watched the others. They were talking and drinking without apparent discomfort. I poured myself a cup of tea. It tasted worse than the whisky and water. I held up my glass and cried, "This tastes awful! How can you drink it?"

My guests, looking relieved and sorry for me at the same time, laid down their cups and glasses at once. I could only admire their tact. The situation reminded me of the story about the courtly gentleman who accepts a bowl of soup in the humble home of one of his tenants. He notices a large fly swimming in the soup. He cannot remove it without embarrassing his host so he swallows the soup, fly and all.

There was nothing wrong with the whisky. The water was at fault, or rather I was at fault running the water through a garden hose. Not all my experiments were successful, far from it!

A few days later, Richard helped me dig up the hose and used it for his own purposes. I replaced it with polythene piping and got a group of young actors to help me lay it with a promise of a day in the country. They were from a small Leicester repertory company playing in a disused Sunday school, ironically called the "Living Theatre", which soon died to make way for an underpass. One of the actors, Kenneth Colley, self-effacing in company, was electrifying on the stage. I used to tell him he would be better getting a steady job as a rat catcher, but he never took my advice for I still see him on television. When the company was disbanded most of the properties were thrown away, except for one which had been made for John Osborne's *Luther*. It was a near life-size figure of Christ. The play begins in the Cloister Chapel of the Eremites of St. Augustine where Martin Luther is being received into the Order. At the back of the stage, behind the altar lit by a spotlight, hangs Christ crucified. He looks startlingly real, head hanging in despair. The figure had been made by a student at the School of Art out of a skeleton of wide-gauge wire wound round with layers of thick, brown, sisal twine. The artist was saddened at the thought of his creation going to the rubbish dump. I offered to keep it until he found a place for it. I never saw him again. I took the Christ to Tilton and crucified him to a tree deep in the wood where the hunters could see him when they rode by. He hung there for more than twenty years until only tangled wire and tattered string remained.

Our nearest neighbour was Mr. Wright, who farmed the fields between the two woods, Tilton and Skeffington. I first made his acquaintance when Pitchou was chasing his ewes near lambing time and I was chasing Pitchou. An irate Mr. W right appeared and told me I was lucky he did not have a gun, for he would have shot the dog. After that we became friends.

He lived happily with his wife, Ellen, in a ramshackle farmhouse. She was a lovely woman, with her white hair and rosy cheeks. She loved the countryside in which she had been born. Every day was a new miracle to her. He was like a piece of gristle, thin and tough, with hardly a tooth in his head. In 1989 Mr. Wright sent us a photograph taken on his eighty-sixth birthday. He had not changed since the day we first met him. He is in his working clothes holding up a bottle of whisky toasting the beholder, because he believes that daily tots of the hard stuff, as he calls it, will see him through to his century.

They had few amenities. A well in front of the farmhouse that tended to freeze in the winter; if going to bed by candle-light was a weekend novelty for us, for the Wrights it was a way of life; in the winter he used a warming-pan, a long-handled brass pan containing live coals from the kitchen grate, to warm their bed. Yet with all this, they were the happiest couple I have ever come across.

In 1984, two years after Ellen died, Mr. Wright caught up with Mr. Edison. I was sitting in his kitchen having a tot with him, when I noticed a small, U-shaped object between the rafters. When I asked him what it was, he went to the lintel of the door, flicked his fingers and the object emitted a glow, hardly stronger than a child's night-light. He demonstrated the phenomenon a few more times, then pointing upwards he said proudly, "Got one in the bedroom too – better than buggering around with candles!"

When I went outside, I could see the small windmill his son had fixed to the top of the barn. He still writes to us in his large scrawl. Sometimes he takes one of our old envelopes, spreads it out and writes on its blank surface. It could be said he lives in the nineteenth century, but he does so with enthusiasm. I have a feeling he will be there to greet the twenty-first in the same way.

From time to time we turn over the pages of the autograph albums our visitors filled with their impressions of the house and the wood. Most are in prose, some in verse and one in morse-code. They write in English, Welsh, Gaelic, French, Dutch, Spanish, Portuguese, German, Afrikaans, Latin, Greek and Hebrew. The cottage is depicted in water-colour, oil

Dr. Mair at Keeper's Cottage, 1984

paint, pencil and crayon. Over the years the same names crop up again and again. Jonathon Taylor, principal dancer and choreographer in the Ballet Rambert and his Dutch wife Ariette, a former dancer with the same company, came with their children from London for the first time in 1971, and thereafter every year until 1976, when they emigrated to Australia. After a brief hiatus, they resumed their pilgrimage from Australia to Keeper's Cottage until we left England in 1986, when the cottage passed into other hands. But that is another story.

Using the cottage as a base we explored a countryside rich in history. In the old days Tilton was the home of the Digbys, for many centuries one of the great families of Leicestershire. They lived in a manor-house standing back on the right of the main street. Today, the Digbys are all gone, save those who rest in the church. Under an arch lies a monumental Sir Jehan de Dygebye (1209), displaying a fleur-de-lys on his shield; clad in chain mail; cross-legged his feet rest on a lion which holds a man's head (a Saracen?) between its paws. Close by lies his wife, Arabella, a lap-dog at her feet. Also in stone, a later Digby lies, a lion at his feet. The last of the Digbys is not here. Sir Everard Digby, one of the handsomest men of his time, was unfortunately not the wisest. He was hanged, drawn and quartered for his part in the Gunpowder Plot to blow up the Houses of Parliament. Today, the Digby manor-house has been incorporated in a modern farmhouse. In the grounds stands an ancient ironstone building called the "The Aviary". When I saw it for the first time it was full of old farm machinery, much of it disused. I had seen other aviaries and this did not look like one in the least. There were recesses in the walls about five feet above the earthen floor that suggested timbers had been set in them to support an upper floor. If that were so, excavations might reveal a stone floor beneath the present earthen one. When I put this to the farmer, he was quite agreeable to let me have a go. When I returned the next week he had removed everything except an old door lying on its side against a wall. When we removed the door we could see a deep triangular recess of dressed stone. The farmer did not remember seeing this before. I lay on my back and was able to wriggle my head and shoulders into the recess. Above me, a wide brick-lined chimney rose to the crumbling roof – a chimney that was not visible from the outside. A week later – for this was a Sunday dig – I returned with a number of volunteers from the laboratory and we began to dig out the earthen floor, removing the soil in a wheel-barrow and sieving it before dumping it. As the digging proceeded it became evident we had found a medieval fireplace large enough to spit a pig, if not a cow. One could step into it with ease. The only object we found with all our sieving was a seventeenth-century memorial ring, enamelled in black and white with a girl's name on it and date of her death engraved on the inside. By this time I had informed the Leicester Museum people about our findings and they had a corrugated iron roof put on the building while they continued with the excavation.

In essence, these exploits, which I pursued for many years, were researches of a different kind. With regard to my work, when people asked me why I had not moved to London where the action is, I took them to Keeper's Cottage.

Chapter 20

Walter in Masada

On the 16th February 1965 I flew to Israel for a working holiday. I was on my way to take part in the archaeological expedition at Masada. For me, this would be the big one. After that I would be content to cultivate my own garden. In August of the previous year *The Observer* had carried an appeal for volunteers from Yigael Yadin, leader of the expedition. With Hélène's enthusiastic support, I wrote to the organizers pointing out that, although I was fifty-two, I was fit, well and laying a road through a wood. I had given up all hope of getting a reply from Jerusalem when I received a letter on the 6th October to the effect that I had been selected to join the Masada Expedition. Enclosed was my volunteer card No. 1259, my "Masada-passport", as from the 19th February 1965. Instructions were brief:

> "The assembly point for transportation to the expedition camp, is the public garden opposite the municipality in Beer-Sheba. You will be expected there at 12.30 p.m. on the date indicated on your card. Bring along sheets, blankets or sleeping bag, working clothes, hat, sunglasses, torch and after-work clothes, including a warm sweater or wind-jacket. Also reading material, musical instruments and anything to keep you busy after work. Leave behind: valuables, 'unnecessaries' and camera."

I learned later that more than 5,000 people from twenty-eight countries had volunteered to take part – far more than the organizers required.

In the wilderness of Judea, between Sedom and Ein-Gedi, on the western shore of the Dead Sea, stands the great rock of Masada. On this rock, Herod, King of the Jews, built his palace-fortress as a protection against his own people and the machinations of Cleopatra, Queen of Egypt, who coveted Judea. After Herod's death, Masada was held for a short time by his son Archelaus, and between A.D. 6 and A.D. 66 by a small Roman garrison. When the Jews rose in rebellion, the garrison was overrun by a band of zealots, who held it for six years until the Roman governor Flavius Silva marched against it at the head of his Tenth Legion with its auxiliary troops and thousands of Jewish slaves. Silva surrounded the rock so that none of the defenders could escape. His slaves built a gigantic ramp of stone, rubble and timber, up which he brought his siege-tower and battering-rams. When the Romans finally breached the wall and entered Masada they found it burning and as silent as the grave. The zealots, about 920 men, women and children had chosen death rather than suffer the humiliation·of a Roman triumph.

During the latter half of the nineteenth century the site was the object of fairly constant attention, albeit brief, because it was a difficult place to reach and the climb to the summit exhausting. With the establishment of the State of Israel, the fortress of Masada began to attract the attention of members of the Jewish Youth movement. In 1955, the government mounted an official expedition. No labourers were employed on the project, all work being done by students and volunteers from various settlements. The Israel Defence Army was responsible for equipment, supply, security and transport. The present expedition of 1963-1965 was mounted along the same lines as the 1955-1956 survey, except that Yadin had called for volunteers from all over the world.

On my arrival in Tel Aviv I stayed with Ann Freemerman, whom I had known in the Young Zionists. She taught English at a secondary school. The children thought her Scottish accent funny: their previous English teacher had been a German refugee. Ann's husband came from Shanghai, where his family had settled after the Russian Revolution. She called him her Chinese Israeli. He drove his own bulldozer and disliked archaeologists and Arab children, the former because they were always making him stop when he turned up something of interest, and the latter because they followed him the way sea gulls follow a ship and when the loader brought an artefact to the surface they swooped on it and were away before he could catch them. Nevertheless, he had managed to rescue a number of ancient oil-lamps and vases, which decorated a sideboard in the dining room. He was often away for days on end. They worked hard to make ends meet. For them, the honey was yet to come.

Ann took me to the British Zionist Federation office where I enquired about Henny and Ray settling in Israel. That always had been his dream. But I was told it would not work out. The language problem and his age were against it. They would find themselves in some vast housing estate surrounded by Roumanians, Yemenis and Persians, and at his age work would be difficult to find. So much for the Land of Promise.

On the morning of the 19th I boarded a bus for Beer-Sheba. Beside me was a young girl from Copenhagen, who had come to Israel to learn Hebrew so that she could take a course in English Literature at the Hebrew University in Jerusalem. By this time I was not surprised because I had met many like her in the few days I had been in Israel. She too was going to Masada. The public garden in Beer-Sheba was strewn with boys and girls, rucksacks and suitcases, all bound for Masada. I could see only one or two grey-beards like myself. Finally we were separated from our heavy baggage, which was taken to Masada by army truck while we went in a convoy of buses by a slightly longer route to the foot of the rock on its eastern side close to the Dead Sea. I do not know if this was done to give us a taste of what was in store for us. Before us was the Snake Path climbing steeply 1,300 feet to the summit of Masada. This is what Josephus, the historian, wrote of it at the time:

"With reference to its narrowness and constant windings: it is broken as it rounds the projecting cliffs and often turns back on itself, then lengthening out again a little at a time manages to make a trifling advance. Walking along it is like

> balancing on a tight-rope. The least slip means death; for on either side yawns an abyss so terrifying that it could make the boldest tremble . . ."

The path has probably been tidied up a bit since Josephus wrote about it, and perhaps he exaggerated also, but it is still a stiff climb and not free from danger when stones loosened by those ahead come tumbling down. Half-way up, where the path took one of the U-turns described by Josephus, I stopped to take a much-needed breather. I thought it was just as well I was making the climb in the relative cool of February. Around me, several young people were congratulating themselves on having got so far, when suddenly the chattering ceased. Coming up the path, carrying not only his pack but the rucksack of a girl struggling behind him, was a distinguished-looking, middle-aged man immaculate in white shirt and tie, three-piece suit and matching suede shoes. Not a hair out of place, casually, nonchalantly he passed us as though out for a morning stroll in St. James's Park. Only the ducks were missing. I could hear, "Englishman, Englishman", as we took up our packs and followed our Pied Piper to the summit, across the plateau and down the Roman ramp to the camp where I was to stay for two weeks.

The next morning I met the man with the suede shoes at a briefing session where we were allotted our working sites. His name was Walter Statham, managing director of one of the largest civil engineering companies in the Midlands. We were practically neighbours. His home was in Loughborough, only ten miles north of Leicester as the crow flies. For the next fortnight, after dinner, we talked. He had left school at fourteen, become a bricklayer, gone to night-school and the local college of technology, and been taken on by the firm of which he was now head. He was a charming man, well-spoken and well-read, with a mischievous sense of humour, as the reader will have already observed. He did not need a camera to record his stay at Masada. His pencil and sketch-pad were enough. One of his impressions hangs in my study; in the foreground is the base camp with its nineteen or twenty large square Army tents, administrative huts, dining hall and workshops, and in the background

Dr. Mair in front of his tent, Masada, February 1965

looms the rock. The camp was run with military precision although, when the day's work was done, there was a free and friendly atmosphere. I shared a tent with eight young men. On the first night I turned in early but a noisy party in the next tent kept me awake so I dressed and joined them. I was greeted warmly by a bunch of Irishmen whose tent was plastered with anti-British slogans.

Reveille was at 04.45 hours followed by quick ablutions, breakfast and up on the rock by 05.45, a look around us at the arid landscape and then at work by six o'clock. There would be a pause at 09.00 hours and a three-hour stint until midday, when we rested in the shade, if it was available, and ate our sandwich-lunch which consisted mainly of hard-boiled eggs, oranges and water. I don't know what we would have done without the boiled eggs and the oranges, particularly the oranges. It was not long before we heard the stock Masada orange joke:

Arab (after attending synagogue for the first time): "Why did the congregation groan every time they heard the rabbi mention Moses?"

Jewish friend: "Because if Moses had turned right instead of left, we would have had the oil and you would have had the bloody oranges!"

After a two-hour break, back to work for another hour, then a race down the ramp to get to the showers before the hot water ran out. After dinner one read, wrote letters, listened to a lecture, attended a sing-song round a bonfire or just argued, a favourite Jewish pastime.

Walter was directed to work with a group of kibbutzniks near the top of the ramp. He got on very well with them, even when they threatened to throw him off the rock, after he remarked, "As an engineer, when I see that ramp, my sympathies are with the Romans!"

I had the good fortune to work with two boys and three girls, all enthusiastic, from England, the United States and Israel. We were taken to a site where we met Yadin and some of his archaeologists. All I could see was a great heap of boulders at the edge of a forty-foot drop which ended in a large cistern carved out of the rock to store rain-water. Yadin said that beneath the boulders there might be a chamber on a road leading to Herod's palace. It was a crucial site and he asked us to be particularly careful. Our supervisor promised to send some labourers to help move the larger boulders but that was the last we saw of him or the labourers. For several days we slaved, pushing the rocks over the cliff, filling one wheel-barrow after another with debris, and sieving until our arms ached. All we could show for our pains were plenty of shards and two bronze coins covered with verdigris. Many of these coins were found at other sites. They bore a vine-leaf design on one side and a chalice on the other. The inscriptions read, "'For the freedom of Zion". They were coins of the revolt.

On Sunday, 28th February, just before lunch – I remember the time exactly because I gave up the lunch-break to pursue my discovery – I was scraping away some sand and loose stones when I came across a length of dressed stone. This was solid, shaped stone unlike much of the stone in Herod's palace, which was rubble covered in plaster painted to simulate marble. I was reminded of the dressed stone in Tilton. But this time it was not a fireplace but a gate that emerged. Within a few days the remnant of a chamber with adjoining gate was revealed, with plastered-covered benches from the Herodian period along three walls. The fourth wall no longer existed, its place taken by the forty-foot drop to the cistern. On page 102 of Yadin's book *Masada*, there are photographs of the site, before and after excavation of what he describes as a "handsome Herodian gate". What he does not mention is the chequer-board scratched in the plaster of one of the benches, a discovery that, for me, bridged the centuries in a moment. I could see the two guards, engrossed in their game, oblivious of the kibitzer. A few days later we had a visit from an archaeologist who had taken part in the 1955-1956 survey. He looked at what we had revealed and he said we should feel proud to be working there as it was one of the most interesting places in Masada. Yadin, who was with him, added that this was one of the places every visitor to Masada would have to see.

On Thursday, 4th of March, I wrote to Hélène and Anneke:

"My last letter from Masada. This morning I looked with affection at the great mass, black against the lightening sky. Yes, it does grow on one, and I am pleased that I lasted out the fortnight and pulled my weight to the last ounce. It was good to hear our archaeologist, who finally turned up, talking to another group of workers about what had been achieved in the last fortnight; that one of the best discoveries in Masada had been 'our' gate.

"Today we finished working just as hard as when we started, only this time lightened by a delightful change. By this morning we were down to just three men, our remaining girl having hit her toe with a pick. There was still a great deal of debris to clear on the site. Over it, the carpenters had built a ramp and a wooden bridge leading to a chute down which we shot our barrow-loads of rubble to fall to the ground a thousand feet below. So we set up time-trials to see who could run the loaded wheel-barrow up the ramp, along the bridge, stop at the barrier between him and eternity, tip the barrow up so that its contents fell down the chute and return as quickly as possible to the starting line. Ira, the American, made it in 48 seconds, Avi, the Sabra, in 45, and I in 35 seconds (in deference to my age my load was distinctly lighter). My record was broken after lunch by Ira . . ."

That night I went with Walter to drink raw Israeli brandy with the Army doctor at his quarters in the camp hospital, something we had been doing for the last few nights. He told us that now Spring was here the snakes, which had been hibernating all winter, would be especially active. One had to take great care when lifting large stones, because the snakes were extremely venomous. For some of them there was no anti-venom so he had arranged for the Army to fly the patient by helicopter to the hospital at Beer-Sheba; the treatment – exsanguination followed by transfusion of compatible blood! We thanked him for telling us this the night before we were leaving and not on the day we arrived.

He asked us what we were planning to do after we left Masada. When we told him we were going to Jerusalem, he said in his very precise English, "Do not go to the King David Hotel. It is too expensive. Go to the Y.M.C.A. It is full of Arabs, but it is clean and cheap. You can always walk across the street and sit in the lounge of the King David."

We went to the Y.M.C.A. Walter was returning to England before me. I asked him to give Hélène a ring when he got home. When I asked him if his wife would be meeting him at Heathrow, he replied, "Nick, it embarrasses me to say so, but my chauffeur will be meeting me."

Our friendship grew closer with the years. He rented and renovated a farm-labourer's cottage at the foot of Robin-a-Tiptoe Hill, barely a mile from Tilton Wood. Of Robin-a-Tiptoe, the locals boasted that if you stood on its summit and looked due east you would not see a higher hill until you came to the Russian Urals.

In the winter of 1980 he had just turned sixty-five and retired from business, when he learned that the stiffness and involuntary movements that had been troubling him for some time was Parkinson's Disease, of which it has been said, "It is not the flesh that is weak, but the spirit that fails to move it." This did not hold for Walter. He refused to let the inexorable progress of the disease deter him from pursuing his usual activities. He continued to cultivate his garden, make wine in season and paint his landscapes. Perched on a scaffold he spent two summers restoring the frescoes of a village church high in the Italian Alps, where his daughter lived with her Italian husband and children. After his wife died in 1983, he travelled the length and breadth of Australia, explored the Great Barrier Reef and was rescued from a rip-tide by life-guards at Bondi Beach.

I saw him for the last time when he came to stay with us over Christmas '87 at our new home in British Columbia. He challenged his increasing disability with long walks along the beach and demonstrations of agility like standing on his head. Mentally he was still very much alert. I shall always remember how he punctured a few egos at a dinner party where most of the guests were university graduates. Asked which university he had gone to, Walter replied, "I didn't go to a university" (pause), "but I built one." From the window of his home he could see much of his life's work – Loughborough University.

Finally he wound up at the Yoga for Health Foundation at Ickwell

Bury in Bedfordshire. He had found meditation and other Yoga practices a considerable help in his battle against Parkinson's. It was not long before he was actively engaged in the role of the Foundation's honorary director of works and happily engaged to Susan, a lovely American woman half his age. But time was running out. On 12th December 1990 he sent us a calendar for the coming year, with pen and ink drawings of Ickwell Bury and the Foundation. With it was a note: "I am afraid my Parkinson's is a little worse and writing does not come easily – hence the infrequency of my letters. The calendar I enclose may seem to contradict that last statement but I'm afraid it is my 'swan song' – at least until the medicos have moved on a bit!.."

On 25th April I sent him the pages of this chapter to check for accuracy and to learn, at the same time, how he was keeping. On 27th May, at a quarter to five in the morning I was awakened from a dreamless sleep by a voice over my right shoulder saying, "Santiago de Compostela is dead!" I was startled and even more startled when the message was repeated. I could not understand it. I had never gone on the pilgrimage. Indeed, I had never even been to Spain, although I nearly got there at the time of the civil war. I got up. Hélène was also awake and I told her about the message, which neither of us could understand unless the voice was referring to a computer disk I had wiped out by mistake the previous night! At 10.00 a.m. I collected the mail from our box which stands at the edge of the road. Hélène read the first letter. She looked up and said, "Walter is dead."

The letter was from Susan. On 1st January, three weeks after sending us the calendar, he had had a mild stroke and gone rapidly downhill. On 4th March he had suffered a second stroke, become comatose and died on 27th March, his seventy-fifth birthday – of old age.

Chapter 21

A Miscellany

I. Cloak and Dagger in Moscow

In my study there is a faded, sepia-tinted photograph of seven men standing in the courtyard of the Pasteur Institute in Paris. Behind them is the statue of Joseph Meister, the little Alsatian boy who was bitten by a mad dog and was the first human being to receive Pasteur's rabies vaccine. On the left of the group is Werner Knapp, the German microbiologist whose paper on pseudotuberculous mesenteric adenitis Hélène and I translated on the beach in Lerici; next to him the Frenchman, Henri Mollaret, head of the plague Centre at the Institute; then the Englishman Tom Burrows, a scientist at the Microbiological Research Establishment at Porton Down in Wiltshire; then the American W. D. Lawton from Fort Detrick in Maryland. The semicircle is completed by Thal from Stockholm and Wilhelm Fredriksen from Copenhagen. I am at the centre, as the smallest and newest member of the group. We have come together because of our interest in the family of bacteria known at that time as *Pasteurella* and later called *Yersinia* in honour of the young French bacteriologist, Alexandre Yersin, who discovered the plague bacillus in Hong Kong in 1894.

When I look back on it, we were uneasy bedfellows. With the exception of Burrows and Lawton, we were medical microbiologists who had taken the Hippocratic Oath in one form or another. Both Burrows and Lawton were scientists working in what were popularly known as bacteriological warfare centres.

By the 1960s Porton Down was concentrating almost exclusively on defensive work. Nevertheless, the techniques used in the manufacture of vaccines could be used also to make biological warfare agents. Fort Detrick, a much bigger establishment than Porton, was openly committed to developing microbiological agents for offence. Later, Burrows and Lawton co-operated in successful experiments involving the transfer of genes between strains of *P. pseudotuberculosis*. These experiments created quite a furore. By applying a similar technique to *P. pestis*, the plague bacillus, it would be possible to tailor-make an organism with the most powerful possible characteristics as a disease-carrier, more fearful than any found in Nature. They were on the way to creating a Doomsday Bug.

In the summer of 1966 our group met at the XI International Congress of Microbiology in Moscow. For Hélène and me it was to be a busman's holiday, part conference, part sight-seeing, with the emphasis on the latter. It was a novel experience, which began when the air-attendant on the Aeroflot plane at Gatwick offered us a chess-board with our vodka. Some soccer fans wearing the colours of the Soviet team that had just been eliminated from the World Cup competition were already laying out chessmen on their boards.

The Congress was being held in the Lomonosov Memorial State University. Constructed in the monumental architectural style of the Stalin period, the new university with its imposing thirty-two-storey central tower, eighteen-storey wings and sixteen-storey contiguous building, dominated the Lenin Hills. The whole complex, we were told, contained ninety miles of corridors and 45,000 rooms and halls housing lecture theatres, laboratories, refectories, concert halls and convention centres, students' halls of residence and apartments for instructors.

The British contingent was billeted in one of the halls of residence. Accommodation for two persons consisted of a small vestibule with a toilet and wash-hand basin on one side and a shower unit on the other. Off the vestibule were two single bed-rooms, clean and simply furnished. On the ground floor was a refectory. At the time it crossed my mind that, in the matter of facilities, the University did well for its students.

Things were a bit chaotic to start with, as an international dental conference had just finished and we had to wait until the last of the dentists moved out. In the end everything was sorted out and we were able to register and collect our Congress material.

The *Pasteurella* committee met and its members read papers to one another and to a small but enthusiastic audience of interested bacteriologists. In private, we discussed the future work of the committee.

Outside of the Congress, we took part in a number of organized visits to a kindergarten, a factory crèche, and a virological institute where we were wined and dined. There was the obligatory visit to the Kremlin. We were overwhelmed by the magnificence of the cathedrals and palaces within its walls, and the opulence of the regalia in the State Armoury. We attended a performance of *Spartacus* by the Bolshoi Ballet on the vast stage of the Palace of Congresses.

For the most part, however, Hélène and I went out on our own. We admired the "honour" system on the buses where there was no conductor and the passengers put the appropriate fare in a box near the rear-end of the bus. More than once, on the crowded platform when the box was not within reach, our money was passed along until it was deposited in the box.

We stood in the queue that wound round Red Square like a serpent to look at Lenin in his tomb. Ahead of us I saw a face which looked familiar to me. I went up to the man and said, "Didn't you work in a bookshop in Churchgate, Leicester?" He replied, "Yes. I left about five years ago and went to London. I work in a bookshop in Charing Cross Road, now." I came back to Hélène, pleased that, in the middle of Russia, I had confirmed once more that I never forget a face!

We went to the Tretyakov State Gallery with its famous collection of Russian art of the eleventh to the twentieth centuries. We enjoyed the visitors as much as the paintings – besides the tourists, there were soldiers and sailors, workmen and old ladies in their babushkas trailing their grandchildren behind them. It could never have been mistaken for the Tate.

On the fifth day of the congress we were coming away from breakfast when we were accosted by Mollaret. I could see he had something important to tell us. In a voice rich with revelation he said, or at least I thought he said, "The Russians do not believe Burrows is Burrows!"

It is not easy to lip-read someone who has difficulty with his English. I looked at Hélène. She said, "The Russians do not believe Burrows is Burrows!"

Was Mollaret telling us the Russians believed the British would never allow their plague expert to visit the Soviet Union? I thought it was a lot of nonsense. As I have already indicated, Tom knew more about the virulence factors of *P. pestis* than most people working in that field, but it was inconceivable that our hosts could see us as part of a conspiracy to deceive them. Nevertheless, the seeds of doubt having been sown, I remarked that I had not seen Tom for a couple of days. Perhaps he was unwell. We knew he was not staying in the same building as the British delegates. Hélène and I set out to find him. At the office where he would have registered we were told he had been allocated a room in a hall which, from a plan we were shown, appeared to be a considerable distance from the convention centre. When I asked why he had been sent there, I was told he had arrived late and there were no more vacancies in our building or any others near the convention centre. I found this hard to believe but I had to be satisfied with the number of his room on a piece of paper and instructions on how to find the building.

Moscow University boasted an enrolment of over 70,000 students but most of them must have gone home for the summer because many of the buildings we passed through were empty, except for caretakers and cleaners. It was a strange experience walking along the silent corridors.

Finally we arrived at our destination. Burrows' room was on the fifth floor. We climbed the stairs without meeting anyone. We came to a door that bore two numbers, one of which was on the piece of paper. The long corridor was deserted. I turned the handle of the door which opened easily. We found ourselves in a vestibule similar to our own. Hélène opened the door to the corridor slightly to keep an eye on anyone who might come along unexpectedly. With infinite care I opened the door to

Tom's room. A mattress, rolled up and tied with string, lay on a sagging wire base. A chair lay up-ended in the centre of a table as though someone, after scrubbing the floor, had forgotten to replace it. Wardrobe and drawers were empty. Whoever had occupied this room had left no trace of his existence. Then I moved the chair that was lying on the table. Underneath it was an English paper-back!

When I recovered from the shock I signalled Hélène to come and have a look. All I wanted to do was to get out as quickly as possible, but she, having had more experience of this sort of thing than I had, pointed to the door of the other bedroom. I could only open it a few inches. There seemed to be some obstruction on the other side of the door. I pushed harder and almost fell into the room. The place was a shambles. Clothes, books and newspapers were strewn everywhere. Although it was near midday an electric light was still burning. I must have disturbed him, because Burrows sat up in bed, holding his head between his hands lest it fall off. He groaned, and between his groans I learned he had been out on the town the previous night with Dr. Martinevskii, an eminent microbiologist from the Anti-plague Centre, in Alma-Ata, Khazakhstan. I doubt whether Martinevskii, a member of our committee, learned anything from Burrows he did not know before, and vice versa. I was too embarrassed to tell Burrows the purpose of our visit. I did not tell him he was in the wrong room. We left him with our hope that he would be well enough to join us at the next meeting of the *Pasteurella* Committee.

By the middle of the seventies the British Ministry of Defence decided to get out of the bacteriological warfare business. In 1978 the Government invited the P.H.L.S. to accept responsibility for a new civil institute, using the buildings and equipment of the Microbiological Research Establishment. The P.H.L.S. accepted with some reluctance, provided its activities would be in those fields relevant to a national public health laboratory service. On the 1st of April 1979, the new Centre for Applied Microbiology and Research began operating. Long before then, Tom Burrows had phoned to tell me that his laboratory was closing down and he would have to look for a new job. Could he use my name as a reference? I said, of course he could, but I did not hear from him again.

II. Anniversaries

Other than my brother's barmitzvah – and the memory of that occasion has all but vanished – I cannot recollect celebrating birthdays in my Glasgow family. I never knew the birth-dates of my parents and as for my siblings, I know that Ray was born in March and is about three years older than I. Henny, six years older was born on the 1st April, All Fools Day, the only date I can remember with certainty. Hélène's birthday comes next in that order, but those of my daughters and grandchildren require confirmation from time to time. Except for childhood deprivation I cannot account for this block. I sometimes rationalize my aversion for birthday and anniversary cards on the grounds that one is merely buying someone else's sentiments and a florist's bouquet as a once-a-year expression of love.

For Hélène on the occasion of her Fiftieth Birthday

> Why fifty?
> Half an unlikely hundred years -
> Bisect a surer three-score years and ten.
> One day, remembered in a forgetting year,
> Mottoed with love,
> Summered with flowers,
> I?
> I celebrate your birthday every day.
>
> 17 October 1968

III. In Search of St. Roch

On my desk beside the sepia photograph of the *Pasteurella* Committee stands the figure of yet another doctor in the form of a manikin about twelve inches high. His name is Dr. Schnabel and he is a caricature of a seventeenth-century plague-doctor. He wears a wide-brimmed black hat, beneath which protrudes a mask in the shape of an eagle's beak, supporting incongruously large crystal spectacles. When the beak is filled with aromatic spices it will, he believes, repel the contagion and the spectacles will protect his eyes. He is clothed from top to toe in black. In his right hand he carries a long white stick to take the pulse and at the same time to keep him a safe distance from the patient. The manikin's hat and coat are made of cloth, but the real Doctor Schnabel's were made of smooth Cordovan leather, because, he was convinced, smooth leather was less likely to trap the contagion than rough wool.

The manikin was one of the trophies that Hélène and I collected in our search for the patron saints of the plague. For twenty years, armed with guide books, cameras and catalogues, we travelled the length and breadth of Europe. We explored museums, art galleries, great houses and innumerable churches (I told our Catholic friends we had heard more masses than they had). Two publications proved invaluable in our search; Raymond Crawfurd's *Plague and Pestilence in Literature and Art* (Clarendon Press, Oxford) and *La peste, source méconnue d'inspiration artistique* by Henri H. Mollaret and Jacqueline Brossollet (published in 1965 by the Royal Museum of Fine Arts, Antwerp). (The same Professor Mollaret who had sent us to look for Tom Burrows was now acting as our guide in a search of a different kind.)

Between the Black Death of 1348 and the final and terrible visitation at Marseilles in 1720, plague dominated Europe. For 400 years epidemics of the "Great Dying" were so frequent that every generation must have thought them inevitable. Today, it is difficult to conceive of the terror under which people lived in the shadow of a disease that seemed inexplicable, irresistible and incurable. Writers and artists, who express the feelings and aspirations of their generation, have left their testimony.

Petrarch and Boccaccio were eye-witnesses of the Black Death; Pepys and others, of the Great Plague of London; in our own time, Camus's *La Peste* presents the tyranny of foreign occupation in the form of plague in a modern city; the theme of plague, particularly in the depiction of its patron saints, is found in the works of many of the great masters of the Renaissance. In almost every country of Europe and Asia, plague has become part of legend and folklore.

When Dr. Schnabel's nostrums were found to be useless people either fled from the plague-stricken areas or turned to the Church for succour. The Church taught and the faithful believed that plague was God's instrument for the punishment of sin. A similar view was held by the fourteenth-century Scottish historian, John of Fordun, who could not understand how Scotland had escaped an earlier plague because, "great sins were not wanting among these people." The people turned in repentance to the Virgin and the saints to intercede with God on their behalf.

Local saints like Genevieve in Paris, and Charles Borromeo in Milan were invoked as protectors against the plague. Job of the Old Testament was revered as St. Job by Christian communities in the East, and St. Anthony had quite a vogue in South Germany. But two saints were especially invoked – St. Sebastian, who was universally recognized as the patron saint of pestilence but gradually became identified more particularly with plague, and St. Roch, who was regarded from the beginning as the most effective intercessor against the plague.

It was not difficult for us to find representations of St. Sebastian, martyred for his Christian beliefs at the hands of the Emperor Diocletian whose archers transfixed him with arrows, the symbols of pestilence. He is invariably shown thus or carrying an arrow in his hand. His was one of the few nude figures permitted to Christian art and this accounts for his appearance in a multitude of pictures. It is not surprising that in this day and age he has become the patron saint of gays.

St. Roch, the most revered plague-saint of the middle ages, was born in Montpellier towards the end of the thirteenth century. Having distributed all of his earthly belongings among the poor, he set off on a pilgrimage to Italy which was being ravaged by the Black Death. There, he tended the sick in one city after another until he was stricken with the plague in Piacenza. A horrible ulcer broke out on his left thigh. So great was his pain, and fearing to disturb the inmates of the hospital, he dragged himself to a solitary hut outside the gates of the city and there laid himself down to die. But a kind Providence watched over him. An angel came to tend his sore, and each day his little dog, that had followed him faithfully in all his travels, went to the city and brought him back a loaf of bread. When he finally recovered, France was at war with Italy, and when he returned to Montpellier he was arrested as a spy and thrown into prison, where he languished for five long years. One morning when the jailer entered his cell, he found it filled with a supernatural light. St. Roch was dead and on the wall above his head were the words: "He who is seized by the plague, and seeks refuge in St. Roch will gain relief from his disease."

Such is the legend of St. Roch, whose effigy can be found in great cathedrals and humble street shrines all over Europe. He can be recognized readily by his attributes. He is generally represented as a man in the prime of life in the garb of a pilgrim with staff, scrip and rosary. The scallop shell on his hat signifies that he has made the pilgrimage to the Holy Land or to the shrine of St. James the Greater at Santiago de Compostella in northern Spain. Less often, the crossed keys of St. Peter on his cloak indicate he has made the journey to Rome. He raises his cloak to show the plague sore on his naked thigh. The angel tending his sore and his dog with a loaf of bread in its mouth are portrayed less often.

The cult of St. Sebastian seems to have been confined to the Continent, while thanks to the iconoclasts of the Reformation the memory of St. Roch has all but vanished in England, except for one Sussex place-name (St. Rokeshill) and screen paintings in Devon and Norfolk depicting him as a pilgrim with a sore on his leg and accompanied by a dog with a loaf of bread in its mouth. When I was a boy there was a Catholic school in Glasgow called St. Roch which had an effigy of the saint standing in the hall. If I remember correctly there was a football club of the same name.

Denis Rice, my friend and mentor on matters Catholic, tells me that, when he was a student at a seminary, St. Roch was invoked for good health. With such a paucity of surviving relics of the saint it was with great surprise and excitement that I discovered a hitherto unrecognized St. Roch hardly four miles from Keeper's Cottage.

Launde Abbey lies in one of the prettiest and most sequestered spots in Leicestershire, or so it must have seemed to the rapacious Thomas Cromwell, arch-confiscator of the monasteries, who so much liked what he saw that he wrote in his diary, "Item to remember, myselfe for Launde." But he did not enjoy his plunder for long. He fell rapidly from King Henry's favour and was beheaded in 1541. Today little remains of the monastic building except the much-restored fifteenth-century chapel. A rare feature of this church is the east window with much of the pre-Reformation stained glass intact. Above three large figures are seven smaller ones in the tracery lights. How often had I looked at these without being aware of the man on the extreme right in the garb of a pilgrim. One morning it seemed to me the rising sun illumined him as it had never done before. Through my binoculars I could see the crossed keys of St. Peter on the upturned brim of his hat and a brown dog leaping up towards him with a loaf of bread in its mouth! There are approximately thirteen saints, most of them obscure, whose emblem includes a dog, docile, mad or dead, but only St. Roch can lay claim to a dog with a loaf of bread in its mouth. I must confess that my discovery of the Launde St. Roch gave me as much, if not more, pleasure than anything that came out of my laboratory. But it had an unfortunate sequel. Henri Mollaret and his wife were staying with us, and I took him along to see the window. There was a service in progress and, I am afraid, our arrival and subsequent discussion must have disturbed the congregation, because I received a letter from the warden to the effect that I was no longer welcome at the Abbey, a proscription which lasted until the warden retired.

One Sunday afternoon in May 1978 I came upon the Place du Grand Sablon, one of the pleasantest squares in Brussels. For three days the antique dealers of the city had set up their stalls on its cobblestones, and this was the last day. The square was alive with restaurants, cafés, tourists and optimistic collectors. I did not see myself as one of the latter. I was browsing around without anything in mind, when I came upon what I can only describe as an ecclesiastical stall. The woman behind it was beginning to pack up her wares, the stone cherubs in cardboard cartons, the brass candlesticks, the crucifixes and the Virgins each rolled separately in cloth, when I noticed one statue apart from the others. It was a wood-carving of a man, about a foot high. He could have been a pilgrim, except that his staff and the right arm which might have held it were missing, leaving an empty socket. It was an exquisite carving. His long hair curled over his shoulders, his moustache and beard had been trimmed with care. He had the air of a man in the prime of life. His eyes were closed as though he had looked upon horrors. With his left hand he pulled up his cloak to expose the sore on his naked thigh. The dealer did not know who he was. Her husband had brought it from the Philippines. She gave me the impression she would be glad to get rid of the broken statue. I could not believe my luck. I examined him again. There were flecks of gold all over his cloak. If he had once been a saint he had been a golden one. We settled on a price, only to find I was several hundred francs short. Frantic, I asked her to wait while I found Hélène and the money. Then I went away with my St. Roch. When I returned to England I took it to the Victoria and Albert Museum, where the wood-sculpture conservator declared it to be a fifteenth-century Spanish carving.

In September I was in Munich for a meeting of the *Pasteurella* Committee. I told Mollaret about my recent acquisition from the Philippines. He asked me two questions.

"Are the feet broken?"

I thought for a moment, visualizing the statue on its pedestal. I told him the feet were broken – the right foot was reduced to a pointed piece of wood and the left foot was broken across the instep. The pedestal was a block of rough wood that did not belong to the statue. Then he asked me the second question.

"Has the nose been flattened?"

"Yes," I replied. "The nose has been rubbed flat."

"Then," said Mollaret "It probably comes from the Philippines."

I asked him how he had arrived at that conclusion. I felt as though I were playing Dr. Watson to his Sherlock Holmes.

"It was all a matter," said Mollaret, "of supply and demand."

The third great pandemic of plague broke out in Yunan in 1892. It reached Bombay in 1896. In India it is believed to have killed some six million people. When it struck the Philippines, the Catholic population, as in earlier centuries, turned to St. Roch. His effigy was in great demand and in Europe there were those who, for profit, were prepared to meet that demand by fair means or foul. My St. Roch was one of many which were stolen from churches and shrines. In wrenching the statue from its pedestal, which was probably fixed, the thief broke its feet, and in the Philippines when the plague went on unabated, the Filipino, whose prayers apparently fell on deaf ears, turned St. Roch into a more receptive native saint by flattening his long Spanish nose!

I was able to confirm Professor Mollaret's hypothesis when I obtained a second St. Roch from the widow of a missionary who had spent many years in the Philippines. It had been carved by a local artist at the turn of the century, at the time of the great pandemic. It is primitive yet it has a reverent air. Beneath the raised cloak a copious flow of bright red blood flows down the right thigh. The left forearm, raised in blessing, is nailed to the shoulder. In all respects the face is uncannily like the effigies of St. Roch we have seen in Europe, except that the nose is unmistakably flat.

IV. Off with the Old and on with the New

By the beginning of the seventies, our laboratory had reached saturation point. The shabby old ward was bursting at the seams. Any attempt to install a new piece of apparatus involved us in a tortuous game of musical chairs with existing equipment. Short of hanging the odd incubator or two from the ceiling, there was a limit to the number of moves we could make. Headquarters had vetoed any suggestion of a new laboratory at Groby Road, and to make matters worse, it was rumoured that a reduction in the number of laboratories was planned, and I feared that Leicester might be on the "hit list". The future looked hardly promising.

At that time, on the other side of town, the University was making plans for a new Medical School. They included a Medical Sciences building on the main University site for pre-clinical students, and a Clinical Sciences building at the Leicester Royal Infirmary where the students would learn the practice of medicine and surgery. An important feature of the Clinical Sciences building was the pathology block, which would be one of the largest in the country. As it happened the top floor of this block proved to be our salvation.

Professor Cramond, the Dean of the Medical School, after hearing my views on the possibility of the public health laboratory transferring to the Clinical Sciences building to the benefit of both, wrote to Sir James Howie, and there followed a procession of people from the P.H.L.S. headquarters, culminating in a visit by the Director himself and Mr. Whittaker, Secretary to the P.H.L.S. Board. I met both men when they stepped off the London train. After the usual greetings, I said, "There's been so much brass coming from London, I don't know whether to feel flattered or afraid."

Sir James replied, "At headquarters we divide our laboratory directors into the stronger brethren and the weaker brethren. You are one of the stronger brethren."

This was encouraging. As we drove to the University, he asked me how we were managing at Groby Road. I did not answer him directly. I told him instead about the time I went to Israel to dig at Masada. I flew El Al from London. I managed to get a window seat and a moment later was joined by a tall man in black. He wore a round, wide-brimmed black hat, long ringlets, a long black beard, a long black coat down to his ankles, and black soft leather boots. Behind the long beard lurked a young man. He kept leaning over me to look out of the window, so I asked him if he would like my seat. He replied in an American accent, "I would consider it a real favour if you did – you see, I was davening (praying) when we came into London this morning."

He turned out to be a Canadian living in New York, fitted out in the trappings of an eighteenth-century Polish Ghetto scholar. He was a Hassid, on the way to an important Hassidic wedding in Israel. On his lap were two tattered brown-paper grocery bags, bursting at the seams, filled with his worldly goods. All the way to Paris he kept taking objects out of one bag and putting them in the other, or vice versa, evidently in the hope that by some Hassidic miracle he would end up with two capacious grocery bags. As it happened, the bags became more tattered and torn and, at one point, his phylacteries fell on the floor. When we arrived in Paris I found a large "duty-free" bag and gave it to him.

At which, Sir James said, "All right, Mair. I get the message."

The meeting was held in the ante-room to the Vice-Chancellor's office. Like Howie, Fraser Noble was an Aberdonian. Another thing they had in common was that they were both keen golfers. Although the tenor of the meeting was in favour of the proposal to include the public health laboratory in the new building, Howie was concerned about the financial costs to the P.H.L.S. When we seemed to have come to an impasse on this matter, Fraser Noble got up and invited his fellow Aberdonian into his office. The rest of us sat there quietly, wondering what was happening behind the closed door. Five minutes later they returned, both smiling broadly. They had evidently come to an amicable arrangement. We were going to have a new laboratory after all.

In the summer of '77 I met Sir James at a meeting in Aberdeen. He had retired four years before and was living in the Highlands. He asked me if I remembered the meeting in Leicester. I told him I often wondered what Fraser Noble had said to make him change his mind. With a twinkle in his eye, Howie said, "Would you like to know what really happened?" Not waiting for my reply, he went on, "Fraser Noble did not say anything. He went over to a golf-bag standing in a corner of the office and took out a driver and a putter he had just purchased and asked me what I thought of them. We had a few practice swings and pushed a ball along the carpet with the putter and we both agreed he had made a good buy and that you should have a new laboratory."

Although I helped in the planning of the new laboratory, like Moses, I did not enter the Promised Land. That privilege fell to my successor who took over when I retired in '78, two years before the building was completed.

Nineteen seventy-eight was an eventful year for me. On the 1st of January I wrote to Professor R. E. O. Williams, who had succeeded Howie as Director of the Service:

> "Dear Robert,
> On 15th December last, the Vice-Chancellor on behalf of the University of Leicester invited me to accept an honorary degree of Doctor of Science at a Congregation to be held on July 14th. Needless to say, I accepted before he could discover his mistake. The official announcement has just appeared in the University Bulletin.
>> With best wishes, etc.

Among letters of congratulation was one from Dr. J. W. G. Smith, head of the National Institute for Biological Standards and Control, who subsequently became Director of the P.H.L.S. He wrote:

> ". . . and I think the University is extremely fortunate that you have honoured them by accepting this degree. It is a very fitting recognition of your outstanding contribution to British Bacteriology.
>> With best wishes to you and Hélène . . ."

With that letter, I knew that the ghost of G. S. Wilson had finally been laid to rest.

On the morning of the 14th July, clad in borrowed robes, I took my place on the platform of De Montfort Hall with Sir Rex Richards, Vice-Chancellor of Oxford University, who was also to receive a D.Sc., and Mr. Albert Deller, whose doctorate was in music. I was called first. The Public Orator sought to find an analogy between me and George Eliot's Mr. Lydgate, "the most convincing physician in English fiction . . . who arrived in another Midlands town in 1829 planning to do good small work for Middlemarch and great work for the world." He went on to explain briefly why Lydgate had failed and at greater length why I had not. I could not make out a word he was saying. The platform in the De Montfort Hall is very wide. I stood in the centre of the stage while he stood in the wings, too far for me to read his lips. I must have looked very solemn because a lady at the luncheon after the ceremony asked me what was passing through my mind as the Public Orator heaped praise upon praise while the whole congregation listened. I told her that while I appreciated the solemnity of the occasion I kept wondering if Julie, my four-year-old Canadian grand-daughter who had come all the way from British Columbia, was going to fall off the balcony at the back of the hall.

A month later, I was knocked down by a car in front of the Medical Sciences Building at the University, spent eleven days in hospital, and recovered sufficiently to fly to Munich for my last meeting with the *Pasteurella* Committee. On the 10th September, on my sixty-sixth birthday, I retired from the Public Health Laboratory Service. Within forty-eight hours of leaving Groby Road I was installed in the Department of Microbiology at the University. The Vice-Chancellor, Mr. Maurice Shock, who was visiting the Department, stopped to have a word with me. I told him I had said goodbye to my staff two days earlier, promising to return as a very junior lecturer. The V-C said, "You will be the first lecturer to become a 'Reader' in the space of two days." (A Reader in the academic hierarchy is a step below the Professor.)

I enjoyed my new honorary status. Instead of the stress of running a busy hospital and public health laboratory, I was surrounded by students, enthusiastic young men and women, the latter as numerous as the former. (I recalled the eleven women among 150 men when I was a student.) I was free to come and go. From time to time I was asked, "But what does an Honorary Reader do?" I could only reply, "For the little he does, he gets paid nowt!"

Hélène, meanwhile, was still at Groby Road. We had planned to retire together, as we had worked together, so I had stayed on an extra year, but, when the time came a replacement could not be found for her and she went on for another twelve months. On a voluntary basis I continued my *Yersinia* reference work, with one foot in the University and the other in the Royal Infirmary to which the P.H.L.S. had moved.

Another legacy from the P.H.L.S. was my collection of strains isolated from abortion in sows and septic infection in piglets. With the tests available to me I had been unable to classify them, although I was convinced that they differed from those recognized as causing porcine abortion. As I had always done, I made a point of treasuring my exceptions, keeping the strains preserved by freezing them, until the time was ripe for additional tests. That time came when Professor Peter Sneath, head of the Department of Microbiology at the University, and a pioneer of numerical taxonomy – a complex method of computer analysis – identified my strains as a distinct new species to which he gave the name *Pasteurella mairii.* At last I had achieved minuscule immortality, my name italicized with Louis Pasteur!

In the summer of '85 we decided to leave England and join our two daughters and their growing families in Vancouver. It was our intention, like old soldiers, to fade quietly away in the wake of our Pickford container, but both Sir Robert Kilpatrick, Dean of the Medical School, and Professor Alan Buchan, Director of Public Health, had other ideas – no less than a farewell dinner at the University. I reminded the latter that he had attended our farewell dinner seven years ago when we retired from the P.H.L.S. Why another one now? "This time," he replied, "we want to make sure you are really going."

And go we did. Fourteen days after the dinner we landed at Vancouver Airport shortly before midnight on the 31st January 1986.

We may have set foot in a new land, but the problems of the old one were still with us. In October Henny was found to have inoperable cancer of the lung, a legacy of the sixty cigarettes that had seen him through each day. I flew over to see him. He was much diminished but as argumentative as ever. He still insisted on walking down to the village nearly a half mile away to do his morning shopping, though he had to stop from time to time to recover his breath. He had always dreamed about settling in Israel – his country right or wrong. Any criticism on my part had usually ended up in bitter argument with Ray trying to restore peace. But now we talked of his other love, Queen's Park, the Scottish amateur football club, and of the time he had played for the Glasgow University Jewish team. After a week I returned to Canada.

Seven months later, when he had just turned eighty, Ray phoned to say he was dying. I was swimming at the local aquatic centre. I was still damp behind the ears when I was on my way to Glasgow. Seventeen hours later Henny looked up from the scrabble board at 20 Woodlands Road and said to me, "We were expecting you an hour ago."

He had gone down-hill since I had seen him last. He was in pain but refused to take morphine because, he said, it made him more confused than he was already. That night I could not sleep at all and it was five o'clock in the morning when I dropped off. The next thing I knew was Ray waking me up and beckoning me into the hall. It was eight o'clock. Stuck to the bathroom door with a drawing pin was a notice which read:

"AM TAKING A HOT BATH"

"I can't get him out," said Ray. He was sitting in the cold empty bath, one arm hanging outside it and his head resting on his shoulder like David's "Marat" without the blood. I stepped into the bath and tried to lift him. It was a terrible job, he had no strength in his arms and legs. Finally I got him out of the bath and into his bedroom, where Ray helped to get him into his pyjamas. The trousers were all right, but he baulked at the pyjama top. It did not match the trousers! Henny had always been most fastidious about his clothes. All the time he kept asking for the morning paper. Ray went to the front door where the *Daily Express* lay. On the front page was a picture of the Glasgow Ranger's manager and his wife. "Not a bad looking woman," said Henny, confirming what I had read somewhere that the sexual urge is the last to go. He kept asking, "What time is it?" He did not trust his own watch but he did not think it was worth getting anything done about it at this stage.

The next morning he brought me in a cup of tea! He wished "it" would come soon. He said he was bored doing nothing. But later in the morning he looked as though he was really going. With a little smile on his hollow face he said, "I must keep going until tomorrow night." That was the night television was showing the first round of the European Cup.

The next day Henny expressed a desire to see the seaside and have tea in a restaurant. I helped him dress. He chose a light brown linen suit and a bright tie. We had a pleasant drive to Largs while Henny read the *Jewish Echo*. We went to a tearoom where Henny had half-a-cup of tea and read the *Jewish Echo*. He asked for an ice-cream. The waitress brought it. He said he wanted to eat it outside. I asked the waitress if that was all right. She disappeared and returned to say it was all right. I helped Henny outside with his glass bowl of ice-cream. He sat on a bench facing the sea, ate his ice-cream and read the *Jewish Echo*. To my surprise, he asked me to go back and join the others in the tea-room. Evidently he wanted to prove he could cope by himself, but after a few minutes we joined him. He felt cold. We wrapped him in a tartan blanket and went home.

Henny's euphoria engendered by my visit soon disappeared. The pain was becoming too much for him. He got some relief from the morphine tablets I doled out to him from time to time. When he asked me where I kept them, I knew what he had in mind. A physician who cuts the life-support system of his patient may be accused of playing God. I believed if I refused Henny's request I too would be playing God. I told him where they were. He began swallowing them like sweets and fell into a deep sleep. Henny was always a fighter. He fought the morphine for two days and two nights. At 3.00 a.m. on the third day, the 14th May, the District Nurse who was on night watch, woke me to tell me Henny was dead.

I have two mementoes to remind me how near he was and yet so far; on my bed-side table a book about the surgeon Lord Lister, awarded to him by Archie Young who ploughed me in surgery, and a large bronze medal presented to him in his fourth and last year as a medical student. On the obverse is a portrait of William Hunter the famous Scottish surgeon, and on the reverse the inscription,

IN ACADEM. GLASGUENS.
FACULTAT MEDICA
DISCIPULUS
INGENIO AC LABORE
INSIGNIS
PREMIUM HOCCE
MERITO CONSECUTUS EST

(The Medical School, Glasgow University; this prize has been awarded to the student for his outstanding intelligence and hard work.)

After Henny's death Ray continued to live in Woodlands Road, but she was now seventy-nine and, small though the house was, it was beginning to take its toll. I flew over again in October '88 to see what I could do. She still wanted to live independently. An old-age home held no attraction for her. I found a purpose-built complex, small flats designed for senior citizens with community facilities. I took her to see it and she was delighted. She signed the appropriate forms and I told her she must see her lawyer to complete the arrangements. The next day, 1st November, I flew back to Vancouver. Hélène met me at the airport. All the way home I told her about Ray's new flat and what a difference it would make to her. When we entered our home, the phone was ringing. It was my friend Morris phoning from Glasgow. Ray was in the Royal Infirmary fighting for her life. She had been on a pedestrian crossing when she was knocked down by a petrol tanker. She fell between the wheels and apparently suffered no serious injury until a car following behind the tanker ran over her right arm. The surgeons, fearing that an attempt to salvage her arm would endanger her life, amputated it below the shoulder. After a stormy recovery she made excellent progress and when I saw her again she was learning to cope with having to use her left arm only. Shortly after her discharge from the convalescent home she entered Newark Lodge, the Jewish Old Age Home for Scotland, where, she complained, there wasn't enough to do.

Coda

For the last six years we have been living in our new home at Boundary Bay, in British Columbia, where the sea-birds come in their hundreds of thousands from the North to winter in the Bay or after a pause continue on their way south to warmer climes. Come late November. when the alders at the back of our house have shed their leaves, the bald-headed eagles perch on the top-most branches tearing at the fish they have plucked from the sea, while around them the crows wait for the crumbs from the rich man's table. We have added a new dimension to our lives.

> Twenty years on, and half a world away,
> Woods become forests, streams a tidal sea,
> We share the brooding eagle and the loon,
> And children's children in the afternoon.
>   (For Hélène on her seventieth birthday)